The Australian Gamble

The Australian Gamble

Organized Crime Down Under

Paul Bleakley

ROWMAN & LITTLEFIELD
Lanham • Boulder • New York • London

Published by Rowman & Littlefield
An imprint of The Rowman & Littlefield Publishing Group, Inc.
4501 Forbes Boulevard, Suite 200, Lanham, Maryland 20706
www.rowman.com

86-90 Paul Street, London EC2A 4NE

British Library Cataloguing in Publication Information Available

Library of Congress Cataloging-in-Publication Data
ISBN: 978-1-5381-7708-2 (cloth)
ISBN: 978-1-5381-7709-9 (electronic)

For Taylor—the best partner in crime a guy could ever ask for.

And for Shaggy—my favorite co-worker and best friend.

Contents

Acknowledgments

Writing this book was an adventure that would not have been possible without the assistance of so many people. A huge thank you to Rowman & Littlefield for taking a chance on a story about a relatively unknown figure on the fringes of the Australian crime story—this book required something of a leap of faith, and I will be forever grateful that you were willing to take that leap with me! More specifically, a massive thank you to my editor, Becca Rohde Beurer, for shepherding me through the entire process and believing in this book from the outset. Every author needs an editor like you, and I am so happy we got the opportunity to work together to bring this project to life.

Telling these stories would not have been possible without the efforts of the individuals and organizations who have worked over the decades (centuries, even) to preserve the historical record. This book grew out of a desire to take the enigmatic character of Jack Rooklyn and bring him out of the shadows for the first time—a task that simply would not have been possible without the assistance of state archives, libraries, historical newspaper collections, court records, and similar documents. A special thanks to the Queensland State Archives, the Queensland State Library, the National Archives of Australia, Trove, and the City of Sydney Library. The historians, librarians, and archivists working at institutions like these (among others) are truly the unsung heroes of projects like this, and too often go uncelebrated.

I am well aware that I am in a very fortunate position in that I work in a profession that not only allows me to work on passion projects like this book, but actively *encourages* it as well. I began this book while working at Middlesex University in London, and I want to thank the team there for always giving me the space to be creative and to dream. In particular, I want to thank the researchers at Middlesex's Centre for Abuse and Trauma Studies (CATS), who continue to give me the opportunity to develop my skills and grow as an academic. I ended up finishing this book at the University of New Haven, in the United States of America. I also want to thank my colleagues from the Henry C. Lee College of Criminal Justice and Forensic Sciences, who are unquestionably the best in the field. I have learned so much since joining UNH, and look forward to learning (and contributing) more in the years to come.

I genuinely believe that the best thing that any writer can do to improve their work is just to write, as often as possible. I have been privileged enough to work with some great research and writing collaborators on this journey, each of whom I have learned from in different ways, the lessons of which you can see shine through this book. Notably to Matt Allen, Tom Kehoe, Elena Martellozzo, Paula Bradbury, Emma Short, Stewart Frost, and Daniel Sailofsky—it has been a pleasure working with each of you, and thank you.

Within academia, historical criminology is a relatively recent addition to the pantheon, but I truly believe it has one of the most supportive research communities that exists. I have been lucky enough to work with the Australian and New Zealand Historical Criminology Network, and want to give thanks to Vicky Nagy and the rest of that team for doing such a great job at ushering in historical criminology in my home country. I also want to thank David Churchill for his tireless support, and for everything he has done for the field as well. Similarly, I want to thank the executive board of the American Society of Criminology Division of Historical Criminology, who I have worked with as vice chair over recent years. Brendan Dooley, Matt Vogel, Alex Tepperman, Lizzie Seal, Chris Mullins, Bonnie Ernst—you all rock, and are doing great things to champion historical criminology in the States.

On the home front, you cannot embark on a project like this without the support of friends and family, who listen to you rant and rave, encourage you to keep going, tell you straight up that you need to take a break, or even (sometimes) try to help you put the pieces of the mystery together. This book was also written on the tail end of the COVID-19 pandemic, during which time I discovered just how much the people that fate puts in your path can become a family. So, in no particular order, this is to John, Rosie, Luke, Naomi, Rima, Jacqui, Myrna, Kristina, Jake, and the many others who were there when I was writing this. Also deserving of a thank you here are my family, all of whom are my biggest cheerleaders. There are far too many of you to mention, but I do legitimately appreciate all the support. One that does earn a specific mention is my mother, Cindy Bleakley, who is my biggest hype man, the Flavor Flav to my Chuck D, on every occasion. Thank you for always backing me, and then asking, "What's next?" You asked, and this is what came next.

The final person I want to thank is the most important in a lot of ways, not the least because she is obliged to deal with me on a daily basis. Taylor, you are such a major part of everything I do. You keep me on track, carry the load when I am on a mad writing binge, and now probably know far more about the inner workings of the Australian organized crime scene than you ever thought you would (or, let's be honest, would like). Thank you for listening. Thank you for helping shrug off every setback. Thank you for asking the questions that need to be asked. Thank you for all of it. Thank you for being *you*.

Introduction

A Cigar-Smoking Enigma

In the end, it took the jury in the trial of Israel "Jack" Rooklyn just over a day to reach its verdict. It had been a long journey to arrive at this point. Initially charged with several counts of official corruption in July 1989, his first trial had been abandoned in August 1991 after the Brisbane District Court determined that media reports about Rooklyn had potentially prejudiced the jury.[1] To be fair, press coverage was hard to avoid. This trial was the latest in a cavalcade of events that had captivated the Australian public for more than four years before the first trial collapsed. In May 1987, an explosive report broadcasted by ABC's *Four Corners* program had sent shockwaves through Australia's "Sunshine State," Queensland. Informed by the stories of a litany of whistle-blowers from the state's seedy underbelly, journalist Chris Masters painted the picture of a society where graft and corruption were rampant, and where powerful vice peddlers were given free rein to operate by paying into a protection system referred to as "the Joke."[2] Then managed by retired Licensing Branch officer Jack Reginald Herbert, some version of the Joke had existed since at least the late 1950s in a Queensland Police Force (QPF) where vice was tolerated and corrupt police held positions of authority. The revelations of *Four Corners*' "The Moonlight State" report triggered a formal inquiry into the allegations of misconduct in the QPF, and, over the course of two years, the Fitzgerald Inquiry revealed the scale of corruption, not just in the police force but in Queensland society more broadly.[3] Perhaps the biggest scalp claimed in the aftermath of Fitzgerald was that of Police

Commissioner Terence "Terry" Lewis, charged with more than a dozen counts of official corruption (and a couple of perjury charges as well).[4]

Although Lewis may have been the most high-profile figure to face court as a consequence of the Fitzgerald Inquiry, Rooklyn was not far behind him in terms of public prominence. Charged with bribing Lewis via Herbert, his role as a corruptor of senior Queensland police (and politicians) belied his reputation as an iconic Australian sportsman, a multiple winner of line honors in the classic Sydney to Hobart yacht race.[5] For observers from the neighboring state of New South Wales, the revelation that Rooklyn was involved in bribery in his business dealings may have been less of a surprise, though, as over a decade earlier, such claims had placed him at the center of the Moffitt Commission's investigation into the alleged penetration of the New South Wales club scene by organized crime. Moffitt was told that Rooklyn's employer, the American poker machine manufacturer Bally, had been deeply infiltrated by the US Mafia and that, through Bally, American organized crime figures had struck a corrupt bargain with local criminals to take over the clubs by threat or, if necessary, force.[6] Moffitt never could prove that Bally's push into New South Wales's clubs was part of a concerted Mafia plot, but did offer strong criticism of Bally Australia's managing director Rooklyn, who he said made attempts to (and, likely, succeeded in) bribing the detectives tasked with investigating the company's criminal links.[7] Despite this exposure, Rooklyn survived and was never charged with any offenses related to the Moffitt Commission. It would not be for another 18 years after Moffitt warned of Rooklyn's alleged habit for corruption that the Australian amusement machine czar would finally sit in that Brisbane courtroom on the evening of Friday, May 22, 1992, anxiously waiting to learn his fate.

There is a long-standing fascination with local true crime stories in Australia, grounded in foundational narratives of convict heritage and the veneration of the much-mythologized bushranger archetype. Rosalind Smith asserts that "crime has a particular significance in historical and contemporary constructions of Australian nationalism . . . a tradition of national mythmaking surrounding criminal figures . . . indicate[s] the centrality of true crime and its narration to formations of Australian national identity."[8] Smith goes on to note that the cultural capital of these stories goes beyond a macabre interest in "the dark side" and is instead "defined by a set of truth claims coupled with the detailed re-creation of lived experiences of crime . . . beneath their detailed, singular histories of a specific set of events—the lines in the book—they are haunted by a diffuse, unresolved and suppressed set of stories."[9] In a sense, the true crime genre speaks to an Australia grappling with its own, sometimes uncomfortable, past. However, it is more than just a recount or (in the view of some detractors) glorification of historical criminals. When done well, the true crime genre can provide a gateway for its audience into a distinct period of Australian history, used as a vehicle to chart the growth of a nation that has often proven to be prone to corruption and criminality in its institutions. Throughout Australian history, we see the cultural imaginary of an idyllic, isolated island nation shattered by revelations that beneath the surface there lies an undercurrent of crime where even those most trusted to keep us safe, our police and politicians, are clandestinely working in conjunction with the very criminals they purport to stand against.[10]

Both Fitzgerald and Moffitt, in their own way, represented a challenge to the perspective that Australia was immune to the social problems facing places like the United States, but they were not alone in doing so—they were just two among a cavalcade of people to expose the *real* state of Australian society in the 20th century, a roll call that includes the likes of Frank Costigan, Donald Stewart, Philip Woodward, Barry Beach, Robert Kennedy, and James Wood, to name but a few.[11] The recurrent nature of the somewhat ritualistic cleansing that occurs via such public inquiries begs the question of whether the imaginary of Australia as an idyllic safe haven is truly the most prevalent, or if our fascination with criminality and true crime stories exposes a more complex side to our shared cultural identity. John Scott attributes this phenomenon at least in part to "the space of national mythmaking . . . shift[ing] from the colonial space and the outback to the post-colonial spaces of beach and suburbia" where new narratives emerge that demonstrate "a sense of discomfort—isolation and disorientation—with being in the Australian landscape."[12] Especially in the post-Menzies era wherein suburban normalcy became aspirational, true crime stories serve as testament to Australians that their country is *not* as idyllic as the establishment would have them believe and, in doing so, vindicates their own contentious relationship with the country they live in. Gregg and Wilson support this view on the cultural resonance of true crime in Australia in their more recent coverage of the popular true crime television drama *Underbelly*, a series they argue "constitutes a televisual history of Australia's present that countervails the official pieties of the ordinary that characterized the Howard years."[13] This idea that the popularity of true crime in Australia is the product of an enforced mundanity promoted by conservative political regimes recurs in the literature. It is a theory that is also validated in the judicial inquiries that captured public attention, like Fitzgerald, which took place under an ultraconservative traditionalist government that—when exposed as being riddled with corruption—provided a great degree of *schadenfreude* to a critical public.[14]

If the Australian canon is littered with true crime stories, what then does Jack Rooklyn's story add to the existing landscape? Indeed, prominent individuals that appear throughout this story, like Lennie McPherson, George Freeman, and Abraham Saffron, have all been well covered in Australian true crime literature to the point that, in some respects, they have assumed the status of modern-day Ned Kelly figures—mythologized to such an extent that they now exist as an essential part of the cultural zeitgeist.[15] This makes the Rooklyn enigma even more curious. Though at the center of events like the Moffitt Commission and the Fitzgerald Inquiry, he nevertheless remains a largely elusive figure—a bogeyman on the fringes of the true crime narrative whose presence is often mentioned, but rarely explained. Rooklyn is treated by much of the extant literature on the subject as a sort of caricature who embodies the feared incursion of American organized crime. He is described as "a tough cigar-chomping" gaming czar in the archetypal Las Vegas style, and has even been apocryphally described by some as "an expatriate American."[16] Such a basic error in Rooklyn's backstory may simply be the result of a mistaken understanding; however, it also underscores the importance of a closer examination of his history in order to develop a stronger understanding of a man who, one way or another, operated at the nexus of organized crime in Australia for decades.

On closer look, Rooklyn's story cannot be reduced to a myopic recount of one of the inquiries he was central to, such as Moffitt or Fitzgerald, although it does seek to discuss these events with Rooklyn's role pushed to the foreground, rather than lingering in the shadows as he has tended to do in the past. When Rooklyn is thrust out of the shadows of the conventional true crime narrative, what we discover is a sweeping tale that goes far beyond the seedy clubs of Sydney or Brisbane; instead, a story emerges that spans four continents over more than eight decades, from Rooklyn's birth in England's industrial northwest to Capone's Chicago and the dynamic postwar landscape of Southeast Asia.[17] On a personal level, it charts the rise of a young Jewish immigrant in New South Wales as he hustled and worked his way up in society to become an entertainment impresario in Depression-era (and, later, wartime) Australia. It answers the question of how someone like Rooklyn could become enmeshed with an American gaming company like Bally in an association that came to define the rest of his life.[18] Not only that, Rooklyn's story is not just one of a rise, but also a reinvention. After the Moffitt Commission and other events occurring in the United States torpedoed his career with Bally, Rooklyn was forced to carve a new path in Queensland that put him on a collision course with the likes of Terry Lewis, Tony Fitzgerald, and, ultimately, that verdict in the Brisbane District Court in 1992.[19] Rooklyn's story does not have a positive outcome, but it nevertheless is an intriguing tale of triumph tarred with corruption, and of a person so important in the story of Australian crime that has, for too long, been neglected.

Though Rooklyn's story is interesting enough on its own merits, it is even more valuable because of what it tells us about Australia and its place in the world over the course of more than eight decades. Our story begins with a family like so many others in the early 20th century, leaving the United Kingdom for Australia to start a new life—from there, Rooklyn's rise (and eventual fall) can be traced against the singular backdrop of the period, impacted by events of a much bigger scale, like the Great Depression and World War II. Historians have routinely written of the

1940s as the time when Australian society began to turn away from Mother England and toward the United States as a dominant cultural influence, prompted (in part) by the influx of American troops stationed in the country during the years it played host to the General Headquarters of the Allied forces in the Pacific.[20] Amid this shift in the cultural zeitgeist, Rooklyn emerged as a preeminent entertainment impresario, at the cutting edge of the boom in such "American" habits as arcade culture and machine-based gambling, like poker machines. Somewhat less favorably, Rooklyn was also central to concerns, warranted or not, of another American invasion, reflected in the fears of a potential US Mafia "takeover" of Australian organized crime. These events did not occur in isolation, instead as part of a transformative era wherein Australia and the United States moved increasingly closer together in so many facets of life, from the cultural (through American music and films) to the political (as partners in the Vietnam War). Understanding the tangible concerns that Rooklyn and Bally were agents of American organized crime must take into account this broader context, and the seismic shifts in Australian society that were taking place at the same time. As such, Rooklyn's story represents more than a simple true crime narrative; it speaks to an important time in the nation's history, with far more extensive social and cultural implications.

It would be easy to characterize Rooklyn's story in the context of the rising influence that "the American" exerted on Australian life in the postwar era. In truth, it is much grander. In the past, Rooklyn has been treated in a rather functional way, entering the true crime narrative around the time of the Moffitt Commission or the Fitzgerald Inquiry as an archetypal (perhaps stereotypical) corrupter of police.[21] Closer examination contextualizes his actions as the regional representative of a major gambling corporation that was fighting its own battles to shed the perception of being Mafia-controlled, which had become so pervasive that it was actively obstructing Bally's attempts to expand.[22] Just as Bally is a key part of Rooklyn's story, and that of organized crime in Australia, so too is Rooklyn and Australia part of *its* story. It is often an Australian tendency to consider how other countries, in particular global superpowers like the United States, impact domestic affairs without considering how events in Australia resonate outward. It becomes a shock then, when names like Rooklyn's emerge in unexpected places, such as in the Nevada Gaming Commission's 1977 deliberations on sanctioning Bally's operations in that territory.[23] When the events involving Rooklyn are explored with a wider lens, a picture comes into focus that extends beyond illicit payments to police or standing over clubs and forcing them to carry Bally products. Instead, a compelling narrative emerges of a company pervasively affected by the infiltration of organized crime figures including the Genovese Family, Meyer Lansky, and the Chicago Outfit.[24] We see similar links between these American crime figures and the Australian criminal milieu, who sought out collaboration with the Mafia in the 1960s and 1970s in a coordinated campaign to capitalize on the considerable profits to be made from becoming part of the Mafia family. This was not limited to connections with Rooklyn and Bally, but extended to drug trafficking operations like the Sydney Connection, another example of the closeness with which certain sectors of the Australian and American criminal community operated in the 1960s and 1970s.[25] Rooklyn's story is an important piece of the puzzle, and so too are the stories that spin off from it, which provide greater insight into how Australia "fit" in the international landscape of organized crime during the same period.

The genre of true crime has often been criticized as treating illegal acts in a sensationalized way that contributes to glorifying real-world criminals who have done actual real-world harm to others. These are not new critiques, by any means; the persistent mythologization of Jack the Ripper is drawn from this tradition of pulp journalism, and Australia's own Robin Hood-esque figure, Ned Kelly, has become a foundational element of the collective national identity along with his iconic "garbage-can" helmet.[26] More recently, the *Underbelly* series and its coverage of the Melbourne gangland wars made cult heroes of crime bosses like Carl Williams, venerated as a tracksuit-wearing suburbanite who rose to power by taking on the establishment—in this case, eliminating Melbourne's traditional criminal hierarchy in a bloody, drug-fueled revenge-fantasy.[27] In this context, these reasonable criticisms directed at true crime explain the reluctance of many researchers to engage in such forms of storytelling. However, there is a growing movement within criminology that champions the essential role that stories play in society's understanding of criminality. As Presser and Sandberg describe it: "[W]e know ourselves and others in the world in large part through stories: they inform and animate us and thus guide our actions."[28] In the same way that a sensationalized (or glorified) narrative like that of Carl Williams in *Underbelly* may have a criminogenic effect, so too can a well-constructed narrative influence the public's relationship with crime in other ways. Aspden and Hayward argue that "as long as society has recognized the concept of crime, a shadow process of making sense of criminal transgression has followed," using narratives as a vehicle for negotiating complex and confronting ideas.[29]

There are tangible implications that arise from the specific way stories are told, and the motivations of the people telling them. Take the story of police corruption in Queensland, for example. In the late 1980s, the Fitzgerald Inquiry was a seminal event that revealed long-standing, entrenched rackets that had existed in the state's police force for at least a decade and stretched all the way to the commissioner's office. Fitzgerald's version quickly became the definitive story of the Queensland Police Force, so it is easy to forget that this was not always the case. Fitzgerald was not the first to examine similar claims of police corruption, but previous inquiries were stymied by a variety of factors, from intentional interference to restrictive terms of reference.[30] Had Fitzgerald's predecessors, like Harry Gibbs or Geoffrey Lucas, been provided the same (generally) unobstructed mandate to tell the story of police corruption in Queensland, the very history of the state itself may have changed as a result. Instead, it took a *specific* person to tell that story within a *specific* sociocultural and historical context, underscoring the importance of appreciating not just the narrative itself, but also the broader context in which stories are told.

Narrative criminology acknowledges that the concept of objective truth is a challenging (maybe impossible) goal to achieve in the storytelling process. However, as Sveinung Sandberg points out, while "for many researchers, eliciting the truth from participants is a hallmark of sound research . . . discerning the 'truth' is not always important." Instead, it is the "multitude of stories people tell [that] reflect, and help us understand, the complex nature of values, identities, cultures and communities."[31] Just as we cannot take at face value the findings of Moffitt or even Fitzgerald, mediated by the terms and conditions (and limits) of their position, neither can we take the direct autobiographical account of people like Rooklyn as gospel. The precise reality of what is detailed here may never be truly known, and yet taking in the different "versions" of reality provided by various actors is helpful in its own right. Not only does it allow for a more holistic and complex portrayal of events and the people involved in them, but it also gives some level of insight into the ways that the people in this story sought to construct (and control) their own identities as "characters" in the true crime canon.

To tell this story, it was essential to approach events with a process that examines the narrative's sociological and criminological foci using historical methods and methodology. In previous work with Thomas J. Kehoe, we explained the transdisciplinary field of *historical criminology* as a fairly broad spectrum (in practice) that stretches from conventional sociological criminology at one extreme to purist historical research at the other, with historical criminology falling at some point or another along this continuum depending on factors like the aims, methods, and methodology (or *way of interpreting*) the research subject.[32] Whereas some research may be concerned predominantly with the historical and others may lean more toward the contemporary (drawing on the past in a limited fashion), the historical criminologist essentially aims to interpret their foci with a sense of temporal awareness, accounting for the context within which both historical and contemporary events take place so as to better understand them and (in some cases) project or predict how lessons from the past can be applied to current or future practice.[33] When it comes to conceiving of historical criminology as a spectrum, this book undoubtedly falls closer toward the historical than it does the contemporary, focused as it is on telling Rooklyn's story and positioning it in the broader context of the period in which events occurred. However, there is doubtless a certain utility in understanding this story for those working in the contemporary. Aside from providing a more multidimensional perspective on events in our recent past, it also highlights the importance of examining organized crime and corruption through a wider lens. To this day the opaque and impenetrable connections between organized crime and legitimate business, as well as the international scope and scale of organized crime, continues to confound researchers. The narrative here offers insight into the numerous opportunities in the 1960s, 1970s, and 1980s to conduct a thorough investigation into recurring accusations of criminal activity occurring across New South Wales and Queensland. In doing so, it emphasizes the challenges and sensitivities of addressing covert organized crime—particularly in a sociopolitical context in which corruption is proven to be rife and widely tolerated. Here, the basic tenets of historical and narrative criminology agree: Telling stories like this is necessary, both in terms of understanding where we are coming from, how it impacts on the way we operate today, and, further, how it may influence the direction we travel in the future.

The research conducted to pull together this account of Rooklyn's life and the lives of those who came into his orbit was directed in large part by engaging with materials produced as part of the judicial inquiries in which he featured, such as the Moffitt Commission and the Fitzgerald Inquiry. In addition to the final report of these inquiries, the raw archival data was examined wherever possible, including transcripts and evidence exhibits presented at the time of each commission. In doing so, it was possible to construct Rooklyn's story from a multitude of perspectives. Though fundamentally unreliable, it is crucial to include the voice of crime figures like Lennie McPherson at the Moffitt Commission as he denied involvement in any standover activity, in the same way it is essential to engage with the story told by former police officer Jack Herbert as he outlined the systems and structures of corruption in Queensland. As noted, however, the persistent issue when it comes to Rooklyn is the fairly basic depictions of who he was in these inquiries, relegating a truly multifaceted individual to cardboard "villain" status on too many occasions. Constructing Rooklyn's past beyond Moffitt and Fitzgerald demanded a systematic search of local and international news media, from the local Hunter Valley newspapers in the small town where he grew up to media sources in Singapore where he made his fortune, and even digitized versions of amusement machine trade magazines from the United States in the 1960s, which helped fill gaps that were otherwise elusive.

Other gaps were filled by digitized recordings of conversations with Rooklyn himself, returning some degree of agency to him in the retelling of his own life story.[34] Personal accounts were used where possible to others who previously went on the record to tell their side of the story, such as US mafioso Jimmy "The Weasel" Fratianno, whose autobiographical account of his time in the Mafia was highly useful to contextualize some of the fringe elements of later events involving Australian criminals in the 1970s.[35] Finally, as the story extended to places like the United States, the archival research was greatly aided by the release of investigation files by agencies like the FBI and CIA, where the monitoring of organized crime figures like Fratianno, Dino Cellini, and Meyer Lansky offered a different perspective on their activity during the same period that they became involved with the Australian milieu, shedding a different light on the variables that influenced either their involvement with Bally or their decision to go into business with Australian criminal syndicates. As mentioned, too many previous accounts of these events have cast Rooklyn as a shadowy organized crime associate without considering that such characterization demands further exploration of exactly who his associations (if they existed) were with and, importantly, what this meant for Australia and Australian crime in real terms. By conducting a more expansive archival research, it has been possible to bring a more developed context to these events and relationships in a way that has not been achieved to such a comprehensive level before.

Previously, the telling of Rooklyn's story has been largely compartmentalized, with researchers either looking almost exclusively at his role within the Sydney milieu and the events around Moffitt or, for those more concerned with Queensland, focusing predominantly on his connections to former police commissioner Terry Lewis and his role in police corruption in that state. Similarly, the narrative to follow comes in two phases—encompassing Rooklyn's time in Sydney and his activities in Brisbane—however, just as Rooklyn worked between both states for most of his career, so too does the narrative dip back and forth between the two as it progresses, more concerned with detailing what Rooklyn and those associated with him were doing than creating arbitrary delineations between "the Sydney period" and "the Brisbane era." In Chapter

2 we explore Rooklyn's origin story in its early stages, picking up with his birth in the industrial northwest of England and following him through his formative years as a young Jewish immigrant in New South Wales during the Depression era, finally making his name as a vaudeville promoter and amusement machine czar in the midst of World War II and, later, in Southeast Asia. From there, Chapter 3 sees Rooklyn's return to Australia in the late 1950s and introduces some of the people who later became closely linked to his story through the Moffitt Commission, like Sydney criminals Lennie McPherson and George Freeman and (importantly) American Mafia associate Joseph Dan Testa. The events leading to the Moffitt Commission and the events of that inquiry are detailed in Chapter 4, which explains how Moffitt came so close to unraveling an organized crime plot to infiltrate the Sydney club scene, but stopped just short of bringing together all the pieces of the puzzle.

By and large, Chapter 5 leaves Rooklyn aside for a moment to recount how others mentioned at the Moffitt Commission continued to cultivate links with the US Mafia after the inquiry with the apparent aim to muscle in on the newly legal casino industry and, in the case of Murray Riley at least, the opportunities of large-scale narcotics trafficking. In Chapter 6 the impact of Moffitt on Rooklyn are laid bare, as he is forced out of Bally as the company attempts to salvage its reputation. In turn, both we and Rooklyn himself look north to Queensland, a state where corruption was already endemic in the late 1970s. Chapter 7 explores Rooklyn's battle with local poker machine manufacturers in the early 1980s, as well as one of his most successful schemes: bribing the state police commissioner to ensure that gambling machines remained *illegal*, giving him the opportunity to corner the local market with his own products, under the corrupt protection of Queensland police and politicians. Finally, we arrive at the Fitzgerald Inquiry in Chapter 8 and see how the corrupt system that Rooklyn was a part of in Queensland was unraveled, ending in the once triumphant gaming czar in front of a jury, charged with corruption.

However, before this story begins in earnest, it is important to recognize that while Rooklyn is the focus of this story, there is another character that is just as important as he is, if not more so in some respects:

the Bally Manufacturing corporation. Though Rooklyn was a proactive businessman who no doubt would have found success regardless, it was through Bally that he attained much of his power and cachet as a businessman and, indeed, the connections to Bally that inextricably linked him to the American Mafia in the collective public consciousness. Thus, to understand Rooklyn's story we must first turn our attention to Bally to understand where its reputation for (and proven association with) organized crime came from and assess the company's own claims at the Moffitt Commission that it had purged itself of Mafia influence by the mid-1970s. While we will return to Rooklyn soon, this story truly begins in late 1931, in an office in downtown Chicago where another entrepreneurial figure named Ray Moloney was about to release his new pinball machine the *Ballyhoo* onto the market, and into the world.[36]

I

All the Bells and Whistles

Sitting in his fourth-floor office at 310 West Erie Street in Chicago's downtown River North neighborhood, Ray Moloney truly believed that he was onto a winner . . . he just did not know what to call it yet. For around six years, Moloney had been managing Midwest Novelty Co., a subsidiary of the Lion Manufacturing Company, which he had played a role in running since arriving in Chicago from Cleveland in 1921.[1] Initially, Midwest had been focused on the production of punchboards, a lottery-style game that was popular at the time, but under Moloney's leadership Midwest (and Lion Manufacturing) were becoming increasingly involved in a new trade: coin-operated amusement machines. Throughout the mid- to late 1920s, Midwest became a major distributor of such machines, and so were already tapped into the market in mid-1931 when a new coin-operated pastime called pinball began to experience a boom in popularity in the United States.[2] That amusement games like pinball attained a certain level of popularity in the early 1930s is both shocking and unsurprising. Though so many Americans were experiencing the poverty caused by the economic turmoil of the Great Depression, it was this same climate of austerity that drove many to seek out parlor games like pinball, a simple pleasure during Prohibition when the very act of going for a beer was criminalized.[3] Not that the Volstead Act stopped the people of Chicago, though—less than 500 yards from Moloney's office on West Erie Street was one of the city's oldest speakeasy bars, the Green Door Tavern, known as a preferred watering hole for some of the city's most notorious gangsters, like (by then deceased)

North Side Gang boss Dion O'Banion.[4] The persistent success of places like the Green Door showed that, despite the hard times Americans were facing, there was always a market for entertainment.

Moloney had jumped on the pinball craze a few months earlier and started purchasing machines to distribute, called Baffle Ball, from David Gottlieb. However, while Gottlieb's factory was producing as many as 400 units of Baffle Ball per day, the manufacturer simply could not meet the public demand, putting Moloney in a position where he could not satisfy all the requests he was receiving to purchase the game.[5] This posed a serious problem: Moloney wanted to corner the market early, and if buyers came to him and he did not have any games to sell them, they would simply go elsewhere and Moloney would see his monopoly quickly vanish. The shortage forced him to make a logical, yet consequential, decision: He needed to go into the coin-operated machine manufacturing business. It took some time to convince his silent partners from Lion Manufacturing, Joe Linehan and Charlie Weldt, but in October 1931 (around the same time Capone was being sentenced for tax evasion only a few blocks away) Moloney was given the go-ahead to pursue his plans for domination of the coin-operated industry.[6] Within a month, Moloney sourced a new machine design from a pair of designers in rural Illinois, and production was set to begin. All that remained as he sat in his River North office was to give his new creation a name, something that people would remember and would become shorthand for pinball machines in the same way the brand name Band-Aid became synonymous for medical plasters in the decade prior.[7] Moloney's mind wandered to the then-popular magazine *Ballyhoo*, which debuted that same year and was widely credited for revitalizing the satirical genre in the United States.[8] The word was already on everyone's lips. In November 1931, Moloney's "Ballyhoo" machine was born. Ballyhoo was not just the name of Moloney's first manufactured machine, it also provided the basis for his new business name. In early 1932, Moloney founded a new company as a subsidiary of Lion Manufacturing, with the sole purpose of developing and selling coin-operated amusement machines. Moloney called it the Bally Manufacturing Company, a name that would come to dominate the world of gambling, both in the United States and farther afield.

Ballyhoo was notable as Bally's first real foray into the gaming business, but it did not stop there. By the end of the 1960s, it was the largest supplier of coin-operated amusement machines in the United States, its products making up 90 percent of the total Nevada market, including gambling mecca Las Vegas.[9] It is important to note, though, that just as Moloney did not invent the pinball machine, nor did Bally invent slot machines. As early as 1876, inventors were dabbling in the creation of a mechanized forms of gambling. "Guessing Bank," built by New Yorker Edward McLoughlin, was a simplistic early version of amusement machine gaming where a punter would insert a coin that would, in turn, cause a dial to spin and land on a random number—if the gambler guessed the correct number, they would win a prize.[10] For the next fifteen years, this rudimentary gaming device remained the most popular form of machine-based gambling, but it would soon be supplanted with the evolution of the poker machine, in the early 1890s. Though working on the same general premise of a mechanical spinning reel (or, in this case, a set of reels) producing randomized results, the complexity of the poker machine went far beyond the first "guessing games" like that created by McLoughlin. When a coin was inserted, the poker machine's five reels would spin, each landing on a random playing card. This set of cards would constitute a "hand" (as in traditional poker), and when a player received a "winning hand," a payout was made by the venue where the machine was located.[11]

The poker machine was a major advancement in the coin-operated industry, yet it remained an imperfect device for hospitality businesses; because of the need for attendants to monitor the machines and offer manual payouts, the original poker machine required more human investment and, thus, was not built for the sort of high-quantity operations seen in gaming venues today. To achieve this, a merger of technology was needed, combining the entertainment value of the poker machine with the easy automation of another coin-operated amusement game, the slot machine. The slot machine was a much more intuitive prospect. Invented by John Light in upstate New York in 1892, when a gambler inserted coins, they would either fall straight into the game's cash box or, alternatively, trigger a secondary mechanism where both the original coin *and* a second would be released, effectively doubling the player's money.[12] Unlike the problem with poker machines, the issue with slot machines was not the time that went into operating them, but rather the simplicity of the gameplay—it was, in short, boring. It was not until amusement machine pioneer Charles Fey, experienced in both poker and slot machines, developed the "Liberty Bell" in the final years of the 19th century that a machine similar to the modern slot machine was created. Cutting the number of reels from five (in a poker machine) to three enabled Fey to successfully create the required mechanisms to allow for automatic payout.[13] He replaced the playing cards painted on each reel with various images like stars and bells, which, when aligned, resulted in a payday for gamblers. Fey's creation became the new industry standard, copied and imitated by various other companies as the 20th century dawned and the era of automated slot machines arrived in earnest.

There was a stigma associated with slot machines from (almost) the very beginning of their existence, and a big part of this stigma came from their associations with organized crime. In places where they were popular, like Fey's hometown of San Francisco, the machines were considered a predatory way for shopkeepers and bar owners to cheat their patrons out of money—the furor led San Francisco to ban slot machines altogether in 1909, a policy that would extend to the entire state of California by 1911, with other jurisdictions following suit in the years that followed.[14] Existing concerns about the impact that slot machines had on the vice trade were only exacerbated when Prohibition came into effect in 1920, banning the production and sale of alcohol in the United States by way of constitutional amendment.[15] In theory, this policy would have had disastrous knock-on effects for slot machine purveyors, who relied heavily on venues like bars and saloons to purchase and host their games. By now, though, the lessons of Prohibition are well documented; rather than stem the flow of booze in the country, Prohibition put control of illegal alcohol firmly in the grasp of organized crime, which operated and protected speakeasies like the Green Door Tavern for a hefty profit.[16] It is perhaps unsurprising, then, that the gambling machine industry found a home in Chicago, Illinois—a city where organized crime syndicates like Capone's Chicago Outfit and Dion O'Banion's North Side Gang held sway over the same venues where machines were being bought and played. Indeed, some linked these infamous gangsters to the origins of Lion Manufacturing and, in turn, Bally itself. In his memoir, gangster-turned-government witness Jimmy "The Weasel" Fratianno (who will assume a much more significant role later in this story) recalls prominent Chicago Outfit mafioso Johnny Roselli telling him that "the Chicago family controls Bally and has controlled it right from the beginning . . . going back now to Capone and [Capone's lieutenant and eventual successor Frank] Nitti."[17] Though Roselli's contention has never been proven, there is little doubt that, in chasing his fortune in the games business, Moloney was operating in the same circles as the legendary "Scarface" Capone and his crew.

Like Capone, Ray Moloney was not a Chicago native. He was born in Cleveland, Ohio, in November 1899 as one of nine children to Irish immigrant parents.[18] At first he followed his father into the steel business, but Moloney was a natural operator with an entrepreneurial spirit and soon left the Midwest to achieve the American dream, a life that was something more than his parents had. From the oilfields of Wyoming and Oklahoma to agricultural work in southern California, and even working as a cook in New Orleans, Moloney tried his hand at whatever he could, but ultimately his luck ran out and he hitched a ride on a freight train back to Cleveland.[19] Moloney was therefore young, but experienced in life, when as a 21-year-old he left home again, this time heading to Chicago on the hunt for work. He found it with a pair of Irishmen like himself, Linehan and Weldt, who first worked with Moloney at a printworks in 1921 before the duo struck out on their own the next year, bringing him with them as a foreman.[20] Linehan Printing had a profitable business producing gambling punchboards, and, impressed with Moloney's enthusiasm, the business's owners put him in charge when they decided to separate the punchboard trade from their regular printing work by forming a new subsidiary division in 1922.

The new division of Linehan Printing did not have an identity of its own until Moloney asked Linehan for some stationary to get started. His boss handed him a stack of papers the printers had been commissioned to produce, but had never been picked up. It was an expedient move, and a fateful one. The stationary was for a company named "Lion

Manufacturing," and thus Moloney's Lion was created based on no more than reused stationary.[21] Soon, Lion consumed the original Linehan Printing, which was no more. Moloney, on the other hand, was given even more opportunities to show his skills in the entertainment trade. When Linehan and Weldt decided to form a separate company to handle the manufacture and distribution of novelty goods and amusement games like the punchboards in 1925, Maloney became a partner in the new enterprise, Midwest Novelty Co.[22] At Midwest, Moloney continued to grow the business, exploring new avenues like the marketing and distribution of slot machines for the first time. It would be six years before Midwest would develop its own machine, the Ballyhoo, but as Prohibition stretched on seemingly without end, Moloney carved a position for himself as one of the top amusement men in Chicago, one of the top markets in the nation.

Bally's entry into the coin-operated machine market could not have come at a better time; on March 19, 1931, the same year that Moloney decided to move into games manufacturing, the western state of Nevada voted to legalize gambling. The decision was to some extent a last-ditch effort to bring capital to the state, which had been suffering for more than a decade through a collapse in the commercial viability of the local mining industry. That precarious state, combined with the impact of the Great Depression, which arrived with a thud in the 1929 stock market crash, may have been the death knell for Nevada if not for Governor Fred Balzar's push to legalize almost all forms of gambling, from table games to slot machines.[23] The first casino license under the new laws was issued to the Northern Club, on Fremont Street in Las Vegas, in 1931—many others soon followed, cashing in on the liberalized gambling regulations and the boom of (mostly male) workers flocking to the region for the construction of the nearby Boulder Dam.[24]

The sudden prosperity (and opportunity) of Las Vegas did not escape organized crime figures who, in most major cities in the United States during the Great Depression/Prohibition era, controlled illegal gambling in some form. The first property known to be acquired by organized crime was the El Cortez resort and casino on Fremont Street, scooped up for $600,000 by Jewish mobsters Benjamin "Bugsy" Siegel and Meyer

Lansky in early 1945 when the Los Angeles Police Department began to crack down on their existing gambling rackets in that major market.[25] The El Cortez was the first case of Mafia infiltration in Vegas, but far from the last. Seeing the city's gambling culture as an opportunity for (legal and illegal) profits, Siegel muscled in on struggling entrepreneur Billy Wilkerson and took over his project to build The Flamingo Hotel and Casino on the Vegas Strip.[26] The Flamingo was a seismic step in the mob's campaign to take control of Vegas, but a fatal one for Siegel himself. Suspected of skimming profits from the project even before the casino opened its doors, Siegel's longtime friend and business partner Lansky greenlit a hit on Siegel. He was shot to death at his Beverly Hills home on June 20, 1947, just six months after The Flamingo's grand opening.[27]

Siegel's death marked the start of a transitional period in organized crime's control of Vegas. Though Siegel and Lansky enjoyed close ties to the Italian Mafia via their connection to bosses like Charles "Lucky" Luciano and Frank Costello, as Jewish men they were not permitted to be members of any particular "family."[28] Vegas's inherent profitability plus the lack of an existing, traditional organized crime presence and the removal of Siegel's early control over the city created a situation where it was seen as open territory. Even though mobsters from all over the United States soon had a stake in Vegas, it was the Chicago Outfit that used its superior financial resources and power to take the most advantage of the situation. With The Flamingo still struggling after Siegel's death, its new manager, Gus Greenbaum, received a $1 million loan to turn its fortune around from Tony "Joe Batters" Accardo, who had recently risen to lead the Chicago Outfit after his colleague Paul Ricca's forced retirement in 1947.[29]

Accardo was a stalwart gangster with a tough reputation. He reputedly received his nickname from Capone himself after murdering three traitors to the Outfit with a baseball bat. He was also allegedly one of Capone's gunmen in the 1929 St Valentine's Day Massacre, which virtually ended the rival North Side Gang.[30] Accardo was ruthless: When a new casino acquisition, the Riviera, failed to make money in its first three months of opening in 1955, he demanded former Flamingo manager

Greenbaum come out of retirement to turn its fortunes around. When Greenbaum at first refused, Accardo allegedly had the reluctant manager's sister-in-law murdered in her own bed—Greenbaum soon changed his mind.[31] It was, perhaps, Greenbaum who unwittingly helped Accardo consolidate his control of Vegas even further. On December 3, 1958, Greenbaum and his wife were found murdered after being accused of skimming from the Riviera.[32] It was after this that Accardo demanded order in Vegas, with a single "coordinator" overseeing organized crime operations in the city to look after everyone's best interests and ensure that another Greenbaum situation was avoided. As the dominant power in Vegas at the time, it was naturally up to Accardo's Chicago Outfit to choose this Vegas coordinator. In his seemingly benevolent effort to protect the interests of all mobsters in Vegas, Accardo secured control of the city for Chicago.[33]

While it was open season for gambling in Nevada, the rest of the country continued to restrict operations like a still-young Bally. At first, Moloney had jumped headfirst into the pinball industry with machines offering automatic payouts. In fact, the release of one such machine called Rocket in October 1933 was so profitable that it gave Moloney the capital he needed to buy out his partners Linehan and Weldt, taking full control of both Lion and Bally.[34] For the next decade, unrestrained by the more prudent nature of his former partners, Moloney became one of the biggest gambling machine producers in the country. In 1951, however, the US Congress passed the Johnson Act, which prohibited the interstate trade in gambling machines, broadly defined as anything from roulette wheels to slot machines and, later, payout pinball machines as well.[35] The Johnson Act "struck hard at manufacturers of the devices in Chicago, which long has been the center of the slot machine industry."[36] Two years later, an even more critical blow: the state of Illinois, where so many amusement machine companies were based, banned the production of slot machines entirely.[37]

While many coin-operated amusement operators suffered and began to lay off staff because of falling sales, Bally's Herbert Jones told the *Chicago Tribune* on January 3, 1951, that the Johnson Act would have a limited impact on the company, as they had "quit making the devices some time ago."[38] Jones was right, to an extent: Bally had allegedly found a way around the new laws by constructing a series of non-payout amusement games with many of the same working parts as the criminalized gambling-oriented alternative. Shipping these games was legal, but their design also allowed a skilled mechanic to strip the new machines for spare parts upon arrival, either fixing old games or even constructing new ones by cannibalizing the machines sent by Bally.[39] The Johnson Act remains in force in the United States, preventing the construction, sale, possession, and transportation of gambling machines in (or through) states where they are not specifically made legal, though increasing liberalization has meant that the industry does not suffer from the same pressures it did when the laws were first introduced in the early 1950s.[40] While Bally did experience a fall in profits because of the governmental intervention in gaming during this period, Bally remained one of the few coin-operated amusement companies to survive the 1950s, even when forced to abandon slot machine production and transition back into the amusement-only pinball business.

The Johnson Act and other laws regulating the gaming industry were not the only concern of organized crime in the late 1950s. At around the same time that Siegel was establishing the Mafia presence in Las Vegas, his partner Lansky had been focusing on setting up a similar racket in Cuba, just 90 miles off the coast of Florida. Lansky had negotiated a deal with dictator Fulgencio Batista at a meeting in New York City in the late 1940s; he and his criminal cohorts would take control of Cuba's racetracks and casinos and, in return, Batista would receive financial kickbacks.[41] Lansky called a meeting that became known as "the Havana conference" on December 22, 1946, just days before Siegel opened The Flamingo (in fact, it was at this meeting that it was decided Siegel had to be killed). Assembled were the most prolific mobsters of the era, from Luciano and other bosses of New York's Five Families to Accardo from Chicago and Santo Trafficante Jr. of the Tampa Family.[42] Here, Lansky laid out his plans for the future of mob-controlled gambling in Cuba, and the potential profits for all if they cooperated . . . and, for a time, Lansky's plan worked. Cuba became a gambling mecca off the east coast of the United States where both criminal and government profited—it is estimated that Batista "plundered Cuba to the tune of three hundred million dollars" in total during his time as leader, including millions in kickbacks from Mafia-owned gambling operations.[43]

Lansky's dream came to an end on New Year's Eve 1958 when a communist movement led by Fidel Castro toppled Batista and brought an end to gambling in Cuba. Lansky's casinos were looted and destroyed by revolutionaries, and Lansky himself only just managed to flee Cuba the day before Castro completed his march into Havana on January 8, 1959.[44] Lansky alone reportedly lost $7 million from his Cuban investments and was now forced to rely on residual profits from his Las Vegas operations, overseen by Accardo's Chicago Outfit in the aftermath of the Greenbaum affair.[45] The mob's experience during the Cuban Revolution is important to this story for several reasons: For one, it highlights the profits to be made from international expansion for companies like Bally, and the active steps being taken by mafiosos to take their rackets not just to Vegas, but to other countries as well. It also reveals a connection between the Mafia and the US government, who found a shared purpose in their hatred of the Castro regime. Central Intelligence Agency (CIA) documents released in 2007 confirmed that the government approached organized crime figures in a plot to have them assassinate Castro in 1960. The approach was made through an asset in Las Vegas, who went to the Chicago Outfit's then-overseer Johnny Roselli—Roselli, in turn, put the asset in touch with acting Chicago boss Sam Giancana and Tampa's Trafficante, who made several foiled attempts to poison Castro using pills supplied by the CIA.[46] The Castro plot was not the only contact the CIA had with the Mafia in the period that followed and, more pertinently, not the only contact the agency had with gangsters associated directly with Roselli, Giancana, and Trafficante. One example of this contact would take place a world away, in the bars and office buildings of Sydney, but would be consequential to the fate of several associates of Bally's Jack Rooklyn in the years that followed.

Ray Moloney did not live to see the Cuban Revolution; the Bally founder died on February 26, 1958, of a sudden heart attack at age 57.[47] His death was not expected, and there is little doubt that Moloney thought he would have more time, both to turn Lion (and Bally) around financially and to put in place a solid succession plan. He did not have a chance to do either, and consequently the entire company fell into the hands of an administrator, the American National Bank and Trust Company.[48] At first, the trust put long-serving executive Joseph Flesch in charge, but soon after, he handed control to Moloney's sons Ray Jr. and Donald. The Moloney boys saw slot machines as the only way to turn the company around, even with the repressive Johnson Act and state bans on production in Illinois, but these factors and the perceived threat of organized crime infiltration made the American National Bank and Trust Company nervous about the prospect of getting into the business once again. Instead, they suggested liquidating Lion and Bally, paying off its debts and calling time on the failing business.[49]

The Moloney brothers may have had no choice if not for the ingenuity of William T. O'Donnell. O'Donnell was born in 1922, around the time Moloney first came to Chicago looking for work. He was forced to drop out of school at 17 to support his family when his father passed away, finding work on the construction of Chicago's L-train system.[50] He joined Bally in 1946 after returning from serving as a Marine in the Pacific theater during World War II, where he likely spent time in Australia, then a base for American troops operating in the region. O'Donnell caught Moloney's eye early, being promoted to assistant sales manager after six months and, in 1951, to Bally's sales manager. He was named to the board of directors as part of the attempts to salvage the company after Moloney's death, a position from which he began his campaign to take Bally for himself.[51] O'Donnell's problem, though, was that the managers of the trust were right. The potential links between a coin-operated machine manufacturer like Bally and organized crime, plus the laws that had put the company in such a bad financial state, made it a losing prospect for any investors that O'Donnell reached out to. Running out of options, and time, O'Donnell turned to Runyon Sales, a major New Jersey–based machines distributor nominally managed by Abe Green and Barnett Sugarman. Unlike other outside investors, Green and Sugarman knew the business well and were not concerned about the perceptions that a company like Bally would be prone to Mafia infiltration. They helped O'Donnell by bringing in other East Coast associates, like pool table manufacturer Irving Kaye and vending machine executive Sam Klein. Together with two others brought in by Klein, the group formed K.O.S. Enterprises and in June 1963 purchased Lion's assets for $1.2 million.[52] Technically, K.O.S. did not purchase Lion Manufacturing outright; instead, they bought up the company's liquidated assets at a low cost and, later, renamed their company "Lion" in what was a takeover by any other name. O'Donnell, the savior responsible for bringing the investors together, was named president of the new company.

The company's fortunes were boosted not only by its motivated new ownership, but also by a reform to state law. For the first time in more than a decade, slot machines were permitted to be manufactured in Illinois again, letting Bally shift attention to a product that its new owners hoped would be its most lucrative venture yet.[53] It was not long before the unforeseen implications of O'Donnell's desperate deal with his partners from Runyon were revealed. In March 1964 one of the new Lion's chief investors, Sugarman, died. His shares were promptly purchased from his widow by his partner from Runyon, Green, who used them to establish a firmer financial interest in Lion, bringing his ownership to 25 percent.[54] That was on paper, at least. It was around the time of Sugarman's death that O'Donnell claims he first learned where the money that Runyon had fronted to help purchase Lion had come from: top-ranking Genovese family underboss Gerardo "Jerry" Catena.[55] The deal was that Catena, who also had an interest in Runyon, would use Green and Sugarman as a front to control Lion and (more importantly) Bally, with Catena secretly holding half of each man's shares for a total of 12.5 percent ownership. That was not Catena's only link to K.O.S. Enterprises, either. He also had connections with Kaye and Klein, meaning at least half of the eight members of the consortium that purchased Lion were linked financially to a key member of one of the most powerful crime families in the country.[56]

Jerry Catena was born on January 8, 1902, in Newark, New Jersey, just over the water from the emerging metropolis on Manhattan Island. Much of Catena's early life is unknown, but it is likely that he initially came to be involved in organized crime via an association with prominent North Jersey gangsters like Guarino "Willie" Moretti, who ran his gambling empire out of the area.[57] Catena was also associated with Jewish gangster Abner "Longie" Zwillman, who, though slightly younger than Catena, was himself a major player in Jersey's gambling scene alongside Moretti and other Italian mafiosos like Joe Adonis.[58] Catena's criminal record shows his first arrest was for "shooting crap" (gambling) in Newark on August 11, 1923, the start of a criminal rap sheet of more than a decade that featured not just illegal gambling, but arrests for offenses like robbery and bribery of a federal juror as well.[59] He was an associate of Moretti throughout the Castellammarese War from February 1930 to April 1931, where loyalists of Joe "The Boss" Masseria were ultimately defeated by partisans of Salvatore Maranzano, a recent Sicilian immigrant. Maranzano prevailed in this conflict thanks in large part to the defection of Masseria gangster Luciano, with whom Moretti was associated through his cousin Frank Costello. It was in the aftermath of this underworld conflict that the Five Families of Italian-American organized crime were formed, with Luciano taking control of one of these Families, a reward for his shift in loyalty to Maranzano at a critical moment.[60]

Though Catena had been working with Moretti and other Italian gangsters since at least the early 1920s, he did not become a "made" member of the Luciano Family until around 1945, according to FBI phone taps from the mid-1960s.[61] Luciano did not preside over the family that bore his name for long; after just five years, in 1936 he was sentenced to 30 to 50 years in state prison on prostitution racketeering charges.[62] So began two decades of conflict over the Luciano Family's leadership. On one side was underboss Vito Genovese, and on the other, Luciano's *consigliere* (chief advisor) Frank Costello. Initially, Genovese became acting boss of the family when Luciano went to prison, but was forced to flee to Italy to avoid criminal charges only a year later. Genovese's departure left Costello as boss of the Luciano Family, with Moretti rising to underboss—a promotion that undoubtedly benefited Catena.[63] By the time Genovese returned, in 1946, after running a lucrative black market operation in southern Italy throughout World War II, Costello was unwilling to return power, or even to offer Genovese his old position as underboss. Genovese's anger was immediate, and plotting commenced.

Meeting with Luciano (now out of prison) at the 1946 Havana conference, Genovese implored the old boss to take back control and put Genovese in charge of operations in New York City in Costello's place. Luciano turned Genovese down, telling him "right now you work for me and I ain't in the mood to retire."[64] Genovese's ambitions did not cease, though. His first move was against Moretti, in a quest to regain his place as underboss. Moretti, a flamboyant figure by Mafia standards, had contracted syphilis, and there were concerns (stoked by Genovese) that the disease was affecting his brain. He had spoken relatively openly at the 1951 Kefauver Hearings into organized crime, and was suspected of informing to police.[65] On October 4, 1951, Moretti was assassinated while eating lunch at a restaurant in Cliffside Park, New Jersey. Genovese was later reported to have described the hit as "a mercy killing because he [Moretti] was sick."[66] Whatever the reason, Moretti's death had a number of implications for the Luciano Family: While it allowed Genovese to reclaim his former position, it also opened the door for Moretti's ally Catena to take more of an active role in managing his rackets in North Jersey.

It was six more years before Genovese finally consolidated his position. Conspiring with Anastasia Family underboss Carlo Gambino, Genovese made the decision to move against Costello. On May 2, 1957, future boss Vincent "The Chin" Gigante shot Costello outside his apartment building. Costello did not die but, understanding that it was only a matter of time before Genovese tried again, abdicated his position. Genovese took control, and promptly renamed the Luciano Family after himself.[67] On paper, Genovese's rise should have seen Catena's prospects fall as a close associate of the Costello/Moretti faction, but this was not the case. Instead, it seems that Catena assumed the important role of underboss instead. He and Genovese even went together to the November 1957 Apalachin meeting, a conference of organized crime leaders called by Genovese to discuss the Mafia's involvement in Cuba and the narcotics trade, and (importantly) to give Genovese an opportunity to explain his unsanctioned attempted hit on Costello.[68] Catena's continued rise in the new Genovese Family can be explained in a few different ways. It is possible Genovese, fearing potential reprisals from a strong

North Jersey contingent, rewarded Catena to stabilize the Family. It is also likely that he saw the operational benefits in retaining Catena, who was closely involved in the Family's gambling operations, overseeing the Family's operations in gambling hubs like Cuba and New Orleans alongside Costello since at least the 1940s.[69] If there was any tension between the men over the death of Moretti and attempted murder of Costello, it did not last long. After Apalachin, Luciano sought revenge on Genovese, paying a Puerto Rican drug dealer to implicate the new boss in a narcotics deal that in 1959 landed him fifteen years in federal prison.[70] Though Genovese continued to issue orders from his prison cell, the Genovese Family (in effect) was run by a triumvirate of senior members, including Catena.[71] For all practical purposes, Catena had risen to become a boss of the Genovese family by the dawn of the 1960s, a position he held for most of the following decade—including at the time he purchased an interest in Bally.

Not content with being a silent investor, Catena used his connection to Bally to gain a firmer grip on the lucrative Las Vegas market. He did this through an agent named Michael Wichinsky, who was related to Catena by marriage, as Wichinsky's nephew was married to Catena's daughter.[72] Wichinsky was recommended to O'Donnell by Catena's front man Green, and was hired as the exclusive Bally distributor in southern Nevada. It should be noted that Wichinsky was not just a patsy, but had real credentials in the business. He was responsible for inventing a critical piece of machinery, a coin-hopper, which facilitated payouts on the new automated slot machines that Bally was developing in the early 1960s.[73] Wichinsky was ultimately forced to sell his Bally distribution business back to O'Donnell in 1972, after an investigation by Nevada gaming auditors found both personal and financial links between Wichinsky and Catena, as well as Wichinsky and a man named Dino Cellini, another Bally distributor with questionable associations.[74] Wichinsky's legacy at Bally, though, was the hopper invention that capped off the new electronic slot machines that Bally started to mass-produce, beginning with Money Honey in 1964, just a year after the Illinois ban on manufacturing slot machines was rescinded. Money Honey was just the first in a line of electronic slot machines that revolutionized the business and allowed

Bally to dominate the market, especially in Wichinsky's turf of Las Vegas. Thanks to the company's development of electronic slot machines, estimates suggest that Bally products made up 90 percent of the Las Vegas market by the end of the decade.[75]

O'Donnell claimed that as soon as he found out Catena was a silent partner in Bally after Sugarman's death in 1964, he began the process of purging his influence from the company. In a later court case, he points to an agreement signed in July 1965 where O'Donnell purchased some of Green's shares in Lion, nominally representing O'Donnell's purchase of Catena's shares.[76] However, Catena was a silent partner using Green and Sugarman as a front and, as such, his name is not on any of the paperwork—thus there is nothing to prove that the shares O'Donnell bought were actually Catena's, and not just part of the Green/Sugarman holdings. Indeed, Green (and other Catena-linked investors) remained with Bally throughout the 1960s, and Bally even retained Green and Catena's Runyon Sales as the chief distributor of Bally products in the highly profitable New York-New Jersey-Connecticut market, despite knowing of its links to organized crime.[77] These factors alone cast doubt on O'Donnell's claims that he was proactive when it came to excising Catena's influence as soon as he learned of it, but there is also the matter of Bally's atmospheric rise in the mid-1960s to consider. Catena, an influential mafioso and leader of the powerful Genovese Family, had invested in Bally right at the time that its profits began to boom with its entry into the electronic slot machines market. What would have made him give up this substantial line of profit simply on the demand of a business executive like O'Donnell? The answer is, nothing. A court later found that Catena did not actually sell his stake in Bally until 1970, when he sold it to his front man Green after being jailed for refusing to testify to the New Jersey State Commission of Investigation. Initially, Catena was held as a coercive strategy designed to get him to talk—five years later, in 1975, Catena still refused to testify.[78] He was ultimately released when the New Jersey Supreme Court determined that, after five years, it was unlikely that any further detention would ever make Catena talk. Catena's imprisonment is instructive about his character, and casts further doubt on the likelihood that he divested his holdings in Bally on

O'Donnell's request in 1965. If Catena was a man who was not intimidated by the State of New Jersey, even after five years in prison, there was likely nothing O'Donnell could do to make him walk away from Bally unless he chose to do so.

The hiring of Dino Cellini is another indicator that Bally was not actively shedding its Mafia ties in the mid-1960s. Born on November 19, 1914, in Steubenville, Ohio, Cellini began his career in organized crime as a "bust out" man for the rackets in his hometown, hustling gamblers and making sure winning streaks did not bankrupt the operation.[79] At one of these gaming joints, he worked with another Steubenville local, Dino Crocetti, later known as singer Dean Martin. Cellini became associated with leading mafiosos in the 1940s and, by the 1950s, was representing the interests of Meyer Lansky in Cuban casinos like the Riviera. He also worked with Tampa Family boss Trafficante at his establishments in Cuba; however, intelligence suggested "Trafficante was a front man for others. . . . Dino Cellini did most of the talking."[80] If the intelligence was correct and Trafficante was fronting for a wider consortium, it is likely that Cellini was working for Lansky, with whom he was closely linked. When the Cuban Revolution took place in the late 1950s, Cellini was forced to flee the country. Avoiding the United States after a shooting in Washington, D.C. (where he previously ran a gambling establishment), Cellini went to Europe where he opened the Colony Club in London's Berkeley Square. He ran the Colony Club as part of a group with actor George Raft and Cyril Schack, Bally's principal distributor in the United Kingdom. It was through this connection that Cellini ended up working with Bally. O'Donnell said he turned up unannounced at the company's head office in 1964 or 1965 on Schack's referral, and told the Bally boss that he would have "the authority to select slot machines for a new casino in the Bahamas."[81] After traveling with Cellini to the Bahamas to investigate the prospect, O'Donnell set up the Bally Bahamian Company with Cellini at the helm. This joint venture did not last long, as Cellini was soon banned from The Bahamas due to his past involvement with Lansky's operations in Cuba; exclusion from the United Kingdom soon followed in 1967 for the same reasons.[82]

Once again, O'Donnell's later protestations that he worked to remove organized crime's hold on Bally is rendered doubtful by his actions with Cellini. Even after Cellini's Bahamian scheme collapsed due to his organized crime links, O'Donnell continued to pay Cellini commissions for selling Bally products in Europe and the Caribbean into the late 1960s. Worse still, O'Donnell paid Cellini through a third party, a move later criticized as a way to avoid Cellini being paid by Bally "on paper," in a similar way that Catena used to avoid being officially linked to the company.[83] In 1969, O'Donnell recommended Cellini for employment to the head of Bally Continental, Alexander Wilms.[84] He remained a Bally employee in Europe until 1973, when his employment was finally terminated after Lansky and Cellini were both charged with tax evasion related to their involvement with the Colony Club in London.[85] By then, Wilms had also become a part-owner of the Colony Club, along with Catena associate and Bally part-owner Sam Klein.[86] The question is why, if O'Donnell was concerned about organized crime involvement with Bally, was Cellini given so many opportunities to continue working with the company? The connection, indeed, may be Catena. Through his work with Lansky in Cuba, it is probable that Cellini came into contact with Catena, who assisted in managing the Genovese Family's interests on the island during the same period. There is also a long-standing connection between Lansky and the Genovese Family, dating back to Lansky's youthful friendship with the Family's founder, Luciano. Genovese informant Joe Valachi testified in 1963 that "anywhere that Meyer Lansky is, there's Genovese . . . they do everything together."[87] It was also Catena's relative-by-marriage, the southern Nevada distributor Wichinsky, who admitted to recommending Cellini to O'Donnell.[88] This link would, of course, be dependent on Catena's continued involvement with Bally after the supposed buyout of mid-1965. Otherwise, it would not explain Cellini's transfer to the European market after the collapse of the Bahamian deal. Again, there are strong indications that Bally continued to be compromised by its affiliation with the Genoveses and Lansky associates into the early 1970s.

The links to Catena and Cellini were not the only criminal problems that Bally was forced to deal with in the 1960s. O'Donnell was personally accused of funding an attempt by a Bally distributor to bribe legislators in Kentucky in early 1968 to change the state's laws prohibiting bingo games. O'Donnell admitted to paying $4,000 to the distributor; however, he claimed this was a "loan" despite letters sent to him strongly implying that the money would be used as bribes.[89] This was not the only bribery case that O'Donnell found himself implicated in around that time: In 1971, he and Bally were indicted for illegal transportation of gambling equipment to a distributor in Louisiana, Louis Boasberg, in contravention of the Johnson Act. While O'Donnell and Bally were ultimately acquitted in this case, Boasberg pleaded guilty to a connected charge of bribing public officials to turn a blind eye to illegal Bally machines operating in New Orleans.[90] This subsequent case achieved national prominence when district attorney Jim Garrison was accused of receiving bribes indirectly from Boasberg and others. Garrison had earlier achieved notoriety from his attacks on the US government over its handling of the inquiry in the assassination of former president John F. Kennedy, which he argued was a plot hatched in New Orleans and connected to the New Orleans crime family led by Carlos Marcello.[91] Garrison asserted innocence in the Boasberg bribery case and, later, was vindicated when former investigator Pershing Gervais, the key witness against him, claimed that he had fabricated evidence at the behest of the US Justice Department to discredit Garrison and force him out of office.[92]

Between the persistent links to organized crime and the consecutive bribery cases involving the company, Bally entered into the early 1970s with a questionable reputation that was impacting O'Donnell's ability to grow the business. In 1971, just as the Boasberg case and Cellini's involvement with Lansky were coming to light, Bally made inquiries to the state's gaming commission about purchasing Wichinsky's Nevada operation. O'Donnell was told the connection with Cellini would be a problem, and soon the Boasberg case put his efforts on the backburner.[93] When the Boasberg case resulted in an acquittal in 1973, and Cellini was terminated in May of the same year, O'Donnell resumed his efforts to acquire Wichinsky's subsidiary operation. Eventually, the company received a probationary license in 1975 on the proviso the company cut all ties with Boasberg, by then released from prison. The commission also demanded that Alexander Wilms, the Bally Continental boss, resign from the company within nine months, and that Bally do no further business with Catena front Abe Green and Runyon Sales, due to their links with organized crime.[94] At a review of this probationary period conducted two years later, the Nevada Gaming Commission found that Bally had failed to comply and had maintained a professional relationship with Boasberg in direct contravention of its orders.[95] In another flagrant disregard for the commission's orders, Bally had also continued to distribute its products in the New York–New Jersey area using a company called Coin-Op. This distribution business was run by Green's son and determined to be "virtually indistinguishable from Runyon Sales."[96] Nevertheless, despite these breaches, Bally's probation was extended another three years.

The end for O'Donnell did not come in Nevada, where he had come up against so many problems in licensure, but in Bally's efforts to secure a license for a casino called Bally's Park Place in Atlantic City, New Jersey. The $300 million project was under threat when the New Jersey Division of Gaming Enforcement (DGE) came to the decision that, due to Bally's continued flouting of orders by the Nevada Gaming Commission and its links to organized crime, the only way a permit for Bally's Park Place would be issued was if O'Donnell stepped aside as president, chairman, and director of Bally. It also ordered that Wilms, still a major shareholder in the company, resign as director and (like O'Donnell) put all of his holdings in a proxy trust that would not permit him to be involved in the active operation of the company.[97] O'Donnell agreed, at least temporarily, in early December 1979, pending a further investigation to determine whether he might be found suitable to return to his position. As promised, a temporary licence was granted and Bally's casino opened on December 29, 1979.[98] If O'Donnell hoped to return, he would be sorely disappointed. When the Casino Control Commission of New Jersey considered making Bally's temporary license permanent in 1981, it confirmed the initial decision that if Bally were to continue operating in Atlantic City, O'Donnell, who "did not demonstrate good character," was not a fit person to be involved.[99] After wresting for control of Bally and rescuing it from liquidation in the early 1960s, O'Donnell's time leading the company came to a conclusion at the hands of a state that refused to ignore the company's tattered history. As Attorney-General John Degnan said at the time, "[I]t's fair to say [New Jersey is] the strictest casino regulator in the world now."[100]

The deliberations about Bally's licensing, both in Nevada and New Jersey, revealed much about the inner workings of the company during O'Donnell's tenure. The Nevada Gaming Commission pushed Bally to cut ties with the likes of Abe Green, Jerry Catena, Mickey Wichinsky, Dino Cellini, Alexander Wilms, and Louis Boasberg. In some cases the orders stuck, while in others Bally did whatever it could to hide the continued involvement of these characters (with limited success). In spite of O'Donnell's involvement in maintaining these prohibited relationships and other affairs like the Kentucky bribery scandal, he survived the Nevada Gaming Commission's efforts to challenge Bally's attempts to gain licensure in that state, but in New Jersey there was a clear line drawn in the sand. With $300 million on the line, there was nothing for O'Donnell to do but to resign his post if Bally were to survive, which he did, albeit not without a protracted legal battle with the Casino Control Commission. That battle only resulted in the commission confirming the decision that he was not fit to lead Bally into its new era of casino ownership, having failed over a period of almost two decades to eradicate organized crime's involvement in the business. However, among the familiar names like Catena, Lansky, Cellini, and others, there was another inclusion in the Nevada Gaming Commission's list of prohibited Bally associates that was less familiar. In the 1974 decision not to consider Wilms for a license, the commission referred (in passing) to the discovery that he had written a report while serving as a director of Bally suggesting that the company could participate in the bribery of Southeast Asian officials through a local distributor so that "[t]he Bally image would remain clean."[101] Later, in 1977, the Nevada Gaming Commission ordered Bally to terminate the same local distributor Wilms had mentioned due to concerns he was involved in illegal gambling in Southeast Asia. There may have been other, unspoken reasons for this decision. The man that Wilms had named was Jack Rooklyn, Bally's top man in the Asia-Pacific. Only three years earlier, Rooklyn had been at the center of a public inquiry in New South Wales that largely focused on the coin-operated machine industry. A major focus of that inquiry? Whether or not Rooklyn and Bally were part of a scheme by the American Mafia to take control of organized crime in Australia.

2

Rooklyn Rises

In a feature shared by so many destined for greatness (or, more aptly here, notoriety), Jack Rooklyn's story is one of humble origins. Rooklyn was the third son of Abraham and Rebecca, a married Jewish couple who both worked as tailors in Blackburn, an industrial city in northwest England.[1] The arrival of the Industrial Revolution in the mid-19th century had been a boon to the city. The combination of improvements to the mechanical loom and the construction of a new railroad line allowed Blackburn to become the center of the cotton trade, making it the perfect place for a couple of hardworking tailors like the Rooklyns to make a life for themselves.[2] Like so many in the Jewish community during the period, the Rooklyns were driven to leave their native Russia by a rising anti-Semitic sentiment leading to large-scale, violent anti-Jewish riots dubbed "pogroms." The first wave of pogroms lasted from 1881 to 1884, with a second wave taking place from 1903 to 1906. In this latter set of pogroms, thousands of Russian Jews were killed in "scenes of horror . . . the Jews were taken wholly unaware and slaughtered like sheep."[3] The knock-on effect of the pogroms had lasting implications for other nations around the world. More than 2 million Russian Jews fled the violence between 1880 and 1920, with many (like the Rooklyn family) relocating to places like the United Kingdom.[4] It was Jack's grandparents who made the decision to leave Russia for the United Kingdom in the late 19th century. He described them as "Russian peasants" who "hated" Russia as a result of the persecution they experienced, and rarely spoke of their lives there.[5] In any case, their immigration was timely; in doing so, the Rooklyns were able to avoid the second brutal wave of violence that erupted only a few years later.

The first of Abraham and Rebecca's children, Hyman "Harry" Rooklyn, was born on January 9, 1904, not long after the first pogrom began. He was soon followed by another boy, Maurice, on April 1, 1905. A few years later, the couple's only daughter, Kitty, was born and, finally, young Israel "Jack" Rooklyn arrived on March 11, 1908.[6] Though once home to a thriving textile industry, Blackburn had started to experience a severe economic decline by the time the last Rooklyn child arrived. Twenty years earlier, the city's chamber of commerce warned against the town "only having one string in their bow" by focusing almost exclusively on the cotton business, arguing that not diversifying put Blackburn at great risk if there were any downturns in that trade.[7] The prediction of calamity came to pass only a few years into the 20th century and, by 1908, more than forty of the city's mills were forced to shut down, reflecting around a quarter of the city's production.[8] This dire economic outlook would have been of great concern to the Rooklyns, a young couple with four children to support in a city that now seemed to be inevitably committed to a spiral of declining fortunes. What the family needed was a change, the kind of which presented itself when Rebecca's brother, who lived overseas, got in touch. He spoke of a country where the Rooklyns could take hold of endless opportunity and raise their family without the cloud of impending poverty casting a shadow over them. It was in pursuit of this promise that the Rooklyns packed their bags in 1911, headed for Australia.[9]

The Rooklyns were like many immigrants in the sense that their Australian dream began in the urban inner city, in this case Sydney. The family settled initially in a suburb called Haberfield in the inner west, just a stone's throw from the Parramatta River, which in turn spilled into the iconic Sydney Harbour.[10] Jack was three years old when the Rooklyns settled in Sydney, and soon after started school at nearby Haberfield Public School. The relatively small size of the Australian population during this era might explain the often strange synchronicity in places like Sydney, where individuals who are destined to later cross paths in more consequential ways first make each other's acquaintance much earlier in life. It is possible that Haberfield Public School was the site of one such meeting, between a youthful Jack Rooklyn and a student just one grade level below him named Norman Thomas William Allan. By 1962, Norm Allan would be chief commissioner of the New South Wales Police Force, a role he served in until 1972, coming into contact with (and, in many versions, corruptly dealing with) many of the Sydney noir characters also important to Jack's story.[11] By around 1920, the Rooklyns decided to move to the Hunter Valley, a mining region north of Sydney, where they first opened a general store in the small coalfields town of Greta and, later, a drapery business in Singleton.[12] In his own words, Jack's experience of school was "minor"—although he participated in formal education at East Maitland High School for just over a year after his family moved, Jack chose to leave school for good in 1922, at just 14 years old.[13]

The Rooklyns' drapery store in Singleton was the subject of suspicion and gossip in the small country town after fire swept through the premises on the night of February 25, 1927. The fire began sometime around nine o'clock that Friday night, after daughter Kitty Rooklyn had closed the shop for the evening. When the fire brigade managed to get the blaze under control, they found little evidence of what may have started the blaze, aside from an empty lemonade bottle found on the shop's counter that police initially suspected may have been used as a makeshift incendiary device—Kitty claimed she often bought that brand of lemonade, but could not remember doing so (or even seeing the bottle there) on the night of the fire.[14] At a coronial inquest into the fire held on March 9, the owner of the property testified that just three or four weeks before the fire, he had told Rebecca Rooklyn that her tenancy was only temporary and that he would soon be needing the property back. During the period between giving her this notice and the fire, he had heard that Rebecca had "said things about him . . . he had heard from a reliable source that she had ill-feeling towards him because he wanted her to quit [leave the premises]."[15] The landlord also testified to having seen Rebecca's husband, Abraham, removing a quantity of stock from the store earlier in the afternoon of the fire, implying that the Rooklyns may have started the fire as part of a scheme to falsely claim insurance on products that had already been removed ahead of time. The Rooklyns admitted to removing some property that day, but claimed it was normal in the course of their business. While Rebecca managed the store, her husband was a hawker who often took property to sell on his travels. In the end, unable to determine whether the fire was accidental or deliberate, district coroner Alex Morrison issued an open verdict on the Rooklyn fire, leaving the mystery forever unresolved.[16]

The business interests of Rooklyn's parents may have gone up in flames, but the prospects for some of their brood were far brighter. Their middle son, Maurice, had been fascinated by magicians from an early age, and by 1919, at age 14, he had been hired by a troupe of magicians to join a tour around rural New South Wales.[17] At first, Maurice developed skills in ventriloquy and juggling, and two years after joining the traveling group of magicians, he left to form a partnership with a performer called "the Great Theodore."[18] As he describes it in his self-published memoirs, Maurice's collaboration with Theodore was mutually beneficial. While Theodore was a multitalented and experienced performer with a routine that combined hypnotism, sharp-shooting, and contortion, he "had always been a 'loner'" until Maurice joined him, taking a position that was a mixture of performer, assistant, and manager.[19] Maurice and Theodore were a double act, both on stage and behind the scenes. Maurice recalls one incident at a show in the coalfields of the Hunter Valley, not far from his family home, when a belligerent audience member challenged Theodore that he would not be able to hypnotize him. After a subtle glance from the magician, Maurice went backstage; while Theodore was on stage hypnotizing the audience member to believe he had been stung by a bee, Maurice pricked him with a hat pin from behind the stage curtain. Between the two of them, Maurice and Theodore knew how to put on a good show for even the most resistant of audiences.[20]

Maurice was not the only Rooklyn to be drawn into the entertainment industry. By 1925, he was joined on the circuit by his older brother Harry, performing in vaudeville concerts. Unlike Maurice, Harry was not a magician and, in some respects, took a role similar to his brother's when he joined the Great Theodore. Billed as "the Rooklyn Brothers," it was Harry's job to play the violin while Maurice performed the magic routine that he had continued to perfect under Theodore's tutelage.[21] Just as Maurice later became known as "the Amazing Mr. Rooklyn," Harry too received a stage name, "the Musical Bandolero," in reference to the Spanish-inspired costume he wore on stage.[22] The entertainment circuit was more than just a career for the Rooklyn boys—it consumed their entire life to an extent. Harry was later able to strike out in his own right, appearing regularly on radio as the Musical Bandolero, and expanding his repertoire of musical instruments beyond the violin as time went on. For Maurice, the performing circuit gave him even more: On May 23, 1926, he was married at the Great Synagogue in Sydney to Ethel "Ettie" Weinstein, one of his stage assistants.[23] By the time of the fire at the Rooklyns' drapery shop in 1927, at least two of their sons were well on the way to making a name for themselves in the Australian entertainment scene, something their third son Jack would also soon gravitate to, albeit in a behind-the-scenes capacity.

When Jack left school in the early 1920s, his older brothers were already on the path to success. Things were not quite as simple for Jack, who struggled to find his place at first. He did what many other young men did at the time, taking "whatever jobs one could find, [in] whatever capacity."[24] Following the opportunity wherever it was in the Hunter region, Jack worked various jobs in retail stores, plastics manufacturing, and construction. He was employed in the mines for a time and even as a racehorse trainer, a role he continued in until he became "a little too heavy" to ride the horses.[25] When he was forced to leave his job at the stables, Jack took to training a different kind of beast. In Sydney, he became a boxing trainer for champion fighters like Australian middleweight belt–holder Frankie Yuvan. He claimed to have contested some of his own bouts at the Leichardt and Newtown Stadiums, not far from where his family first settled in Haberfield. According to Jack, his brief tilt at a professional boxing career "didn't last very long" and, soon, he was back on the market looking for a career that would stick.[26]

Now in Sydney, it seems that Jack was hitting a brick wall. Unlike his brothers, he had not found a lasting passion in the (almost) decade since leaving school. It is perhaps this element of professional drift that led Jack to come before the courts in September 1931. Now 23 years old, Jack appeared before the Sydney Quarter Sessions court charged with breaking and entering a retail store, along with a 21-year-old accomplice named Geoffrey Howard Stanley Clare.[27] The men both pleaded guilty to two counts of shopbreaking and were released on a good behavior bond by the court, on the proviso they paid a surety of £50 and made restitution of a further £52 each to the store they stole from.[28] The conditions of these restitution payments again give insight into the state of Jack's life in the early years of the 1930s. While his co-offender Clare was listed as a clerk and ordered to pay the full restitution amount within eighteen months, Jack was listed as a "traveller" and permitted a payment plan for his restitution obligations of £4 each month.[29] The court's decision to tie Jack to a regular series of payments may reflect the fear that, as an itinerant with no stable source of income, he might disappear before restitution was made unless a plan was put in place to avoid it. Regardless, the fact remains that in 1931 the trajectory of the Rooklyn brothers could not have been further removed, even as all three made appearances in the local media, for very different reasons.

His criminal conviction was, quite possibly, the push that Jack needed. From 1931 on, a very different version of the youngest Rooklyn brother starts to emerge in the archival record. There are no more petty theft charges; instead, Jack the entertainment impresario begins to take center stage. After leaving school, Jack had seemed set on taking a different path from his brothers and yet, in the end, it was by going into business with Harry and Maurice that he found success. This is, likely, no coincidence; like many families with a black sheep like Jack, it is probable that the Rooklyns decided to bring Jack into the fold, an intervention to keep him on the straight and narrow after the scare of his court date.

Built to commemorate the sacrifices of Jewish servicemen in World War I, the Maccabean Hall in Darlinghurst was the site of some of Jack's early efforts as a producer. An article in the *Hebrew Standard of Australasia* refers to a concert organized by Jack on Sunday, September 10, 1933, which is described as being "up to his usually high standard . . . the programme was particularly fun and the large audience was unanimous in its expressions of appreciation."[30] It seems that, in the two years since his conviction, Jack had already started to make a name for himself as a go-to person for entertainment in interwar Sydney.

Around this time, Jack also began working with the Tivoli circuit, a highly popular vaudeville theater company established in the late 19th century by English music hall performer Harry Rickards.[31] Though it originated in Sydney, by the 1930s the Tivoli circuit had expanded to incorporate venues in most of Australia's major cities, with prominent performers constantly moving from city to city to perform their acts. Cultivating close ties with the Tivoli, Jack became a producer and sketch writer for established stars like comedian Roy Rene, as well as his own brothers, the Amazing Mr. Rooklyn and the Musical Bandolero.[32] Though Jack was (finally) on the ascendant, the mid-1930s was a time of struggle for Maurice. In 1936, his wife Ettie gave birth to stillborn twins, and, as if that tragedy was not enough, the Great Depression had reached Australian shores and made variety entertainment an unaffordable luxury for many.[33] Under pressure, Maurice tried to think of new ways to draw a crowd, and knew "you had to do something really different to make a living."[34] The "Human Target" was his solution, and almost his downfall. The act was an optical illusion that involved someone firing a gun at Maurice, who would then *appear* to catch the bullet in his teeth. It was risky, and it was exactly what he needed to revitalize his gimmick.

Maurice was right: The Human Target was a success, but not without some close calls. Maurice was wounded twice on stage in just eight weeks in 1934. In the first instance, on March 8, 1934, he escaped with a bullet to the shoulder—in response to the close call, a leading authority on magicians warned that ten people had already died in performances similar to that which Maurice was attempting.[35] The warning fell on deaf (or maybe desperate) ears, and Maurice continued as the Human Target. On May 5, 1934, he was again struck by a bullet during a show at Hoyts Olympia in Bondi. This time the bullet grazed his scalp, coming very close to ending the Amazing Mr. Rooklyn's career once and for all.[36] Despite these palpitation-inducing encounters, the Human Target helped Maurice become one of Australia's best-known magicians once more. By 1936, he had left for three years in London; when he returned, he rejoined the Tivoli circuit as a vaudeville star. Thankfully, because of his public profile, he was no longer required to participate in life-threatening acts like being shot at to sell tickets.[37] His brothers saw similar successes: Harry continued to develop his brand as the Musical Bandolero while Jack, now a success in the vaudeville scene, went to the United States as a scriptwriter, where he reputedly worked on Hollywood films for Westerns star Randolph Scott.[38]

Jack was not content to rest on his laurels and, though becoming sought after as a writer, director, and producer of vaudeville, he also managed a growing coin-operated amusement business. Given the "knack or talent for writing" Jack had demonstrated while working with the Tivoli, he saw it as a natural shift to move into advertising and marketing, and began freelancing as an advisor for a series of sporting goods stores in the Sydney suburbs.[39] He started this sideline consulting at the age of 23, around the same period as his conviction for shopbreaking in 1931. As fate would have it, starting the new business coincided with a boom in the popularity of the pinball machine, largely a result of Lion Manufacturing's rollout of the Ballyhoo in 1932. For Jack, pinball offered an opportunity to get punters through the door of the stores he worked with, which were struggling through the Depression like other branches of the entertainment business. The Rooklyn pinball empire began with a loan of £5 from Rebecca Rooklyn, allowing Jack to purchase his first machine to put into a small store in Rockdale, in southern Sydney.[40] As with his start in the vaudeville business through his brothers, it is likely that Jack's mother was more than happy to loan him the money, hoping this new venture would keep him out of trouble. If so, she was right. Alongside his success at the Tivoli, Jack grew his pinball importation company throughout the 1930s. He did so alongside his brother Harry, and by 1938 the Rooklyn brothers could confidently describe their business as "Australia's largest operator of coin-machines."[41]

Something about pinball that Jack learned early on was that its popularity was fleeting. After just a few weeks, the novelty of the game he had placed in the store in Rockdale had worn off, and he was forced to "move it on" and replace it with a new amusement machine.[42] As the business grew, the Rooklyns began placing an increasing number of machines in other venues and, given the need to turn over the pinball machines regularly to keep their popularity fresh, Jack began importing larger quantities of machines from the United States. It was through these business transactions that he first contacted Bally, then a subsidiary of Lion Manufacturing.[43] Though he may have contacted Bally for its pinball business, this professional connection would become a defining feature of Jack's life. Along with pinball games, Bally also produced poker and slot machines—a corner of the amusement business that could potentially be lucrative, considering the notorious Australian predilection for gambling. Poker machines had started to appear in New South Wales hotels by 1921, at which point they were declared illegal by the state's Supreme Court. However, as John O'Hara notes, "[T]he ruling was sufficiently ambiguous to permit their continued operation in clubs, where the profits from the machines contributed to the club, rather than to an individual owner of a machine."[44]

This ambiguity around the legality of gambling machines continued throughout the 1920s and 1930s, and the machines continued to appear in both clubs and hotels intermittently. The machines, referred to in Australia as "fruit machines," were the subject of a royal commission in 1932 investigating why the Lang government (recently voted out of office) had approved the placing of machines in hotels, despite the precedent set in 1921. The Lang government argued the machines had been licensed on a limited, trial basis in the Sydney metropolitan area, with a percentage of the profits going to the state's hospital fund.[45] Despite these apparently noble aims, the incoming government saw gaming machines as immoral and ordered their removal from all hotels *and* clubs.[46] A petition from club owners in 1939 to reinstate their permissions to host gambling was dismissed by the government, and so, as the Rooklyns' game importation business reached new heights, the status of gambling machines remained largely unresolved. Even so, while they remained illegal, estimates in 1939 suggest that an illicit market was thriving behind the scenes, and it was believed that around 2,500 poker machines were operating in New South Wales.[47] The tolerance of these machines was, perhaps, part of Police Commissioner Bill Mackay's policy of tactical ignorance. As he told a briefing of junior officers around the same time, "[A]mbition and over-zealousness brought down the Roman Empire, and it will bring down the New South Wales Police Force if allowed to be pursued."[48] In Mackay's view, fighting illegal gaming was largely a losing battle that was destined to put his officers at odds with the public if pursued too aggressively. It might, he suggested, be better to ignore the man wasting his own wages in a machine and, instead, focus on crimes like murder and rape committed by dangerous criminals who needed to be brought to justice.

Of course, the fight over poker machines was not the only war being fought in the late 1930s. Hitler's invasion of Poland in September 1939 sparked a chain of events that saw first Britain and then its former colony of Australia declare war on Germany. Initially, World War II was a primarily ideological affair for Australians, so far removed from the horrors occurring on the European continent. Although the Second Australian Imperial Force (AIF) was formed and eventually deployed to the frontlines, the troops did not join the Allied efforts in the Mediterranean and North Africa until early 1941.[49] That year also brought the war to the home front, with the sinking of the HMAS *Sydney* off the coast of Western Australia on November 19, 1941, by German cruiser *Kormoran*, resulting in the death of 645 Australians aboard.[50] The attack on the HMAS *Sydney* was an early indication that the war would not remain in the Northern Hemisphere this time, as it had in World War I. That reminder was reiterated more forcefully less than a month later on December 7, 1941, when Japan entered the war with its attack on the United States at Pearl Harbor, Hawaii.[51] Plagued by an undercurrent of isolationism, the United States had failed to join the war effort to this point, but now was left no choice. The Roosevelt administration declared war on Japan and its allies, Germany and Italy.

As the War in the Pacific began, the first of the AIF soldiers sent to fight overseas started to return in March 1942, called to the home front due to possible threat of a Japanese-led attack. The return of the AIF, plus the impending threat of invasion, made World War II all the more real for Sydneysiders and, in some ways, created an opportunity for men like Jack and Harry Rooklyn. Jack attributed the success of his pinball machines in this period to the need for "wartime escapist activities." The community, and especially returned soldiers, needed an outlet where they could, for a moment, forget the fear and tragedy brought by the conflict.[52] Though a limited form of conscription was introduced, allowing for compelled service within Australian territory, there was (at first) a variety of professions that were "reserved"—where a person in that business was exempt from being conscripted.[53] As the War in the Pacific kicked off, the policy changed, but initially entertainment providers like the Rooklyns were included on this reserved list. It was in this context in January 1942 that the Rooklyn brothers opened their first amusement parlor, Pennyland, at 244 Pitt Street in the Sydney central business district (CBD).[54]

The timing of Pennyland's opening was a double-edged sword: On one hand, the AIF were due to return soon, which would be a boost to business, but on the other, the removal of entertainment providers from the reserved list meant that the Rooklyns might not be around to manage their business through the boom time to come. Having developed an affinity for sailing in the late 1930s, Jack signed up with the Naval Reserve and attained the rank of lieutenant. Signing up with the Naval Reserve may have been ideological, but it was also tactical, as it prevented him from being conscripted into a different branch of the armed services. Nevertheless, in this new role, Jack was destined to see action. In July 1942, Japanese forces landed on the Australian-held territory of Papua and, in response, the Australian government deployed troops to fight the four-month-long Kokoda campaign.[55] Ultimately, Kokoda would come to symbolize the Australian efforts in World War II, as troops fought alongside the Papuans across the mountainous, jungle terrain of the island to push Japan out and, by some estimations, stop the Japanese advance toward the Australian mainland. It was to Papua that Jack was about to deploy in mid-1942 when, at the last moment, he was made an offer that he simply could not refuse.[56]

From 1942 on, Australia played host to the Allied general headquarters (GHQ) in the South West Pacific Area, led by American General Douglas MacArthur. After a brief period in the southern capital of Melbourne, the GHQ in July 1942 moved to the Queensland capital of Brisbane, the northernmost city with the necessary communications infrastructure from which MacArthur could manage the campaign.[57] With MacArthur's shift to Brisbane came an influx of American troops who would be based out of the city for the duration of the Pacific conflict. At the peak of the war, around 80,000 US troops were based in

Brisbane, a massive number considering that the ordinary population of the city was not much over 300,000 in the prewar years.[58] As the Allied forces settled in for a protracted conflict, it became apparent that entertainment infrastructure was needed to satiate American soldiers and, to some extent, keep them out of the way of the Australian troops, with whom they increasingly found themselves in conflict. As more and more Americans arrived in Brisbane over the three years that the War in the Pacific lasted, the cliché that they were "over-paid, over-sexed and over here" became a maxim among their Australian counterparts, who blamed the US servicemen for any number of sins, ranging from the overt segregation they displayed toward African American soldiers to the perception that they were using their superior financial compensation and cultural capital to "steal" Australian women.[59] Partly as a way to head this predicted animosity off at the pass, Jack claimed he was approached by a representative of the US military just before he was due to be sent to Papua, who asked whether he would be interested in coming north to Brisbane and helping set up an entertainment and recreation facility for American soldiers.[60] Faced with the prospect of combat or continuing in the entertainment business, Jack was eager to accept.

The product of Jack's collaboration with the US military in Brisbane was the American Centre, where he boasted that he could provide "home amusements to the US troops."[61] The need for the American Centre was reinforced by the events of the Battle of Brisbane, which commenced on Thanksgiving night in November 1942. Tensions between American and Australian troops led to pitched street battles between the two contingents that left one Australian soldier shot dead by US military police.[62] Located on the site of the old Brisbane Town Hall on Queen Street, the American Centre opened (appropriately) on July 4, 1943. It was a comprehensive leisure operation that was for the use of US servicemen exclusively, fitted out with everything from a dance floor and bowling alley to poker machines, nominally still illegal in Queensland.[63] It was by all accounts a "lavish" facility that reportedly cost an estimated £2,000 to run each week. Later, when the finances of the club were revealed, it was found that the American Centre was a "source of considerable revenue" to Jack Rooklyn, the concessionaire and manager of the facility. He received up to 75 percent of revenue from pinball games at the site, and up to 85 percent of the revenue from other coin-operated games.[64]

In the meantime, the Rooklyns' Sydney interests continued to operate under the watchful eye of Harry. His management tenure was not without controversy. On April 2, 1943, the Pennyland arcade received attention when an 8-year-old boy died after a slot machine fell on top of him, fracturing his skull.[65] The amusement machine industry also came under fire in the New South Wales Police's annual report for 1943, where police claimed to have spoken to 1,079 young girls "of tender years" who were found loitering in amusement arcades and other similar places, often in the company of military men.[66] Life for Harry could have been worse than this negative attention, though; other Tivoli performers, like George Bradshaw, had been conscripted into the military and ordered to develop an entertainment show to deliver to troops on the frontlines. In fear of the prospect, Bradshaw killed himself on November 27, 1943, before he could be deployed.[67] Meanwhile, Harry was working to build the Rooklyn brand even further. On April 24, 1944, he applied for a permit to open a new amusement arcade, Happyland, just down the road at 148 Pitt Street.[68] Apparently, not only was trade strong, but it was also strong enough to support two competing enterprises only a matter of blocks from each other.

By October 1944, the shifting sands of the War in the Pacific saw General MacArthur make the decision to move the Allied command's GHQ once again, this time out of the country entirely to a forward position in Hollandia, New Guinea.[69] With the American soldiers leaving en masse, the American Centre announced that it would close on January 2, 1945, after a brief (but profitable) eighteen months of operation.[70] There was some discussion in the early months of 1945 about the Australian Army taking over the vacated facility for local troops, but the plan was rejected.[71] Although the American Centre would not continue, the experience was a highly positive one for Jack; not only did he manage to avoid being deployed on active duty for the entirety of the war, but he made a lot of money while doing so. Perhaps even more importantly, Jack made contacts and established himself as *the* premier entertainment provider in Australia, with the cachet from his work with the American military only strengthening his existing connections in the coin-operated machine industry in the United States. Though it was winding down, the war was not even officially over before Jack was once again in the United States, on the hunt to purchase the next hot pinball (and, probably, slot) machines to bring back to Australia. A short note in the August 20, 1945, edition of the *Cash Box*, an industry magazine, mentions that Jack was "still in the U.S. and is expected back in Chi[cago] to complete the buying he started when he was last here before he returns home again."[72] There was seemingly no rest for the Rooklyns, already looking forward to the next opportunity to grow their business.

While he was still actively buying new machines in the United States, the postwar years were nevertheless a period of consolidation and change for the burgeoning Rooklyn empire. By the end of 1946, the brothers' first arcade, Pennyland, was closing, selling off machines in an advertisement in the *Sydney Morning Herald*, in spite of the still-dubious legality of the products.[73] Just over a year later, Harry's Happyland was also selling off all of its machines and games, advertising that "everything must be sold" on April 19, 1948.[74] The Rooklyns did not divest from amusement arcades completely, and Harry continued to run the Big Top arcade on Lower George Street, a role he held with the venue well into the 1980s.[75]

Meanwhile, Jack was finding a new passion: sailing. He had first got the sailing bug in the prewar years of the late 1930s, purchasing his first yacht, *White Wings*, around this time. A decade later, in 1949, *White Wings* (with Jack at the helm) was one of seven contenders in the inaugural Brisbane to Gladstone yacht race, a forebear of his later success in the iconic Sydney to Hobart race in subsequent decades.[76] Rooklyn's lackluster performance in the inaugural Brisbane to Gladstone race was, in many respects, an aberration. There was much more success in Jack's future as a skipper. On the water, he would make just as much a name for himself (if not more) as he would in the amusement trade.

For Jack, this period was not solely about Sydney amusement arcades and yacht racing. It was in the late 1940s that he would make his first forays into taking his business international, a campaign for success that started with a trip to his birth country, England. Ever the networker,

Jack was quick to make the acquaintance of one of the most successful entertainment entrepreneurs in British history, Billy Butlin. The South African–born mogul started his career operating fairgrounds across Great Britain, which later transformed into the Butlin's holiday camps, which holidaymakers could visit to enjoy all entertainment and activities provided on-site. The first Butlin's camp opened in the coastal English town of Skegness in 1936, followed soon after by another camp in Clacton-on-Sea before the arrival of war in 1939 forced a pause in Butlin's domination of the industry.[77] Butlin's camps were requisitioned by the War Office and used as training camps, but when the military asked him to build more, Butlin spotted an opportunity. He agreed on the proviso that he would be able to buy the camps back from the government when the war concluded, adding them to his holiday camp portfolio.[78]

Just as Jack profited from his involvement with the American Centre, so too did Butlin look past the current conflict to begin planning for a future when his empire-building could resume in earnest. When Jack arrived in England, he set up a machine distribution business and won the contract to supply Butlin's camps with amusement machines.[79] Despite this deal having the potential to set him up for life given Butlin's monopoly of the British entertainment trade, Jack later described the environment in England as challenging. Though remembered as a pioneer of the industry, the postwar era was tough for Butlin, too. His new camp in the Republic of Ireland in 1948 was met with resistance from a republican population who saw holiday camps as an English concept that had the potential to corrupt the Catholic population.[80] Another venture to expand into The Bahamas fell apart in 1950 after four years of planning and a US$5 million investment. Despite his best efforts, Butlin needed more money to complete his vision and was unable to attract new investors, putting an end to his Caribbean dreams.[81] With Butlin facing these struggles, it is not surprising that Jack felt that his British business was underwhelming. Though he kept his interests there for a few more years, Jack saw the writing on the wall and decided to turn his attention elsewhere, somewhere he could make his fortune without quite so many obstructions.

Jack was back in Australia by 1950, where he was once again working with the Tivoli circuit. The entertainment industry may not have known it, but these were the dying years of vaudeville. The invention of television in the mid-1950s was a death knell for live performance and, by the end of the decade, the profits to be made by theater companies like the Tivoli had shrunk into insignificance.[82] In late 1950, Jack found himself going head-to-head with the Actors' Equity union over his management of the Tivoli ballet girls. The flashpoint was a proposed appearance at a military recruiting drive in Sydney's CBD, with the union denying the request for the ballerinas to dance without being paid.[83] The union threatened to fine members who performed £10 each, a move that Rooklyn publicly criticized as unpatriotic. In the end, the union won this tug-of-war and other, non-union performers from the Tivoli took the place of the ballet at the rally. The incident seems to have hit a nerve with Rooklyn, though, and soured his views on the Australian entertainment business where he had made his start. In July 1951, he was once again in Chicago where he told "some stories about APRA (Australian Performing Rights Association) which made music ops who listened to him plenty hot under the collar."[84] His frustration with the state of live performing in Australia may have had something to do with his next move in 1952, one that would bring him one step closer to Bally and, in turn, notoriety.

His great British adventure had not lived up to expectations, and he was at loggerheads with the industry in Australia. It was in this context that Jack Rooklyn decided to take a new route to success, this time in the far more foreign terrain of Southeast Asia. Once a British bastion in the region, Singapore had fallen to the Japanese during World War II and now was in a period of rebuilding, along with so many other Asian countries that had also been caught up in the Pacific conflict.[85] Setting up a base in Singapore, Jack entered the Asian market with Harry once more in tow. The June 8, 1954, edition of the *Straits Times* refers to Harry as "an Australian businessman, prominent in the entertainment trade," touring Malaya in pursuit of the introduction of coin-operated radios (jukeboxes) there while Jack remained in Singapore, keeping watch over Rooklyn business interests there.[86]

The Rooklyns' expansion into Asia was not limited to the amusement machine business, though that remained a core part of their portfolio. In 1955, Jack was making waves in Singapore through his campaign to introduce greyhound racing to the country. Under Rooklyn's proposal, his company Rooklyn Amusements would "bring dogs and trainers from Australia . . . we hope to get about 10,000 to 15,000 people to a weekly night meeting."[87] The profits projected by Jack were indeed persuasive: He claimed that the Singaporean government could pocket between $3 and $5 million a year from betting, taxes, and admission fees alone. This was Jack's first foray into the racing industry, and he was potentially influenced by his earlier association with the Butlin empire in England, which had ties to greyhound racing. Butlin's partner in his failed Bahamian camp was a man named Alfred Critchley, head of the British Greyhound Racing Association and the man "who first brought dog-racing to Britain."[88] Supporting the idea that it was Jack's British connection driving his plans in Singapore is the fact that he told local media he was working with an architect in the United Kingdom who was helping design his proposed racetrack, a connection he likely made through his dealings with Butlin.[89] Whatever the case, Rooklyn's plans for greyhound racing did not come to fruition, stymied by a Singaporean population who were increasingly moving toward the adoption of "Asian values" that looked down on "the mentality of taking unreasonable chances" promoted by gambling.[90]

In the mid-1950s, Jack continued to work alongside some of the most prominent names in the Australian entertainment business, like boxing promoter Harry Miller. Like the Rooklyns, Miller had immigrated to Australia as a young man from England and, also like Jack, had worked a variety of odd jobs through the peak of the Depression era until being hired as the manager of Sydney Stadium in 1936.[91] The parent company of Sydney Stadium, Stadiums Ltd., had been owned (until his death in 1953) by Melbourne entrepreneur John Wren, a former bookmaker and media mogul reputed for capitalizing on his political connections to get ahead—former New South Wales premier Jack Lang once pejoratively described him as a "champion wire-puller."[92] Though accused of suborning corruption on numerous occasions over the course of his career, Wren was never proven to have paid for political favors. In any case, in the early 20th century Wren's Stadiums Ltd. enjoyed a virtual monopoly on boxing promotion in eastern Australia.[93] When French fighter Robert Cohen won the bantamweight title in Bangkok over Thai police lieutenant Chamroen Songkitat in September 1954, it was Jack Rooklyn who was dispatched from Singapore to Thailand as a representative of Stadiums Ltd. to invite Cohen to defend his title in Sydney.[94] Jack's ability to assist Miller in this way, due to his physical presence in Asia, was not the extent of his dealings with Stadiums Ltd. Years later, he would continue to work with Miller and another iconic entertainment industry figure, Lee Gordon, to bring some of the world's biggest musical stars, such as Frank Sinatra and Sammy Davis Jr., to Australia.

Apart from his thriving amusement machine business and continued dabbling in the live entertainment sector, Jack's life changed in other, more personal ways during his time in Singapore. He also found the woman who would become Mrs. Rooklyn. Joan Johnson had come to Singapore from Sydney for a holiday around 1956, meeting the enigmatic young impresario from her own hometown. Having met Jack, Joan extended her holiday—in the end, her trip to Singapore lasted fifteen months, and when she returned, she came with a new last name as well. Jack and Joan were married in a civil ceremony in Singapore on August 27, 1956, later renewing their vows in a Jewish ceremony at the Woollahra Synagogue when the couple returned to Australia toward the end of 1957.[95] Jack and Joan's marriage was to be a lasting one, surviving all of the later upheaval in Jack's life. The union resulted in three children: a son (who followed his father into the world of sailing with great success) and two daughters.[96]

Jack's gamble to try his luck in Asia, even after being burned by his less successful European endeavors, had paid off. In the five years or so that he operated in Southeast Asia, Jack had developed a reputation as a key distributor of amusement machines—as well as someone who could get things done in what was, at times, a challenging environment. This was, in no small part, due to Jack's willingness to grease wheels and cut corners where needed. When journalist Evan Whitton interviewed Jack about his time in Asia many years later, he asked him outright, "[Y]ou'd have to do a bit of slinging [paying bribes] in the East, wouldn't you?" Jack rejected the accusation, before qualifying his statement: "No . . . we might pay unofficial taxes here or there, but slinging we never do." In spite of this damning admission, Jack did not stop there, going on to give even more insight into the way the Rooklyns operated during their time based out of Singapore. He told Whitton that "perhaps we've sold a portion of the business, a few shares to a relative, or something of that nature, but never any open bribery."[97] Was it this shrewd method of doing business that led to the Rooklyns being so successful in their Asian business, where they failed in Europe? It is hard to say, but what is clear is that Jack would be accused decades later, in the 1970s, of using the same tactic—offering a stake in his business in lieu of cash bribes—to corrupt police looking into his ties to organized crime in Sydney. Whether he learned this skill in Asia or not, Jack Rooklyn seems to have recognized the enduring value of the "Singapore sling."

Things were changing for the Rooklyns' business interests by 1957, for the worse in Singapore and (hopefully) for the better in New South Wales. Once a British colony, Singapore was now firmly on the path to self-governance and, within a few years, would become an autonomous state. Part of this transition to independence included an emerging party politics in Singapore, increasingly dominated by the People's Action Party (PAP) and its leader Lee Kuan Yew, who would become the first prime minister of Singapore when the PAP won the May 1959 elections in a landslide victory.[98] Lee's PAP had campaigned on an Asian values platform, which would see Singapore institute a prohibition on gambling that would have stymied the Rooklyns' business there considerably.[99] The election of a values-oriented government, no doubt, also made the Singapore sling much harder to accomplish. At the same time that regulations on gambling were tightening in Singapore, they were liberalizing in New South Wales. The state had legalized poker machines on July 31, 1956, just one month prior to Jack's marriage to Joan in Singapore. Though machines had always been an illicit presence in the New South Wales pub and club scene to some extent, legalization meant that the coming years were certain to be highly profitable to any person who had the connections and ability to step into the marketplace. Indeed, by the end of the decade, there were an estimated 7,000 machines in New South Wales, across 1,100 different venues.[100] Jack could no doubt see that his position was becoming ever more tenuous in Singapore, just as his fortunes in New South Wales were again starting to rise. With a new wife, also from Sydney, and the potential to make a large amount of money by using his connections to reenter the Australian market, the decision was obvious. After five years away, Jack Rooklyn was coming home.

3

Family Vacations

Jack Rooklyn was returning from Asia triumphant. He was anything but a certain bet when he had left to seek his fortune abroad in the early 1950s. Then, he was coming off the back of a largely failed attempt to conquer Europe, and was mostly known for his involvement in a vaudeville business that was on its way toward being made redundant with the advent of television. Now, Rooklyn had proven himself as a *real* businessman—not just on the relatively sedate streets of postwar Sydney but also navigating far more complex markets in exotic locales like Bangkok, Manila, and Saigon.[1] Rooklyn's move into Asia after the war came at the best possible time, too: It was not long after that Singapore would pivot to a more restrictive stance on gambling, and other nations in which Rooklyn operated in Southeast Asia would experience the brutal impacts (both direct and indirect) of the Vietnam War. Rooklyn had been a chief distributor for Lion Manufacturing and, more pertinently, Bally since he set up shop in Singapore in 1952. For five years he had helped establish Bally's presence in what was expected to be a growth market, just as other company agents had done in Cuba and, later, attempted in The Bahamas. These international markets could not have been more crucial to Bally's future growth, considering the far more dire (comparatively) situation on the home front in the 1950s. The Johnson Act, banning interstate transport of slot machines, was passed into law in 1951 and, shortly after, a ban was placed on the manufacture of slot machines entirely in Bally's home state of Illinois.[2] In the United States, the noose was tightening around Bally's business in a way that would have made Rooklyn's Asian distribution empire seem even more appealing.

The appeal only grew on July 31, 1956, when New South Wales legalized the use of poker machines in non-proprietary clubs, essentially opening the gate for their widespread rollout for the first time in New South Wales history. Liberalization was largely the product of a royal commission presided over by senior Supreme Court judge Allan Victor Maxwell from 1951 to 1954, tasked with examining (among other related subjects) the state's liquor laws and existing processes for managing licenses for hotels and clubs.[3] Arguably, the most significant direct impact of the Maxwell commission was that it brought an end to the six o'clock closing laws, which, since 1916, had forced hotels and pubs to stop serving alcohol at 6 p.m. in an effort to prevent public drunkenness and a general decay in public morality.[4] Maxwell's findings prompted the New South Wales government to hold a referendum on the issue in 1954, which, when passed, saw serving hours extended to 10 p.m. There was a knock-on impact for those with more of an interest in slot machines than booze, as well. Another of Maxwell's recommendations was to amend the Liquor Act to provide for additional club licenses, which were at that time tightly restricted. Arguing successfully that clubs across New South Wales were responsible for more than 2,000 jobs in 1956, which were funded by slot machines, the state's club lobby successfully convinced the state government not just to expand licenses, but to permit gaming machines to be placed in a far greater variety of venues than before. The windfall for clubs was enormous, with the profit margins on some machines as high as 80 percent in favor of the venue.[5] Though venues across the state had always had illegal machines, the industry was no longer a clandestine affair, and, naturally, a provider (or providers) would have to step into the gap to supply the newly legal slot machines that clubs were clamoring for. Just as companies like Bally were struggling at home, their fortunes were turning around in faraway Australia.

When he came back to Australia in early 1957, Rooklyn did not focus exclusively on his slot machine distribution business at first. Instead, he fell back into a familiar role working with an old colleague, concert promoter Lee Gordon. Born in Detroit, Michigan, Rooklyn's partner had arrived in Australia in 1953 as a salesman before identifying a major gap in the country's live entertainment scene: Whereas the vaudeville industry in which Rooklyn made his career was flailing, there was a strong appetite for international acts and, especially, performances from rock 'n' roll and pop stars from the United States.[6] Though an ambitious idea, Gordon soon succeeded in his plan; within two years, by January 1955, the entrepreneur had partnered with Stadiums Ltd. to bring music icon Frank Sinatra to Australia for the first time ever. It was a successful endeavor and, years later, Sinatra would serve as best man at Gordon's wedding. Gordon's star only continued to rise from there, with his performers playing to packed crowds in Stadiums Ltd. venues around the country throughout the late 1950s, including tours in 1957 featuring the likes of Bill Haley and the Comets and Little Richard.[7]

It is likely that Rooklyn would have worked on these major cultural events. He said that immediately after leaving Asia he began working with Gordon in Melbourne, part of the usual touring circuit.[8] How Gordon and Rooklyn came to meet each other is unclear, as Gordon only arrived in Australia in 1953, after Rooklyn had relocated to Singapore. What is clear is that the duo worked together prior to Rooklyn's 1957 return to the country, however; earlier, he had acted as Gordon's agent in Asia and assisted to bring his acts there in yet another of Rooklyn's many entertainment industry sidelines. Indeed, it is possible that Rooklyn was connected to Gordon via Harry Miller, the boxing promoter and manager of Sydney Stadium. Gordon and Miller worked together to put on Gordon's concerts at Miller's venue, and Rooklyn was noted as having acted as Miller's agent in Asia in 1954—it is possible that Miller tipped Gordon off that Rooklyn was a useful man to know, if the music promoter ever wanted to crack the Southeast Asian market.[9] Rooklyn may not have been aware that his new partner Gordon was linked to the American Mafia, though that might have explained why he had found it so easy to attract a big name like Sinatra to Australia with no background whatsoever in putting on major events in the country. In the late 1940s, Gordon had worked as a promoter and booker at Havana's Tropicana Club, operated from 1946 until the Cuban Revolution in 1959 by Mafia interests led by Tampa's Santo Trafficante Jr.[10] In Havana, Gordon would have come across the likes of Bally's European employee Dino Cellini and others who would later be linked to the company, including Jerry Catena, who traveled to Havana as part of the Genovese Family contingent on various occasions.[11]

Gordon's organized crime links did not end at the Tropicana Club, or even the speculation about his relationship with Sinatra. In 1958, he acquired the local rights to Roulette Records, an American company headed by Morris Levy and later found to have strong ties to the Genovese Family, even serving as a front for later boss Vincent Gigante, the failed assassin of Frank Costello.[12] Shortly after Gordon set up Roulette's Australian operation, he disappeared overseas, suffering from a mental breakdown. While he later returned to his business, things never again reached the peaks of the mid-1950s and Gordon fell deeper into drug addiction. He returned to Australia in 1960, sold off the record label and instead focused on the concert tours where he had made his reputation, as well as new ventures like the conversion of a former cinema in Sydney's vice district, Kings Cross, into one of Australia's first discotheques, The Birdcage. Gordon also partnered in opening the Jewel Box Revue Club, the first drag club in Australia, which would later become the infamous Les Girls. His partner in both was not the American Mafia, but a local man with an equally questionable reputation: the notorious former nightclub owner, Abraham Gilbert Saffron. While Saffron provided the financial backing for the venues, described as Gordon's "paymaster," the promoter was the gregarious face of the partnership.[13] The business relationship between Gordon and Saffron continued until 1963, when Gordon fled Australia after a warrant was issued for his arrest after he failed to appear in court on charges of attempting to obtain pethidine without a prescription. He fled to London where, on November 7, 1963, he was found dead from a coronary occlusion in a Kensington hotel room.[14]

Gordon offers an early connection between Rooklyn and Saffron, a pair whose relationship only continued to flourish in the decades that followed—by the early 1970s, their names were almost inextricably linked in the New South Wales press. Even beyond their mutual association with organized crime, Rooklyn and Saffron had much in common. Like Rooklyn, Saffron was born to Russian-Jewish parents, with his father a draper, just like Rooklyn's parents. Whereas the Rooklyns initially settled in Haberfield, the Saffrons were based in another part of Sydney's inner-west, Annandale. Saffron was born on October 6, 1919, the youngest of three sons—though he also had two sisters, compared to Rooklyn's one.[15] In the 1930s, the Saffron drapery business moved into bustling inner-city Pitt Street, just down the road from the Rooklyns' first arcade, Pennyland. During the war years, Saffron dabbled in gambling but mostly focused on fencing black market stolen goods along with a partner he had met on Pitt Street, an American named Hilton Kincaid.[16] Later, Saffron and Kincaid partnered in a (slightly) more legitimate venture, laundering the illicit profits of their wartime stolen goods ring into the purchase of The Roosevelt Club in Kings Cross and, from there, a string of hotels and pubs across the Hunter Valley, north of Sydney. Saffron and Kincaid were frustrated by a state law that prevented a person from holding more than one liquor license at any given time, but quickly found a way around this, using the names of family members and other associates to "front" for them and pose as the owners of their new acquisitions while Saffron and Kincaid pulled the strings behind the scenes. It was this scam, in part, that led to Saffron facing the Maxwell commission in the early 1950s, and being named as one of the worst liquor offenders in Sydney.[17]

Maxwell named The Roosevelt Club as the worst perpetrator of illegal alcohol sales in Sydney, made even worse by the fact that the venue was not permitted to sell alcohol at all—it did not have a liquor license; instead, Saffron diverted alcohol nominally purchased for the other hotels and pubs in his portfolio to the Kings Cross club where it was sold at a considerable markup.[18] The judge went on to call The Roosevelt Club "the most notorious and disreputable nightclub in the city" and accused Saffron, who had denied any wrongdoing when he appeared before the commission, of lying under oath.[19] As a result of Maxwell's accusation, Saffron was indicted for perjury and forced to sell off the illegal hotel interests the commission had revealed. Ultimately, these penalties were short-lived. On the basis of tenuous legal argument, Saffron's evidence to Maxwell was ruled inadmissible in his trial, making it hard to prove perjury took place, and he was later able to restore his business holdings.[20]

By the mid-1950s, Saffron began to expand from illegal liquor sales into other lucrative sidelines, like the hosting of sex parties for the city's elite, which helped Saffron secure his position at the top of the criminal milieu, in more ways than one.

What began as simple parties for a few friends at the palatial home of prominent doctor, and illegal abortion provider, Reginald Stuart-Jones soon became a regular affair hosted at one of Saffron's properties like the Appin Hotel in Kings Cross, a stone's throw from The Roosevelt Club.[21] Saffron supplied the venue, the booze, and the girls and asked nothing in return, ever a benevolent host. However, the orgies were more than they seemed: Saffron rigged his properties with two-way mirrors and secret cameras, taking pictures of those attending his parties (including police, doctors, lawyers, judges, and businessmen) and holding them to use as blackmail if he ever found himself in trouble with the law again. Saffron's reputation for sexual depravity became public in 1956 when he faced charges of "scandalous conduct" emerging from a sex party he and Kincaid were involved in, where he was accused of whipping a naked woman and, later, a separate count of having committed an "unnatural offence" on another woman at a property in Potts Point several months later.[22] Both charges were ultimately dismissed under a cloud of corruption and the suggestion that witnesses were interfered with on Saffron's behalf, and the man now dubbed "Mr. Sin" slipped the net with no more than a tokenistic charge of possessing obscene publications, namely pornographic magazines. The fine for this offense was not enough to dissuade Saffron, who allegedly ordered "four tons . . . of pornographic books" after the case was settled, making a resale profit of around £66,000, equivalent to more than $1.5 million in modern currency.[23] This was the man that Gordon went into business with, effectively acting as Saffron's front at The Birdcage and the Jewel Box Revue. Saffron was also the man who, later, would be implicated with Rooklyn in his alleged attempts to corrupt New South Wales Police officers on behalf of Bally.

Having spent some time working with Gordon after returning to Australia, Rooklyn was ready to jump back into the amusement arcade business in Sydney by the end of the decade. Once again, he set his sights on a glorious return to his old stomping grounds of Pitt Street, where he had set up Pennyland almost twenty years earlier. Playland, the new venue from Rooklyn Investments Pty. Ltd., was located near Sydney's town hall at 252 Pitt Street, opening its doors in early 1960.[24] Rooklyn described the amusement arcade business as a model for success, no matter whether they were located in downtown Sydney or far-flung areas where he also had establishments, like Singapore or Thailand. He told a journalist in 1968 that "regardless of colour or creed, a boy is just a boy . . . the machines attract the boys, though, of course, the boys attract the girls."[25] Ironically, Rooklyn put the blame for any juvenile delinquency at his amusement arcades like Playland on suburban clubs and, in an astounding display of hypocrisy, poker machines. He told the *Bulletin* that he thought "the suburban clubs have a great deal to answer for—Mum and Dad are off enjoying the Thursday night 50–50 dance and playing poker machines and they don't really know or care what their teenage sons are doing."[26] Rooklyn's statement blaming poker machines for social disorder seems counterproductive, not just because of his long connection to Bally and the gaming machine industry, but also because by the time this interview was published in the late 1960s, Rooklyn was no longer just a distributor of Bally, but the managing director of its entire Australian operation.

The company's move into Australia began in earnest not long after Bally changed hands in 1963, when William O'Donnell finally gathered a team of investors in an effort to save the company from liquidation. This last-ditch, desperate move relied on partners Abe Green and Barnett Sugarman from New Jersey–based Runyon Sales, who in turn acted as front men for Genovese boss Jerry Catena's hidden ownership stake in Bally.[27] The organized crime infiltration of Bally was not the only problematic change occurring in the early 1960s, with similar shifts in leadership in New South Wales taking place that would also have implications for Bally's campaign over the next decade to enter the Australian market. On February 28, 1962, Deputy Commissioner Norman Allan was named the new chief commissioner of the New South Wales Police Force. Nicknamed "Norman the Foreman" for his superior administrative talents, Allan had grown up in Sydney's inner-west like so many in the criminal milieu, and was even just a year below Rooklyn at Haberfield

Public School.[28] He had very little experience with on-the-street policing, having been plucked from beat duty to serve first as a police prosecutor and, later, assistant to wartime police commissioner Bill Mackay. Despite his protestations to the contrary, illegal casinos flourished in Allan's ten years at the helm of the police force, as did the careers of senior officers with links to organized crime like Ray "Gunner" Kelly and Fred Krahe.[29] Though unproven, a close associate of gambling czar Perce Galea once told journalist David Hickie that Allan (and his successor, Fred Hanson) received $100,000 each year in bribes.[30] The accusation was supported later by Saffron's son, Alan, who alleged that his father paid Allan between $5,000 and $10,000 each week as the cost for operating, and that Allan was a frequent guest in the Saffron home.[31] If true, Allan would not have been the first corrupt police officer to hold the top job, and he certainly would not be the last.

Norman Allan was not the only person with links to organized crime who rose to power in the state during this era. Three years later, an election was held that elevated Robin "Robert" Askin to the lofty position of premier of New South Wales. Again, Askin was born in Sydney's inner-west on April 4, 1907, the son of a working-class tram driver and railway guard.[32] He enlisted in the Australian Imperial Force (AIF) in World War II, and was deployed on two occasions, in 1942 and 1943, then to Borneo in July 1945, a month before nuclear bombs were dropped on Japan and the War in the Pacific came to a conclusion. In the military, Askin attained the nickname "Slippery Sam" in reference to his less than honorable sideline business as an illegal starting-price (SP) bookmaker for his unit.[33] He became active in the Liberal Party after leaving the military and was elected as Member for Collaroy, in Sydney's north, in the 1950 election. After one failed tilt at forming government, Askin led his party to victory against a long-serving Labor government increasingly seen as out of touch with the average citizen.[34] Askin's time in office is widely considered a time of consolidation and growth for organized crime in Sydney, in part due to the permissive attitudes (and potential corruption) of the premier. A former bookmaker himself, Askin was seen to be tolerant of the illegal gambling industry and uninterested in pressuring police to act against illegal casinos and SP bookies. The same source from the Galea camp who told Hickie that Allan received bribes also implicated Askin in the scheme, and said that "the largest inner-city casinos were run by friends of Askin and [police comissioner Fred] Hanson in return for huge cash pay-offs."[35] Like with Allan, these claims of corruption were never proven, but nevertheless the perception existed that in 1960s New South Wales, organized crime could find both a premier and police commissioner who would look after the interests of the vice trade, for a fee.

It was into this context that the first American organized crime figures began to arrive in 1965. One of the first in this Mafia vanguard was Miami-based Morris Lansburgh, who came to vacation in Sydney only a few months after Askin's May election.[36] Lansburgh did not fly under the radar on this trip, receiving a fawning review in the *Australian Women's Weekly* where the millionaire hotelier was described as a man "with varied interests."[37] One of the "varied interests" the magazine was referring to was Lansburgh's ownership of the world-famous Eden Roc hotel in Miami, Florida. Another was his stake in The Flamingo casino in Las Vegas, first opened by Bugsy Siegel in the 1940s and still operated in the 1960s by Mafia identities like Siegel's old friend Meyer Lansky. Years later, Lansburgh's involvement with Lansky and others in a major fraud centered on The Flamingo would become public. During his time as part-owner of the casino, Lansburgh took part in a "skim" in which they concealed and distributed around $36 million in income from The Flamingo to avoid paying federal taxes on the money. While Lansky fled to Israel in an attempt to dodge prison, Lansburgh pleaded guilty and served five months in prison.[38] While this fall from grace was several years in Lansburgh's future at the time he touched down in Sydney in 1965, his association with mobsters like Lansky was already open knowledge. Not long after his Sydney trip, Lansburgh was put on a British stop list after flying into London with Philadelphia mob boss Angelo Bruno and, in 1967, British territory The Bahamas followed suit.[39]

The ban on Lansburgh in The Bahamas sank his proposed leasing of a casino in the country at the same time that another Lansky associate, Dino Cellini, was blacklisted from the country despite being named Bally's distributor in the region.[40] Lansky himself had been accused of attempting to bribe the Bahamian minister of finance to allow casino gambling, which, combined with Lansburgh and Cellini's moves into The Bahamas at the same time, suggests a concerted campaign to infiltrate the Caribbean nation in the years following the collapse of the Mafia's Cuban enterprise in the late 1950s. With the Lansky group clearly looking to expand their reach internationally, it seems reasonable to suggest that, even if it was not the primary purpose of his trip, Lansburgh would have been keeping his eyes open for opportunity while he was in Australia. If so, he would have liked what he saw. Lansburgh received a warm welcome from Sydney nightclub operators like Denis Wong, a friend of Premier Askin. Wong ran Chequers in Sydney's Chinatown, a club Lansburgh allegedly described as being "better than either the Copacabana or the Latin Quarter in New York."[41] Chequers was a premier venue that hosted American artists who also performed at Lansburgh's Eden Roc, many of whom were brought into Australia by Rooklyn's colleague Lee Gordon. Lansburgh did not (as far as can be told) invest in any projects in Australia as a result of his visit, likely focused on the upcoming and ill-fated Bahamian venture, but the report of his visit would have filtered back to Lansky, potentially planting the seed for later efforts to crack the Australian market in the 1970s.

Lansburgh was not the only Mafia associate to visit Australia in 1965. Not only was Joseph Dan Testa first, but his visit would also prove to be far more consequential. Testa, not to be confused with Gambino/Lucchese Family killer Joseph Testa, was born in Chicago, Illinois, on January 5, 1928.[42] He was not born into the Mafia lifestyle, and first became affiliated with members of the Chicago Outfit after purchasing a savings and loan banking facility, where he was well placed to launder money for organized crime in return for a cut of the profits. Former Testa friend Michael Corbitt testified that Chicago mafiosos conducted large purchases through Testa's bank in order to avoid scrutiny, buying up parcels of land and property in cash, with no questions asked.[43] His ability to legitimize cash made Testa valuable to organized crime and, though he never officially became a "made" member of the Family, he became close to senior Mafia leaders like Tony Accardo and Sam Giancana, both of whom served as boss of the Outfit at one point or another. His closest relationship, however, was reputedly with Felix "Milwaukee Phil" Alderisio, a feared hitman who, it is believed, served as the Outfit's boss for a short period in the late 1960s.[44] Alderisio was tapped into some of the biggest players in Chicago, coming into the Family on the recommendation of his cousin Louis "Cock-Eyed" Fratto, the "Mob Boss of Iowa."[45] He formed a deadly duo with fellow assassin Charles Nicoletti for more than two decades, and was suspected of carrying out more than a dozen murders on behalf of the Outfit. The men were so serious about their craft that they created what they called a "Hitmobile"—a car fitted out with secret compartments to hide murder weapons, and special switches controlling head- and taillights to avoid detection by police and (presumably) their victims.[46]

Testa did not just launder mob money, but also spent his cut on developing an extensive property portfolio including an apartment complex near Chicago O'Hare Airport and a trailer park in the small village of Justice, Illinois.[47] In Justice, Testa used the strong-arm skills learned from his associates in the Mafia to his benefit. Shortly after his first visit to Australia, Testa was accused of intimidating the residents of his trailer park to vote for his ally, James Gualano, as mayor of Justice. Testa allegedly told any of his tenants not willing to vote for Gualano in 1967 that "if you like this place you should honor my local politics, if not you should move."[48] At the time, Testa was seeking to have the village rezone 14 acres adjacent to his Sterling Estates trailer park to allow for expansion, explaining his desire to see Gualano succeed in the election. With Testa's help, Gualano won the election, but that was not the end. Just one year later, Gualano was ousted from office when it was revealed that he had been convicted on several previous occasions of fraud, which disqualified him from running for mayor in the first place (by 1968, Gualano had served in the role for around 11 years).[49] The Gualano affair was not the only case of Testa compromising public officials to get what he wanted. Corbitt, his close friend, was police chief of nearby Willow Springs. Corbitt admitted that he had been purposefully placed in the Willow Springs police department as a young man on the advice of Giancana, who saw benefit in having an ally on the force. Before becoming an officer, Corbitt had worked at an Outfit-run gas station that was used as a place to store stolen goods before they were sold.[50]

Before heading for Sydney in February 1965, Testa first stopped in Hong Kong, where it is believed he was given the name of gambling identity Ronnie Lee by a mutual associate and told to look Lee up when he arrived in Australia.[51] He did just that, linking up with Lee and his associate Reg Andrews, who together with Eric O'Farrell and Perce Galea ran several major illegal casinos in Sydney, such as the Forbes Club and the Double Bay Bridge Club.[52] In 1965, at the time of Testa's visit, Lee and Andrews also were partners in the Kellett Club in Kings Cross with baccarat king Richard Gabriel Reilly, a former doorman at Saffron's Roosevelt Club who was shot dead in his car in a June 1967 ambush. After his murder, Reilly's "black book" was discovered, containing records of every highly placed official that he paid off to do business, causing a stir in political and policing circles.[53] Thanks to his Hong Kong connection, Testa had fallen in with some of the key players in Sydney's illegal gambling trade, all of whom had the kind of local relationships with police and politicians that Testa knew from experience were needed to operate safely and successfully. When Testa left Australia a few weeks later, he surely had stories to tell his associates back in Chicago. In the years after his 1965 visit, Testa was reportedly followed to Sydney in an under-the-radar visit by Alderisio and another Outfit killer, Jimmy "The Monk" Allegretti. While little is known about what Alderisio and Allegretti did in Sydney, it is probable that they also met up with Lee and Andrews, who had hosted the American pair's friend Testa so well in 1965.[54]

What Testa, Alderisio, and Allegretti found in Sydney was an underworld that was less organized than they were used to in Chicago but, nevertheless, was on its way. At its heart was a trio of Sydneysiders who came to supplant Lee and Andrews as the Outfit's key contacts in Australia, building on these connections to the American Mafia to enhance their stranglehold on crime in New South Wales. Most senior of this group was Leonard "Lennie" McPherson, who relished his reputation as the "Mr. Big" of the Sydney underworld. McPherson was born on May 19, 1921, to a working-class family from Balmain, nestled in the same pocket of Sydney's inner-west where Police Commissioner Allan, Premier Askin, and others from the Sydney milieu like Rooklyn and Saffron spent their childhood.[55] McPherson was an early bloomer, receiving a good behavior bond for stealing at age 11 and, by 13, serving a term of imprisonment in the notorious Mount Penang juvenile reformatory. He romanticized the life of crime he was embarking on, and dreamed of building the same kind of reputation as a gangster as his idol, Al Capone. In 1951, McPherson even traveled to Chicago on a false passport in hopes of meeting members of Capone's Outfit, without success.[56]

Back in Sydney, McPherson established himself as a feared standover man through actions like the 1959 murder of George Hackett, a charge he only beat with the assistance of the state attorney-general, Reg Downing, who spiked the case after (allegedly) McPherson "donated" £10,000 to the politician's reelection fund.[57] The most audacious murder McPherson was accused of occurred on July 9, 1963, when rival Robert "Pretty Boy" Walker was killed after being shot at close range while walking to a pub near his Randwick home. In what seemed an homage to the Capone legend, Walker's murder was the first gangland killing in Australia to be carried out with a machine gun. Walker had attracted McPherson's ire by shooting McPherson's associate Stanley Smith in the chest during an altercation (Smith was reputedly McPherson's wheelman for the Walker hit).[58] What made the Walker shooting difficult to pin on the men was that July 9 was also the day of McPherson's second wedding. Shortly before Walker's murder, Smith received a phone call and both men excused themselves from the reception for a short period, rejoining the party after taking the brief break to commit a brutal, public murder.[59] No one was ever charged with the Walker murder, though it was an open secret in the underworld (and among police, like McPherson's "handler" Ray Kelly) that Walker had paid the ultimate price for challenging the city's Mr. Big.

Stanley "Stan the Man" Smith was the second member of Sydney's ruling underworld triumvirate. He was a Balmain boy like McPherson, though born on January 3, 1937, making Smith sixteen years younger than his partner. Working in tough, thankless jobs at the Sydney docks in the mid-1950s, Smith met McPherson at the age of eighteen and was quickly introduced to the business of criminal standover.[60] While McPherson was more than capable of holding his own, Smith was notorious as an enforcer who was set apart by the sheer level of brutality he was capable of—over the course of his career Smith was linked to at least 25 shootings and murders, a record that would have been impressive even for Mafia hitmen like Alderisio and Allegretti.[61] There were rumors in the Sydney underworld that it was actually Smith's penchant for violence that had secured the trio's ties with Testa. An apocryphal story making the rounds recounted that Smith and McPherson had first met Testa before 1965, on a visit to the United States. On this occasion, McPherson and Smith were talking to Testa at a party when another guest was rude to him. Smith "promptly knocked the bad-mannered one down and the friendship with Testa started from there."[62] While it is unlikely that Testa had crossed paths with McPherson and Smith prior to 1965, as with most stories there is often a grain of truth in it. Though this was not how Testa first met the pair, there is little doubt, given his habitual preference for violence, that Smith may have (at some point) defended Testa's honor in such a way.

The third and final man who became close to Testa was George David Freeman, a man with less of a reputation for wanton violence than his peers—though no less dangerous. Another wayward youth from the inner-west, Freeman was a contemporary of Smith, born on January 22, 1935. Like the others, he did time in a youth reformatory for stealing as a teenager. He met McPherson, already emerging as a legend of the local criminal scene, through Smith, whom he had grown up with on the streets of Sydney.[63] Whereas McPherson and Smith were focused on standover and protection rackets (with an occasional sideline in gangland-style murders), Freeman was more concerned with illegal gambling, and worked as a SP bookmaker under the tutelage of "Melbourne" Mick Bartley. In the mid-1960s, Freeman's decision to enter into the illegal bookmaking industry may have seemed short-sighted, with off-track betting legalized by the Labor government in 1964, just prior to Askin's election. These criticisms are misplaced, however, as Australians continued to patronize illegal bookmakers rather than the state-administrated Totalisator Administration Board (TAB) facilities. Not only were local independent bookies easier to access, set up at any local pub on a Saturday, but they had another advantage in that they did not pay taxes in the same way their legal competitors did, meaning they were able to offer better payouts to punters and a more profitable enterprise for the bookies themselves.[64] Later, Freeman would build on his success as a bookmaker, diversifying his business model to encompass related activities like race-fixing and illegal casinos, where even more money could be made.

Just two years after Testa and Lansburgh visited, Sydney was changed forever by an agreement that it would serve as a venue for rest and recreation (R & R) leave for American soldiers fighting in the Vietnam War.[65] As they had in Brisbane during World War II, American troops flocked to Sydney; however, the conditions under which they came were very different. Whereas Brisbane was a working base for the Allied command in the 1940s, Sydney was an R & R port, which meant the soldiers who came had few day-to-day responsibilities and were ready to let their hair down. By 1968, around 1,200 American soldiers were estimated to be visiting Sydney every month.[66] The Americans tended to congregate around the Kings Cross area; as the troops typically only had six days of leave before shipping back to the frontline, basing themselves in an area dotted with bars, clubs, brothels, and strip clubs was a smart logistical decision, if nothing else.[67] The influx was a boon to the likes of Saffron, with his considerable holdings in Kings Cross and, particularly, involvement in the sex trade. It was also a gain for illegal casino operators like Lee, Andrews, and another of Freeman's mentors, Joe Taylor. It no doubt also piqued the interest of Rooklyn, who had seen what the arrival of American troops could do for the profits of his amusement businesses in World War II. The average cost of an American soldier's week of R & R in Sydney was estimated by the US military to be roughly $325, and while many did indeed spend their leave experiencing the Australian wildlife and beaches, many more "looked for a good time in the traditional soldier's sense of women and drink, as well as the less traditional something that stoned you out of your mind."[68]

It is inaccurate to suggest that drugs were not a feature of the Sydney criminal scene before the Vietnam War—indeed, intergang feuds over the supply of cocaine were partly the cause of the Razor gang wars that erupted in 1920s Sydney and resulted in pitched battles between rival groups on the streets of Kings Cross.[69] However, it is fair to say that the arrival of American troops fresh from the battlefields of Southeast Asia was a major contributor to the rising demand for marijuana and heroin in Sydney. In an effort to placate soldiers in the theater of battle (many of whom were conscripted), the American military had decided to turn a blind eye to rampant drug abuse by soldiers. By 1971, officers were reporting that widespread heroin addiction in the rank and file meant that "tens of thousands of soldiers are going back [to the United States] as walking time bombs."[70] This addiction also caused demand for heroin among troops during R & R in places like Sydney, creating a boom market for narcotics where one did not exist before.

In this vacuum, suppliers emerged that could cater to this hunger for heroin. Just one month prior to the announcement that Sydney would be an R & R destination, Texan entrepreneur Maurice "Bernie" Houghton arrived in town, seeming to have the inside line about the boom that was about to befall the city before anyone else did.[71] With stellar personal references from American generals and admirals, Houghton acquired a loan to open the Bourbon and Beefsteak restaurant in Kings Cross, just a stone's throw from the strip clubs, brothels, and casinos that would attract the American contingent when they arrived. The Bourbon became a hub for visiting troops and, in turn, the center of the heroin trade in Kings Cross. Not coincidentally, it was also the hub for a group of American ex-patriates closely linked to drug trafficking. One frequent visitor was George "Duke" Countis, another 1967 arrival with connections to American Mafia figures like Jimmy Fratianno.[72] Another was former American general Michael Hand, a Central Intelligence Agency (CIA) veteran involved in secret missions with the Hmong population in Laos where (it is believed) he was a lynchpin in securing the supply of heroin from Laos to frontline troops in a clandestine effort to ensure soldiers remained sedated and compliant.[73] Both Countis and Hand were intrinsically linked to later efforts by the McPherson, Smith, and Freeman triumvirate to maintain connections with American organized crime in the mid- to late 1970s.

His early 1951 visit to Chicago may have failed, but his rising fortunes and the connection with the Chicago Outfit via Testa had reawakened McPherson's interest in forging ties between his stable of Sydney villains and the American Mafia. In 1968, he decided it was time to try again. There was a catch, however; McPherson could not travel. He had attempted a sea voyage with Smith in 1966 to scope out business opportunities in Asia, but Australian police who were not on his payroll tipped off the authorities in each country on their itinerary. Wherever McPherson and Smith's boat docked, they were met by a welcoming committee who either turned them away or kept a close enough eye on them to prevent any meaningful criminal work being done. Hong Kong police wrote to their Australian counterparts at the time, describing an open conversation with McPherson and Smith where they "seemed rather proud of their criminal background and somewhat boastfully admitted that . . . they would have seized any opportunity to get in on the 'big time' (as they put it) smuggling gold and narcotics."[74] The harassment experienced on this trip showed McPherson that any trip to link up with the Mafia in the United States would be heavily scrutinized, and that he should send emissaries instead. Aside from this, McPherson was also experiencing heat after shooting gangster Raymond "Ducky" O'Connor dead on May 28, 1967, in the Latin Quarter nightclub, just next door to Rooklyn's Playland arcade in Pitt Street. McPherson claimed that O'Connor had tried to attack him and, in the ensuing struggle, shot himself—a claim that was rejected by others in the room, but was supported by two police detectives coincidentally sitting at the next table when the incident occurred.[75] While the coroner ultimately accepted McPherson's version and he was never charged, the attention on him would have increased his paranoia about his American trip being ruined as a result of police scrutiny.

In his place McPherson sent Smith and Freeman to the United States on false passports in 1968, with a mission to link up with Testa and, through him, other organized crime figures. Smith and Freeman set out in mid-1968, destined first for San Francisco, where Freeman engaged in a stint of shoplifting, unable to resist nabbing a cache of gems from an unattended safe in a department store.[76] Before long, they reached out to

Testa, who was more than willing to welcome two friends of his Australian host Ronnie Lee, returning the favor extended during his 1965 visit. For Smith and Freeman, the trip was nirvana. Testa put them up in an apartment block he owned in Schiller Park, near O'Hare Airport. In his memoirs, Freeman recalls arriving there to see the block's residents, many of whom were air hostesses, lounging by the pool. When Testa arrived, Freeman says he asked him which of the women were off-limits, to which Testa replied, "[M]y mother and my sister, and they're not here . . . go for your life." It was not just fun and games, though; Smith and Freeman were there to do business. Telling Testa about his shoplifting score in San Francisco, the mafioso took Freeman to a police station where he handed over the contraband for safekeeping. Freeman claims these "friendly" police later sold the loot for $200,000, taking a cut for themselves.[77]

Testa also took his Australian guests to Las Vegas, where he introduced them to other organized crime figures during a three-day gambling trip. It was on this visit that Smith and Freeman met Danny Stein, an associate of Lansky who would (in many ways) succeed Testa as the Australians' chief Mafia contact in the 1970s.[78] All told, Smith and Freeman spent six weeks in the United States as guests of Testa. They had not intended to stay that long, but Freeman got word through his contacts that police had discovered the false name that Freeman was using on his forged passport, forcing them to spend additional time overseas while they tried to figure out how to return home without being detected. In the end, it did not matter; when they arrived back in Australia, Smith and Freeman were both arrested and fined $200 each on charges of forgery.[79] It was a small hiccup, but did not take the shine off what was a successful trip overall. The six weeks with Testa had cemented the relationship between some of Sydney's most incorrigible rogues and the Chicago Outfit, and was soon followed by a second visit down under by Testa only a few months later.

When Testa and his "bodyguard" Nick Giordano touched down, they were met with the full hospitality of a local criminal milieu hell-bent on showing off its best side. The Americans arrived in Sydney on February 10, 1969, and stayed for a total of 22 days, over which time they were afforded celebrity treatment by what seemed like the entire underworld, led by the firm of McPherson, Smith, and Freeman. The value of selling the city as a satellite territory for the Mafia was such that the triumvirate was able to assemble a casting call of Sydney rogues to welcome their American guests. Testa and Giordano were booked into the newly built Chevron Hotel in Potts Point, just a street away from the bustling "Golden Mile" of Kings Cross. Unlike Testa's previous visit, the Americans were on the police radar from the start of their trip. At the first party thrown for them, held at Denis Wong's Chequers nightclub, a group including Testa, Giordano, Freeman, Smith, McPherson, and several other Sydney criminals had their picture taken by someone posing as a club photographer—in reality, he was a federal police officer tasked with tailing them.[80] Over the next three weeks, Testa and Giordano experienced nights out at Sydney's illegal casinos and parties at the palatial waterfront homes of local identities like Testa's old friend Ronnie Lee. McPherson enforcer Branko Balic even piloted his boss, Testa, and Giordano to western New South Wales in a light aircraft so that the group could go pig- and kangaroo-shooting—a photograph of McPherson and the Americans brandishing submachine guns was later tendered to the Moffitt Inquiry and became an iconic reminder of Testa's trip down under.[81]

The collective push to impress among Sydney's criminals was embodied at a party held in Testa's honor at the Fisherman's Lodge Restaurant, where some of Australia's hardest criminals surprised him with a cake iced with the words "WELCOME JOE." Not only were the triumvirate in attendance (as they were at most of the events held in Testa's honor), but so too were notorious criminals like thief king Arthur "Duke" Delaney and the vicious thug Milan "Iron Bar Miller" Petricevic.[82] Testa may not have kept a low profile on this trip, but it seems doing so was not his intention anyway. While in Sydney, he gave an interview to Australia's *People* magazine that was arranged by contacts prior to his visit. It seems that, for whatever reason, Testa wanted to be seen. The reporter for *People* produced a fawning profile of Testa as "an American good guy" and (wrongly) characterized him as "a millionaire cop from Chicago . . . his official title is Chief of Detectives in the State of Illinois." This was, of course, a lie. The closest Testa came to being a police officer was a part-time police badge given to him by his ally Mayor

Gualano . . . and the police officers he allegedly used to fence stolen goods. Testa's false claims made their way back to Chicago, where his self-promotion was described in the *Chicago Tribune* as "a bold-face lie in boldfaced type."[83] The question remains why Testa, spending his time in Australia with some of the country's most notorious criminals, would attempt to convince the local media that he was "an American good guy." One can only assume that this publicity campaign was a forerunner to further plans where Testa's cultivation of a positive public image would be useful. This is often the case when an associate of organized crime plans to act as a front for a business likely to come under considerable public scrutiny, whether in the press or in state licensing processes. A company that sells poker machines, for instance.

When Testa and Giordano eventually left to return home, they were seen off with a champagne celebration hosted by McPherson at Sydney Airport. Having missed Smith and Freeman's original 1968 trip, McPherson accepted an invitation to visit Testa in Chicago in 1970, traveling under the radar (likely on a false passport, as was typical in his set).[84] It is not certain whether Testa met with Rooklyn during his 1969 trip; however, it is highly possible. Around the same time that Testa and Giordano visited, Rooklyn officially became Bally's chief distributor in Australia and, as such, no doubt would have been an individual that a Chicago-based Mafia associate would be interested in meeting.[85] Later, federal police claimed that Testa presented himself in Australia as a representative of Bally and, in this capacity, assisted in putting pressure on local venues to purchase Bally products instead of alternative locally produced machines. If true, Rooklyn would have been a direct beneficiary of his intimidation campaign, and so it would be unusual (to say the least) if he and Testa had not met. However, Rooklyn maintained a low profile and was not photographed or otherwise noted as being an attendee at the soirees thrown in Testa's honor. Like Testa, who was telling the press he was a high-ranking police officer in Chicago, Rooklyn also had a reputation to protect if he wanted to continue to operate as Bally's agent in Australia and not draw the attention of honest police. As the Swinging

Sixties came to an end, the stage was set for the long-dreamed-of collaboration between Sydney's criminals and the Mafia. There seemed to be limitless potential for all involved to profit, but this house of cards was not destined to last. Within five years, growing fears of a Mafia infiltration erupted in stunning fashion, with Jack Rooklyn's Bally Australia firmly in the crosshairs.

4
Ballyhoo

Joseph Dan Testa and Nick Giordano's trip down under in early 1969 may have been seen by some observers as the vanguard of an American Mafia takeover bid, but behind the scenes another invasion was being plotted from Chicago, this time with more of a veneer of legitimacy attached. The association between Jack Rooklyn and Bally had existed in some form since at least the 1930s, when the burgeoning amusement business Rooklyn operated in Sydney's suburbs grew to the point that he started to appear on the company's radar.[1] Rooklyn had continued to show his prowess and ability to turn any situation (even war) into a profitable enterprise during World War II and, later, consolidated his position as one of Bally's point men in the Southern Hemisphere during his time in Southeast Asia. The five years in Asia had been lucrative, both for Rooklyn and for Bally. Legend had it that, when he returned to Australia in the late 1950s, Rooklyn opened a bank account with an initial deposit of $60 million.[2] He had been back in Australia for about a decade by 1969 and, thanks to the newly liberalized climate toward poker machines in New South Wales, continued to peddle Bally products from his office above his Pitt Street arcade, Playland.[3] Relationships matter in any business, and Rooklyn capitalized on his: He was "sole Australian distributor" for Bally, appearing in the local media in December 1968 to promote Bally's new "cheat-proof poker machines," which he was already rolling out across Sydney's clubs. Rooklyn, then managing director of Pitt Amusements, told the press that "what might appeal to the clubs about our machines is the security measures . . . they are foolproof."[4]

The new machines, of which Rooklyn claimed 50 had already been sold in Sydney at between $1,900 and $2,400 a unit, were fitted with "coin counter meters," which were an extension of the coin-hopper initially designed by Bally's Las Vegas distributor Mickey Wichinsky a few years earlier.[5] By this point, Rooklyn's business aspirations had moved far beyond the sale of individual machines to small-scale operations in the greater Sydney area. He openly hoped his pitch on these "foolproof" devices would convince the consortium behind the newly proposed Hobart casino to consider introducing poker machines at their facility, which they had already rejected. As Rooklyn said, though, "no casino could survive without poker machines . . . [in Las Vegas] poker machines pay the overhead . . . without them the place would go broke."[6] In 1969, Rooklyn began to diversify his business interests, founding a new company called Electronic Amusements, which was solely focused on distributing poker machines, rather than including his interests in arcades and other assorted ventures as Pitt Amusements had. The timing of the new business's creation was interesting. While Rooklyn was at first spearheading Bally's push into the Australian market as part of his Pitt Amusements operation in December 1968, it was after Testa and Giordano's February 1969 visit that he made the decision to treat his Bally distribution lines as separate—a precursor to Bally's decision to buy Electronic Amusements three years later, in 1972, in a deal that formally brought Rooklyn into the fold. He was paid $460,000 for his share in Electronic Amusements, now renamed Bally Australia Pty Ltd., and was retained by the parent company as the managing director of its Australian arm. He also sold his Asian distribution empire for a much higher price, reputedly received $3.8 million in cash and shares in Bally America.[7] It had taken more than thirty years, but finally, Rooklyn was not just working with Bally—he *was* Bally.

Though both Rooklyn and American Bally chief William O'Donnell would later deny that Testa acted on the company's behalf, it is useful to note that several key developments in Bally's push into Australia occurred around the time of a Testa visit: first, Rooklyn's creation of Electronic Amusements to handle his Bally business exclusively just after Testa and Giordano's trip in 1969 and, later, the purchase of Electronic

Amusements in 1972, just after Testa's third visit in 1971. In the absence of concrete evidence, there can only be speculation about the correlation between these events; however, it is nevertheless useful to acknowledge this curious pattern connecting Chicago and Sydney. When Testa came in 1969, his time was mostly occupied by fancy nights out at Sydney's illegal casinos and enjoying the hospitality of the underworld milieu—in 1971, he came ready to do business. Though it was McPherson who (with his idolization of Capone) was most motivated to create ties with the Chicago Outfit, Testa seems to have cultivated the strongest relationship with another member of the trio: George Freeman. The pair even started a new company together in 1971, Grants Constructions, named after Freeman's eldest son. The purpose of the company was to purchase three apartment blocks in Sydney's elite Double Bay and demolish them for new development. Between them, Testa and Freeman sank \$350,000 (or \$4.1 million in 2021) into Grants Constructions, only to discover after the fact that building height restrictions in Double Bay meant their planned development would not be legal.[8] The bad investment in Grants Constructions was not the only thing Testa purchased on his 1971 visit, also acquiring a racehorse called Just U Wait, most likely with the advice of his bookie pal Freeman.[9] More than on his previous trips, it was clear that Testa was no longer coming to Australia simply to vacation—the Mafia associate was putting down roots.

It was on his 1971 trip that Testa's supposed connection to Bally started to become clearer, no thanks to the New South Wales Police. Testa's name turned up incidentally in a federal police investigation, not in Sydney but farther south in Victoria, where officers were monitoring the activities of Italian organized crime in the State of Victoria. An informant told federal police that Testa had brought a briefcase with him to Australia, reputedly filled with \$1 million (now worth around \$11.7 million) as a "gift" for distribution to the "right" people. While this undoubtedly included his friends in Sydney, Testa was reportedly also interested in setting up an arrangement to place Bally poker machines in Victoria, where they were then illegal.[10] The federal police passed on information to their New South Wales colleagues that Testa had met with members of the 'Ndrangheta, a Calabrian Mafia group based in the

Riverina region of New South Wales who held significant control over parts of the Victorian underworld.[11] The details of what Testa discussed with the 'Ndrangheta (if such discussions even occurred) are unclear, and Testa later denied ever meeting with the Australian mafiosos to the Moffitt Commission. That said, he also denied having any connections *at all* with "any mafia organisation or mafia-type organisation, or any criminal organisation or group in Chicago or anywhere else"—an easily disproven lie.[12]

The growing concern over Testa's presence in Australia even prompted action from the usually inert New South Wales Consorting Squad, who took him in for questioning as he left a solicitor's office where he had just signed the Grants Constructions deal. He was taken in for questioning by Detective-Sergeant Doug Knight, at the behest of Consorting Squad boss Jack McNeill. During the course of the interview, Testa claimed that Knight told him that his friend Freeman was a criminal and "insinuated [Testa] was a member of the Mafia."[13] Nothing came from the questioning of Testa, who was released without charge. What is most unusual about the interaction is McNeill's involvement. The Consorting Squad boss had "inherited" McPherson as an informant after the retirement of his mentor Ray Kelly, and was close to Freeman, often receiving racing tips from the bookie.[14] It is not clear, thus, why he would sanction taking Testa into custody and risk disrupting McPherson and Freeman's business arrangements—except, perhaps, as a demonstration to the mafioso that while his new Australian friends ran organized crime in Sydney, McNeill still controlled the streets.

While the New South Wales Police were happy to let Testa go about his business with minimal interference, the Commonwealth Police were determined to get to the bottom of Testa's visits to Australia. Before long, their investigation focused in on Testa's alleged links to Bally, with an informant suggesting that the American was conspiring with Bally and local criminals like McPherson "to attempt penetration of clubs with a view to gaining control of their entertainment, food and liquor services."[15] A subsequent 19-page Commonwealth Police report dated May 19, 1972 (titled "The Bally Manufacturing Company"), highlighted the silent ownership stake in Bally held by Jerry Catena and the Genovese Family for most of the 1960s, and repeated intelligence that an "American crime organizer . . . [had initiated a] campaign against club managers who have refused to purchase Bally products." The report did not specifically identify this "American crime organizer" except to say he visited Australia in 1971. Whoever the "American crime organizer" was, they had purportedly chosen a local expert to spearhead their strongarm campaign: Testa's friend, Leonard Arthur McPherson. Not just relying on intimidation and threats to force clubs into buying Bally products, McPherson also reportedly worked a scam where "professional cheats" were brought in to drive down the profitability of Australian-manufactured poker machines, thus making the "cheat-proof" Bally units promoted by Rooklyn more appealing to club proprietors.

The report also alleged that McPherson was intrinsically tied to an entertainment booking company, Arcadia Top Artists. It was suggested that, while the Americans from Bally (and, directly, Rooklyn) reaped the rewards of having their poker machines forced into Sydney's clubs, the benefit to the locals came from their involvement with Arcadia. It was observed that "once Bally moved into a club, Arcadia follows shortly after . . . if a club installs Bally machines, it apparently obtains the opportunity to secure an overseas act supplied by Arcadia on a cheaper basis than normal."[16] Commonwealth Police believed that Bally and Arcadia were both part of a plot, commanded on the ground by the McPherson crew, to secure a monopoly of Sydney's entertainment industry. Arcadia's country bookings manager, Murray Stewart Riley, was central to McPherson's plan. Not only was he a former New South Wales Police officer, Riley was also an Olympian. He had competed in the 1956 Melbourne Olympics while an active officer and won a bronze medal in the double scull rowing along with partner (and future police commissioner) Merv Wood.[17]

Born in 1925, Riley joined the police in 1943 and was mentored by senior officers close to the McPherson camp, like Ray Kelly. He left the force in 1962 and began working for poker machine distributor Raymond Smith, who he became close to after being assigned to his protection detail years before—Smith had found himself in conflict with rivals who had bombed his car, resulting in Riley acting as his protector and "shadow" for a period of time.[18] Riley was jailed in New Zealand in 1966 after attempting to bribe a police inspector $1,000 to secure bail for the associate of an underworld figure that Riley was acting as an emissary for. He returned to Australia after serving a year in prison and began working as a security consultant for Wally Dean, president of a South Sydney Juniors club empire that boasted a 53,000-strong membership.[19] Dean, who was also McPherson's longtime barber, had only recently taken control of the club, not long after first signing up as a member in 1965. The position gave him almost total control over entertainment contracts at the club, including poker machines, and there is a strong suggestion that his takeover bid was a concoction by McPherson wherein Dean would act as a Trojan horse, opening the door to Bally and Arcadia from the inside.[20] Riley held the dual role as security consultant (and "poker machines supervisor") under Dean at South Sydney Juniors, as well as being a partner in Arcadia, which in turn was the chief supplier of live entertainment to the club. Later, Moffitt would find that although Dean held no official role with Arcadia, "it is almost impossible to think [he] would go unrewarded" for using their services at South Sydney Juniors.[21]

While Dean and Riley were seemingly working to help Bally (and Arcadia) from within, the repeated assertions from Commonwealth Police that Bally was trying to muscle in on the Australian poker machine industry finally forced the New South Wales Police to act. A limited investigation had been carried out in December 1971 on the orders of Jack McNeill, providing an early indication that the Consorting Squad was aware of McPherson's alleged scheme. Notes from a police interview with an unnamed informer state unequivocally that "the American Mafia were in the [Sydney] clubs" and, in part, the racket included a professional cheat instructing others in McPherson's crew how to cheat locally manufactured poker machines. The informer even named Dean and Riley as part of the scam, claiming the duo had "been to the [United] States with the Mafia and met the same people in Las Vegas buying acts" that they were supplying to New South Wales clubs via Arcadia.[22] Despite this early indication that Dean and Riley were involved with a Mafia takeover plot, the New South Wales Police sat on the information until May 1972 when the Commonwealth Police called a meeting to pass on its own report on the issue. Just a few weeks later, on July 1, 1972, the state police published its first report on the potential Mafia infiltration of Sydney clubs and, based largely on the Commonwealth Police findings, indicated that it was a "distinct threat" that required further attention.[23]

Around the same time, the New South Wales press also began to circle the issue. On July 16, 1972, just over two weeks after the first police reports were filed, journalists Tony Reeves and Bob Bottom published a bombshell article titled "The Night the Mafia Came to Australia" in the *Sunday Telegraph* newspaper. It was the first in a series of articles alleging Mafia penetration of the Sydney club scene, and prompted intimidating phone calls to Bottom from McPherson himself, reaching out to express how "upset" he was.[24] In July 1972, Premier Robert Askin told parliament he was gravely worried about Bally's push into clubs, given the concerning reports he was receiving from police. On August 1, 1972, McNeill requested permission to send police to the United States to further examine Bally's links with the Mafia, asserting that although his intelligence to that point was "purely hearsay . . . [he] believe[d it] to be true."[25] A second report on the issue was released on August 16, 1972, affirming the position that Bally's entry into Australia was a matter for concern. Soon after, though, official sentiment on Bally began to shift in a more positive direction. In his final report in November 1972, McNeill appears to have experienced a complete turnaround in his views. Dismissing his previous concerns, he now claimed to "have been unable to find any proof of Mafia influence in the course of [his] inquiries."[26] Touching on Testa, McNeill said he had now been told "the right story . . . [and was] now of the opinion Testa is a normal sort of a fellow who in all probability visited Australia on a holiday with no ulterior motive."[27] As McNeill's confidence in Bally's criminal links (and their plans for Australia) weakened, so too did the statements made by Askin in parliament, though the local press continued to beat the drum with stories about the growing infiltration of Sydney clubs.

Why, then, did McNeill experience such a clear change of heart about Bally between August and November 1972? When the question was considered by Moffitt a few years later, the inquiry found that McNeill was likely not corrupted by organized crime figures during that period. Instead, Moffitt blamed the Consorting Squad boss's "personality and inability . . . to handle this inquiry" for the about-face in the final report. Moffitt said that, McNeill having found no further evidence of Mafia infiltration in Sydney during his investigation, it appeared that he had become frustrated (and embarrassed) by the furor his first report had wrought and, as such, "went out of his way to negative everything" in his final report to counteract it.[28] Here, Moffitt suggests it was McNeill's pride and reputation at stake more than anything else. That said, there was an apparent campaign to corrupt the police investigation from the time of the first report's release in July 1972. Central to these corruption claims was Rooklyn, who allegedly met with longtime business associate Abraham Saffron to discuss the problems Bally Australia was facing. In the early 1970s, the men were more than associates, but actively pursuing a partnership in Rooklyn's old stomping ground of Southeast Asia, where Saffron was actively exploring the idea of opening hotels (nominally, a front for brothels) in Jakarta that were connected to Rooklyn-run casinos.[29] Thus, helping Rooklyn was not only the act of a good friend, but crucial to Saffron's own interests. Rooklyn reputedly asked Saffron if he could use his contacts in police and government "to see somebody in authority to take the heat out of the inquiry."[30] It is unknown if Saffron did exert influence on Rooklyn's behalf but, if the request was indeed made, it must be considered that Saffron had every reason to render assistance if possible.

Rooklyn's actions to scuttle investigations into Bally were not just passive, as seen in his efforts to corrupt McNeill sidekick Doug Knight. Sometime after requesting Saffron's help, Rooklyn called McNeill and Knight to a meeting in which he offered a business partnership to the two investigating officers. While McNeill apparently rebuffed the overture, Knight did not. On November 7, 1972, a new company, Metropolitan Club Services, was registered by Knight's solicitor (who acted as Knight's "on paper" proxy) in partnership with Rooklyn. Knight was not just a silent partner, but was observed in Sydney clubs along with a Bally Australia employee not long after Metropolitan Club Services was formed, in "an alarming spectacle . . . [raising] grave suspicion against Knight."[31] In the end, there was no direct proof that Knight's business arrangement with Rooklyn compromised his work on the Bally case. Even so, it is reasonable to believe that Knight would have been reluctant to contribute to any inquiry that would have an adverse impact on his personal financial interests.

Rooklyn's corruption of Knight seems aggressive, yet he had every reason to believe it would be successful. When working out of Singapore, Rooklyn became adept in this persuasive tactic. About his time in Southeast Asia, Rooklyn denied bribing officials but said that "perhaps [he had] sold a portion of the business, a few shares to a relative, or something of that nature, but never any open bribery."[32] Seemingly, the old Singapore sling was back in action. It was not just Rooklyn's strategy to compromise critical police enemies by bringing them into the Bally family, however. A similar strategy had been employed to deal with former US Justice Department agent William Tomlinson, a "rackets buster" initially tasked with investigating Bally before being swayed to join them in 1971 as a lawyer and lobbyist, trading on his previous role to assure anyone who would listen (including the New South Wales Police) that Bally's links to organized crime had been severed long ago.[33] It appears that Rooklyn and Bally shared the view that it is better to keep your enemies close . . . and, often, on the payroll.

At the same time that the police and Bally were finding themselves at loggerheads in mid-1972, the Sydney criminal milieu was becoming more organized. The commitment to greater cooperation between the city's criminals was, in some respects, a direct response to the promise of working with the American Mafia. For 50 years, the Mafia had routinely gathered to settle their differences, carve out territory, and establish the "way forward" to ensure organized crime continued to be profitable for all involved, without one group stepping on the toes of another. Just as the 1929 Atlantic City conference, the 1946 Havana conference and the (disastrous) 1957 Apalachin conference brought together the factions of organized crime in the United States, so too did the 1972 Double Bay meetings in Australia. The venue was 44 William Street in Double Bay, home of the self-anointed "Godfather" of Sydney's eastern suburbs, Karl Bonnette. News of three such meetings was passed on to the Commonwealth Police by an informant and, in turn, handed to New South Wales

Consorting Squad officer Brian Ballard in early August.[34] Intelligence suggested that meetings were being held to "discuss the current activities re organized crime" and were attended by the trio of McPherson, Freeman, and Stan "The Man" Smith, along with other criminal heavyweights such as Frederick "Paddles" Anderson, Milan "Iron Bar Miller" Petricevic, Arthur "The Duke" Delaney, and Leo "The Liar" Callaghan.[35] Interestingly, the roll call of the Double Bay meeting attendees reflected almost exactly the list of local rogues who had been seen meeting with Testa during his previous visits, and Commonwealth Police believed the summits were at least partly intended to ensure the Sydney crims were prepared for the Mafia's impending arrival.[36] Considering this connection, Ballard passed the information about the Double Bay meetings on to McNeill, then spearheading the Bally investigation.

In a move later described as "almost beyond belief," McNeill disregarded Ballard's intelligence about the Double Bay meetings as being irrelevant to his own inquiry—despite the overlap between the attendees and Testa's Australian associates, and the presence of McPherson, who was (according to rumor) the driving force behind the Mafia's club takeover. Instead, McNeill passed the information over to another ally in the Consorting Squad, Frank Charlton, who promptly showed up at 44 William Street and knocked on the door on the morning of August 4, 1972, less than 24 hours after the intelligence was initially received from the Commonwealth Police. Charlton asked Bonnette outright if criminals had been meeting at his house and, when Bonnette of course denied this, arrested him for receiving a stolen television set. Why Charlton decided it was best to alert Bonnette to the intelligence about the Double Bay meetings rather than monitor the property in the (likely) event of further meetings is unknown. In any case, Charlton's fumbling meant the Double Bay meetings came to an end, and if Sydney criminals continued to hold summits, they did so far deeper under the radar than before.[37] Again, we see a recurring pattern of the Commonwealth Police sending warning signs about the organization of a Sydney milieu with purported links to the US Mafia. Again, we see a recurring pattern of the New South Wales Consorting Squad rejecting that intelligence, either because of deep-seated resentment of the information's source, the Commonwealth

Police, or (perhaps) the vested interest held by some squad members in ensuring certain privileged criminals were able to go about their business undisturbed.

Most of 1972 was spent by McNeill's squad walking back the initial fears over Mafia involvement in the Sydney club scene; however, the clamor in the media persisted unabated into 1973 until finally the Askin government was forced to act, and called an official judicial inquiry to get to the bottom of the allegations. The calling of a judicial inquiry into organized crime and corruption is often, conversely, a useful way for governments with something to hide to take control of a narrative. While giving the appearance of transparency, a well-organized inquiry can have the effect of neutering an investigation by providing limited resources and terms of reference—and, according to Justice Athol Moffitt, this was precisely Askin's initial intention. Writing years later, Moffitt told of how it took a weekend of negotiations with the New South Wales government, where he "insisted any inquiry would have to include a reference to organized crime activities, or as far as I was concerned, there would be no inquiry."[38] Eventually, Askin acquiesced to Moffitt's demands and, on August 20, 1973, the Moffitt Commission commenced with a remit to investigate "certain matters relating to allegations of organized crime in clubs"—not only meeting Moffitt's demands, but inextricably marbling them into his mandate.[39] Moffitt was a judge with more than a decade of experience at the bench when he put his name to Askin's commission, an event that would come to dominate his reputation in New South Wales. He had made his bones as a lawyer in the war years, prosecuting Japanese war criminals responsible for the brutal Sandakan death marches in Borneo where, out of 2,434 Australian and British prisoners of war, only six survived.[40] Returning to civilian life, he had risen through the ranks to join the Appeals Court, a body he became president of the same year the Moffitt Commission concluded. His entire career was dedicated to sounding the warning siren about organized crime and the growing menace of drug trafficking in Australia, and though he was criticized by many as an alarmist, "when the dust settled, few people ever said he was wrong."[41]

Specifically, Moffitt was tasked with investigating three key matters: if the accusations in McNeill's reports had merit, if any person had tried to cover up such crimes, and (later, at Moffitt's own request) if Bally's entry into Australia presented "a risk of infiltration of organised crime into or in relation to Clubs."[42] Assisted by Gregory Needham and Roger Gyles as counsel assisting, the Moffitt Commission began in earnest, issuing subpoenas to some of the key persons of interest to attend, including McPherson. The reputed "Mr. Big" appeared before Moffitt quite early, on September 19, 1973. McPherson claimed he made a living as the maintenance man at his nephew's Balmain boardinghouse where his responsibilities included collecting rent and putting the garbage out twice a week.[43] Later, Consorting Squad detective Charlton (who had botched the Double Bay meetings investigation) told the inquiry that he had known McPherson for 25 years and that "to [his] knowledge" he was no longer an active criminal, something that may have been a surprise to those who were stood over by McPherson and his cronies.[44] In a particularly Kafkaesque statement, Charlton denied McPherson maintained an active standover racket, yet admitted, "I do not think McPherson has to stand over [victims] . . . but I think if McPherson called on this type of person, [they] would give a donation."[45] Rookyn's business associate Saffron appeared before Moffitt as well, indignantly denying that he was sometimes known by the label of "Mr. Sin" as a result of his interests in the sex trade. Despite these denials, the public branding at the Moffitt inquiry stuck, and Mr. Sin became entrenched as a tag that Saffron would battle for the rest of his life. For his part, McPherson told the media that Saffron was not "Mr. Sin" and, in fact, "the loveliest person you could meet"—somewhat contradicting Saffron's own statement to Moffitt that he had never met McPherson at all.[46]

Other local crims felt it was better to dodge Moffitt completely. While Freeman fronted the inquiry, his friend Smith was "missing" at the time of the inquiry, with rumors (peddled by Dean) that he had been "fed to the sharks," which later turned out to be erroneous when he reappeared alive and well after the commission concluded. Moffitt was told that another criminal associated with Testa, Milan Petricevic, had fled the country in October 1973. This too was later disproven, as

Petricevic was openly at work as an enforcer in Sydney's illegal casinos at the same time police claimed they could not locate him to appear.[47] The South Sydney Juniors president (and McPherson barber), Dean, could not escape Moffitt, but his partner Riley did. The ex-police officer disappeared into the ether when the commission was called and, despite Moffitt's strong insistence he be located given his importance to the events in question, police could not seem to track down their former colleague.[48] Unlike the local rogues, the executives from Bally implicated in the accusations presented to Moffitt could not simply "disappear" when the time came for them to front the investigation. Rooklyn appeared and denied all accusations of misconduct, while Bally America boss William O'Donnell and former US Justice Department agent Tomlinson both came to Australia to explain away the company's links to the Mafia and deny that Testa was acting as their agent in Australia. O'Donnell said, "Testa has found it convenient to suggest he represents us in Australia . . . he has caused us great business harm and irreparable damage to our image . . . if Testa sold $10 million worth of slot machines in our name in Australia, we wouldn't honour the sales."[49] O'Donnell acknowledged that, years earlier, Bally inadvertently came under the silent ownership of Mafia figures, but insisted that he had worked to excise this influence immediately after discovering it and, now, Bally's operations were totally legitimate.

On February 22, 1974, a witness appeared before Moffitt who seemed to blow O'Donnell's protestations out of the water. The public gallery was packed that day, with an American contingent from Bally attending along with Rooklyn, Police Commissioner Fred Hanson, and at least nine New South Wales detectives. Testifying was an informer for the US Federal Bureau of Investigation (FBI) and Central Intelligence Agency (CIA) named Herbert Itkin, and he was there to tell Moffitt all about how Bally's executives knew *all* about the company's ongoing criminal links.[50] Itkin told the commission that he had been a CIA asset since at least 1954, and for the past five years had been working as an informant with the FBI. Itkin told of how he had penetrated the Mafia (purportedly on behalf of the FBI) and, in doing so, became privy to the group's plan to take control of organized crime in Europe using Bally as a front. Itkin testified about a meeting held at London's Dorchester Hotel in November 1966, which was attended by Itkin as well as crime bosses from across Europe, the United Kingdom, and the United States.[51] The purpose of the meeting was to discuss the first tourist hotel opening in Spain, and to ensure that the opportunities it brought were divided up in a way that was acceptable to all parties. Also at the meeting was Alexander Wilms, Bally's European director, who claimed to represent the interests of Marcel Francisci, a French Corsican politician and alleged member of French organized crime syndicate, the Union Corse. Francisci was even believed to be the mastermind behind "the French Connection," a decades-old trafficking network in which heroin from Indochina was smuggled to France and, from there, sent on to Mafia allies in North America, hidden in the bodywork of cars.[52] The collapse of the French Connection in the 1970s caused great disruption to the Mafia's narcotics pipeline at the time, providing an opening for entrepreneurial Australians that will be discussed in more detail later.

The Itkin revelations about Bally's cooperation with organized crime first came to light several years before Moffitt, in a 1971 libel case filed in the British courts. The petitioner was Cyril Shack, a part-owner of Bally distributor Associated Leisure, which had assumed exclusive rights to sell Bally products in the country in 1962. By 1968, Associated Leisure was angling to purchase the struggling Butlin's holiday camp empire established by Rooklyn's old friend Billy Butlin. Amid this takeover, the *Daily Mail* newspaper published an article alleging that Associated Leisure was controlled by the Mafia, to which Shack and his fellow directors took great umbrage.[53] Against the advice of several in his close circle, Shack pursued a libel suit against the newspaper, claiming the "Mafia article shattered [him]," and tanked the impending Butlin's deal. The decision to try to clear Associated Leisure's name backfired. Prepared to defend themselves, lawyers for the *Daily Mail* brought evidence of the company's association with the Mafia, including Shack's own part-ownership of the Colony Club along with Meyer Lansky associate Dino Cellini, and a meeting in New York City between another director and Lucchese Family boss Anthony "Tony Ducks" Corallo several years earlier.[54] A later case involving Bally indicated that it was Shack who recommended Cellini to O'Donnell as an agent for Bally in the mid-1960s, with Cellini later going on to work with Wilms at Bally Continental.[55] Importantly, the Associated Leisure case also marked the first appearance of Itkin, who not only told the court about the Dorchester Hotel meeting but further alleged that another Associated Leisure director, Gordon Marks, had met with Philadelphia boss Angelo "The Gentle Don" Bruno in New York City in mid-1967. In the end, Associated Leisure lost the libel case, as the court found more than enough reason to support the imputations of Mafia connections made in the *Daily Mail* article.[56] When Itkin appeared before Moffitt, it was not to offer direct links between the Australian market and organized crime, but rather to show how executives with the company had acted in previous expansion plans, and to draw parallels with the stories the commission was hearing about Bally's ties to organized crime. Itkin's testimony was a major blow to Bally's credibility in Australia, perhaps even more so than anything Testa ever accomplished.

After nearly a year, on August 15, 1975, the Moffitt Commission released its much-anticipated final report. As is often the case when dealing with the complex matter of professional, organized crime, Justice Moffitt's findings were unequivocal in some senses, and elusive in others. Effectively, he determined that there was evidence to support the constituent aspects of his terms of reference, though stopped short of drawing definitive connections between Bally, the American Mafia, and the reported criminal activity in New South Wales clubs. Contrary to O'Donnell, Rooklyn, and Bally's ardent protestations, Moffitt determined that Bally was inherently tied to organized crime and, particularly, the Mafia. He believed that allegations that Dean and Riley preyed on local clubs to "skim" money were, on balance, true. Moffitt also found there was evidence to suggest the Consorting Squad (specifically McNeill and Knight) had been involved in "a deliberate or corrupt" effort to both conceal Bally's links to organized crime and absolve Riley of all criminal accusations, concluding that "if the police inquiry is a fair indication of the police capacity to meet the problems of organised crime, the intelligence and investigation processes of the police are not adequate to . . . initiate serious action against organised crime from abroad."[57] Despite this, while he had much to say about the scruples of Bally and its executives, Moffitt could not offer evidence that the American company (and the Mafia interests he believed controlled it) were behind the actions of McPherson, Riley, and Dean to muscle in on the local industry.[58] The threads were all there, yet still could not be tied together.

He could not definitively prove Bally's guilt in the end, but Moffitt nevertheless had much to say about the risks posed if the company were allowed to continue operating in Australia. The final report is clear that the lack of evidence is not, in itself, proof of innocence; Moffitt notes that "if there has been any attempt to corrupt club officials [by Bally], say by secret commissions, it is extremely unlikely that any trace of such will appear in any records."[59] Moffitt was scathing of Rooklyn's role in Bally Australia, asserting that "Rooklyn lied [about his business dealings with detective Doug Knight] . . . and concealed what occurred by a pretense of lack of memory."[60] Indeed, one thing Moffitt was clear on was his belief that, while serving on the Bally investigation, Knight "was participating in some operation or business on behalf of Rooklyn or Bally."[61] In concluding his summary of this affair, Moffitt states that "it should be bluntly said that in respect of the Australian operation [of Bally], it is directed by a man (Rooklyn) who has lied before me and that the parent company, which gives him his ultimate directions, is presided over by a man (O'Donnell) who has lied before me."[62] In Moffitt's view, between Rooklyn's clear efforts to corrupt police and the tattered criminal history of Bally America, there was a major risk that "any takeover by and any expansion of Bally would constitute a risk . . . [that is] too great to have the Bally organisation trading here at all."[63]

On one hand, Moffitt failed to solidify the connections between Bally and the alleged criminal takeover of New South Wales clubs, yet the findings were still explosive enough to prompt a significant reaction from those involved. Rooklyn was defiant in the face of the judge's criticism of his honesty and business practices, vowing publicly that Bally Australia would do whatever it could to fight on and stay in business. He described the Moffitt Report as a "vicious document with no factual basis" and stood firm in his original protestations of innocence.[64] Dean, another person in Moffitt's firing line, also responded to the report in harsh terms, claiming that the commission had set out to make him a scapegoat and "crucify" him, as well as police officers like McNeill and Knight. For his part, Knight refused to comment, citing police rules—his under-the-radar approach seems to have worked, with the detective most maligned by Moffitt avoiding major sanctions for his conduct, including his concealed business dealings with Rooklyn.[65] McNeill, too, did not respond as he was on sick leave when the report was handed down. Far from being demoted or otherwise penalized for his conduct in the Bally investigation, McNeill had actually been *promoted* during the course of the Moffitt Commission, now holding an inspector rank.[66] Years later, in 1978, he would go on to apply for the role of assistant commissioner, the next step on what seemed to be a march to the commissioner's office. This promotion was scuttled when the New South Wales Police internal affairs unit produced a report claiming McNeill was on a retainer of $1,000 paid by "a prominent racing identity known to control one of the major organised crime syndicates"—a reference to Freeman.[67]

Two central protagonists in the claims of organized crime penetration, McPherson and Riley, had very different experiences with Moffitt—McPherson was a star witness at the inquiry, whereas Riley disappeared and, over the course of an entire year, could not be found and (thus) brought in to answer questions. It was not necessarily that Riley was especially good at hiding, but perhaps more to do with a purposeful disinterest in tracking him down, and Moffitt believed the New South Wales Police's treatment of Riley demonstrated an "undue favour" that was typical in the "blue brotherhood."[68] Once the heat was off, Riley wasted no time returning to the public eye. The day after Moffitt released his report, the ex-police officer "reappeared in Sydney in spectacular fashion, driving his flashy Buick Le Sabre, and threatening to smash the camera of a reporter who tried to interview him."[69] When it came to his alleged co-conspirator, McPherson, no charges were laid as a result of the Moffitt Commission, in spite of Moffitt finding that McPherson's explanation of the source of his income (salary from a motel, supplemented by a small import/export business) was not credible. The reason for this may have been the result of a *quid pro quo* that McPherson was well used to. In his final public address in 2006, Moffitt admitted that McPherson had been a "supergrass" for the commission, a paid informant covertly pointing Moffitt's investigators in the right direction on organized crime.[70] Trading intelligence with police in return for leniency was stock and trade for McPherson, so Moffitt's allegation makes sense in the context of Mr. Big's criminal career. However, it also poses new questions, namely, whether McPherson used his position to misdirect the commission, purposefully steering it away from sensitive areas and obstructing Moffitt's ability to firm up the connections between Bally, the Mafia, and organized crime in New South Wales.

While he was not ultimately successful in striking a death blow to organized crime in New South Wales, Moffitt nevertheless did pose a tangible risk to the state's criminal milieu and disrupted the control of McPherson, Freeman, and Smith, as well as their American partners. The death of gunman Stewart John Regan is reflective of both the weakening of the trio's power and their decisive attempts to regain control as the shadow of Moffitt faded. Regan, 29, was a maverick operator in Sydney's underworld, known as "The Magician" due to his propensity to make enemies "disappear."[71] An independent rogue for the most part, Regan was best known for his alleged campaign to hunt down a gang called "The Toecutters," who stole the rewards of other criminals' illicit conduct. By the mid-1970s, Regan's legend as a brutal killer had struck fear into much of the Sydney underworld and, as such, he was emboldened to challenge McPherson, Freeman, and Smith's dominance when their stranglehold was momentarily loosened while they kept a low profile under Moffitt's spotlight. Regan started to muscle in on illegal casinos like the 33 Club, which was McPherson's turf, and was also believed responsible for killing a bookie who was on Freeman's payroll. On September 22, 1974, Regan arrived at the Henson Park Hotel in Marrickville, reportedly to collect protection payments from a gambling venture operated by Freeman. He never made it. As the story goes, three men ambushed him in the street outside and shot him dead. Police (and criminals) believed the trio were none other than McPherson, Freeman, and Smith, but no charges were ever laid.[72] Ordinarily, it would seem unusual that three heavy-hitters would put themselves at such risk, committing a very public gangland murder together. One explanation is that it was a sign of force; with

Moffitt having ended just a month earlier, Regan's murder was a symbol that the trio were back in action and would suffer no challengers.

The Australian contingent might have survived Moffitt, but it seems that Testa's fortunes were fading. For almost a decade, Testa had been spearheading the connection between the American Mafia and the Australian milieu, even getting into business with Freeman in a clear sign of his commitment to the relationship. However, like Icarus, Testa may have been too ambitious. His name became synonymous with Mafia presence in Australia, attracting much unwanted attention to Bally and essentially ruining the perception O'Donnell was trying to build that the company had shed its ties to the Mafia.[73] Testa was not a "made man"—an official member of the Chicago Outfit—and, thus, was expendable. This was particularly true after the death of his chief patron, Felix "Milwaukee Phil" Alderisio in 1971. Alderisio had risen to serve as boss of the Chicago Outfit in the late 1960s, a time correlating with the peak of Testa's connection with the Australians. He was convicted of extortion in 1969 and in prison for most of this time, dying two years later while still in prison.[74] It may have been Alderisio's death more than the Moffitt Commission that marked the beginning of the end for Testa with the Chicago Outfit. Sources close to Testa claim that, in the mid-1970s, the Mafia came after Testa to repay a loan given to "somebody who had subsequently gone to prison and died"—potentially Testa's close ally Alderisio. When Testa refused to pay, the would-be collectors allegedly blew up his restaurant, his home, and his office, with Testa "unable to . . . get rid of the problem."[75] Testa began spending more time at his properties in Florida, away from his former associates in Chicago. It was in Testa's best interests to keep a low profile, something that would become clear years later in an explosive fashion.

An issue that has been hotly debated is whether Testa could be considered the vanguard of an American Mafia plot to penetrate the Australian club scene, using Bally as a front and with the enthusiastic backing of local allies like McPherson and company. In the 1980s, writer Richard Hall took the position that "the Mafia menace theory" was no more than a scare campaign fueled by the Commonwealth Police in a desperate attempt to carve out a relevance and purpose for the federal force to exist.[76] He disregards the Commonwealth Police's concerns (shared by their partners in the FBI) that the Mafia was moving the profits from its illegal enterprises into legal companies like Bally, arguing that although "the ultimate source of the money was certainly tainted . . . the Rockefeller and Carnegie fortunes were not entirely pure either."[77] On Testa, Hall questions "whether all the connections [with Sydney criminals] were part of a grand plan or whether it was just socializing" and later "assess[es] with confidence" that the American was "not a Mafia takeover man."[78]

Can we make this assessment, though? There is little doubt that Testa was closely connected to top Chicago Outfit mafiosi like Alderisio, Tony Accardo, and Sam Giancana. It is also undeniable that from 1965 on, Testa became increasingly close to leading criminals in the New South Wales milieu like McPherson, Freeman, and Smith. He did not hide his associations, making a splash and even giving interviews to the local media during his visits down under.[79] Testa was actively and openly pursuing business opportunities with the New South Wales criminals. More importantly, he was representing himself as an agent of Bally in Australia, and considering Bally's connections with Jerry Catena and the Genovese Family, it is unlikely Testa would have been permitted to do this without the blessing of the Mafia. While some, like Hall, doubted Testa's role as a Mafia agent, there is no better proof that he was one than the fact that he continued breathing after his actions in Australia were exposed—had his actions not been sanctioned, the repercussions for Testa's false representations would have been fatal.

In the end, Moffitt fired a torpedo at the Mafia's ambitions in Australia. He may not have been able to draw definitive links between the Mafia, Bally, Testa, and the Sydney criminal milieu, but he did find enough of concern to justify a recommendation that the risk of American organized crime infiltration via Bally was too high to risk. As head of Bally Australia, Rooklyn pledged to stay the course in the face of Moffitt's criticism, with good reason. Ultimately, the Moffitt Report was not tabled in parliament after being handed over to Premier Askin, suggesting a willful disregard for its findings.[80] Though its reputation was tarnished, Bally Australia continued to operate, albeit with a slightly less aggressive approach to monopolizing the industry in New South Wales.

To the best of our knowledge, Testa never returned to Australia, though he reportedly remained in contact with Freeman and other Australian friends.[81] Testa may have been relegated to the bench as a result of all the attention, but his absence did not mean that organized crime figures in Sydney stopped pursuing opportunities with their American allies. The late 1970s were a time of reorganization, certainly—but a reorganization that saw the Mafia and the Sydney milieu become closer than ever before.

5

Chasing the American Dream

In 1974, the Moffitt Commission strongly advised against allowing Bally to continue operating in Australia, fearing that it could be used as a vehicle for potential Mafia infiltration. Despite this clarion warning, not a single government in the country—state or federal—took Athol Moffitt up on this recommendation. Not only that, Bally did not even see fit to remove Jack Rooklyn as managing director of its Australian arm. This was in spite of well-publicized claims that Rooklyn had attempted (maybe even succeeded, in Doug Knight's case) to bribe Consorting Squad detectives who were looking into Bally's Mafia connections, as well as had his questionable personal and professional links to vice traders like Abraham Saffron.[1] For anyone else, the level of negative publicity that Moffitt caused may have forced a retreat from the public eye, but Rooklyn had always been a consummate showman and, instead, remained defiant. He even went so far as to take out an advertisement in the September edition of the *Secretaries and Managers Journal of Australia*, just one month after Moffitt's report was released, defending Bally and describing the commission's findings as "based on hearsay, innuendo and fiction."[2] Though he pledged to stay on and continue to pursue Bally's expansion in Australia, even Rooklyn could not deny the negative effect that Moffitt had on the business. Before the commission, Bally's share of the poker machine market in Australia had risen to a peak of 18 percent, but by the time Moffitt ended just one year later in 1974, Bally's share was down to 10 percent . . . and still falling.[3]

In his public statements, Rooklyn gave the distinct impression that he was confident that the bad press would eventually pass, and Bally Australia would soon be on its former path to dominance once more. In private, the tensions of this turbulent period were reportedly showing signs of getting to Rooklyn. In February 1974, John Burney, then a features writer for Sydney newspaper the *Daily Telegraph*, visited Rooklyn's palatial Rose Bay home, nominally to discuss his subject's other passion: his yacht, the *Ballyhoo*. At the time, the Moffitt Commission was still in full swing, though the furor over its initial revelations had started to subside after a quintessential long, sleepy Australian summer.[4] Burney was ushered into a room where the interview was going to take place, where a cigar-smoking Rooklyn poured himself a brandy, which Burney declined, noting it was around 10 a.m. and perhaps too early to start drinking spirits. Journalist Tony Moore later recounted (in a hearsay recount) that Burney initially asked a few questions about *Ballyhoo* before touching on the Moffitt Commission—understandable considering Rooklyn's involvement and the then-ongoing status of the inquiry. Rooklyn's reaction was reportedly one of "immediate anger," in which he called Burney a "bastard" and ordered him out of the house. When Burney argued that he had already cleared this line of questioning with Rooklyn in advance, his hostile interviewee snapped his fingers, at which point a "very large" Asian man appeared and, "taking a very firm grip of Burney's arm, he escorted him through the front door and threw him onto the lawn."[5] When he returned to the *Daily Telegraph*'s offices later, Burney received a phone call from a person identifying himself only as "Smith." He asked if Burney had a family and, when he replied that he did, "Smith" told him "then you'd better stop your inquiries, or they could be in trouble."[6] The caller did not mention Rooklyn's name, but Burney was left to assume that the threat was in relation to his explosive encounter with the Bally boss.

When Rooklyn invited Burney into his home, it seems he thought that the journalist would be asking questions about a part of his life that was much more successful than Bally was at that point. He had been interested in yachting since he was a teenager and loved being on the water, joining the Navy Reserve during the early years of World War II and, later, entering his boat *White Wings* in 1949's inaugural Brisbane to Gladstone yacht race.[7] Rooklyn had continued to pursue his passion in the years since then, perfecting his skills on the water while living in Southeast Asia. By the early 1970s, he was not just a capable sailor—he was one of Australia's best. In 1972, Bally Australia's fortunes were on the rise. Rooklyn was also on the ascendent, beginning his path to glory with the purchase of ocean racer *Apollo* from millionaire businessman Alan Bond. The 58-foot sloop was designed in the late 1960s by maritime designer Bob Miller, who would also go on (under the name Ben Lexcen) to produce 1983 America's Cup winning vessel *Australia II* for Bond.[8] By 1972, *Apollo* had already competed in the iconic Sydney to Hobart yacht race twice, with limited success: It finished toward the back of the pack in 1969, and was forced to retire partway through the 1970 event.[9]

Rooklyn says he first spotted *Apollo* while visiting the marina where it was moored, and was immediately set on purchasing it, something Bond was open to.[10] *Apollo* returned to the Sydney to Hobart race in December 1972, now with Rooklyn at the helm. It came in eighth place on Rooklyn's maiden outing, four places behind Bond's new boat, the unoriginally named *Apollo II*.[11] Soon after, Rooklyn commissioned Miller to design him another yacht. The vessel started in its first Sydney to Hobart in 1974, only a few months after the Moffitt Commission issued its damning condemnation of its skipper. In what was perhaps another example of Rooklyn's characteristic bravado, the name of his new racing yacht did not shy away from the controversy: He named it *Ballyhoo*. In one sense, it was an homage to the company where he made his fortune, and the original machine that put it on the map. But Rooklyn also says it was at least partly a tongue-in-cheek swipe at his critics, with the word ballyhoo serving as "an American euphemism for 'bullshit' [and] that was my opinion . . . of the [Moffitt] royal commission."[12] Rooklyn's place in the Australian yachting scene was enhanced through the purchase of *Apollo* and secured with the construction of *Ballyhoo*. His time on the water would have no doubt provided a nice distraction as he navigated the tumult of Moffitt and its aftermath. However, while Rooklyn spent less time in the office and more time on the water in the mid-1970s, others in the milieu who had also been targeted by the commission were actively looking for new ways to make themselves useful to their American counterparts.

The fallout of Moffitt meant that all eyes were on Bally and its agents, both official (like Rooklyn) and unofficial (like Mafia associate Joseph Dan Testa). For almost a decade Testa had been *the* key contact between local crime figures and the American Mafia. However, Testa was "too hot"; he had drawn too much attention to himself and, if any business at all was to be done, a new intermediary needed to be found. Fortunately, George Freeman knew just the right person. He reputedly first met Danny Stein on his trip to the United States with Stan Smith in 1968, while visiting Las Vegas as guests of Testa.[13] Stein, real name Noah Steinberg, was born on June 7, 1916, in Chicago, the youngest son of a house painter. He left school early, dropping out while still in the fourth grade and becoming a pool hall hustler before later joining the US Army. When he left the army, he returned to Chicago and met the wealthy Virginia Hill, the girlfriend of Benjamin "Bugsy" Siegel. Hill introduced Stein to her partner and, when Siegel went to Las Vegas in 1945 to muscle in on the nascent gambling industry, he brought Stein with him to work as a floor boss at The Flamingo.[14] Of course, Siegel did not last long in Vegas; on Mafia orders, he was shot dead at Hill's Beverly Hills home on June 20, 1947. Stein may have lost his patron, but he found a new one in Siegel's old friend (and, reputedly, the man who sanctioned his assassination), Meyer Lansky. Looking to build on Siegel's early work in Las Vegas, Lansky was among the silent partners in the new Sands Hotel and Casino on The Strip, which opened in 1952—around that time Stein transferred to The Sands and became a pit boss, then shift manager.[15] Stein was a star on the rise. After more than a decade at The Sands, he moved to the opulent Caesars Palace ahead of its 1966 opening, where he assumed "executive duties."[16]

Although he was said to have first met Freeman and Smith in 1968, Stein's first known visit to Australia was in early 1972, where the Australians returned the hospitality experienced on their earlier trip to Las Vegas. Freeman introduced Stein (who he described as "one of the nicest guys I ever met, and one of the most honest") to his criminal colleagues, and the American commenced regular visits down under.[17] Interestingly,

Stein's visits to Australia began more than a year *before* the Moffitt Commission began, bringing an end to the plot (seemingly involving Testa) to use Bally to muscle in on Sydney clubs.[18] While this does not in itself prove that Freeman and the others were already looking for new American opportunities outside of their existing relationship with Testa, it certainly was fortuitous timing for them to solidify a relationship with Stein and, through him, gain access to the Lansky machine. While Stein downplayed his links to Lansky, his professional success at casinos where Lansky held a financial interest indicated otherwise, and the fact that Stein purchased a racehorse in Australia that he named "Lansky" certainly did not help his argument either.

Of all the Australian criminals, Stein became particularly close to Freeman. He used Freeman's addresses when in the country and was photographed aboard a boat on Sydney Harbour with Freeman and other local "identities." He even featured briefly in the Moffitt Commission, caught up in the club scams run by Murray Riley and Wally Dean. Somehow, the American had been named "entertainments manager" at the Associated Motor Club in Sydney, an organization that Riley and Dean had "raided . . . and took what they could."[19] Realistically, there are few logical reasons for Stein to have become associated with Riley and Dean in the Associated Motor Club other than to reap the profits of their criminal enterprise. In fact, there are indications that Stein *was* receiving profits from Australia, one way or another. In June 1974, in the later stages of the Moffitt Commission, Stein sent a letter to Freeman complaining that he "[has] been having a problem with mail lately . . . you [Freeman] know I always drop you a note as soon as I receive the money and I haven't gotten it for June yet."[20] Based on this correspondence, it can be presumed that Stein was already deeply involved in affairs in Australia by the end of the Moffitt Commission, with Freeman acting as his agent. It is likely that these interests in Sydney went beyond minor rip-offs at local clubs with Riley and Dean. With the laws on gambling in New South Wales moving toward reform, the playing field was about to change in a way that might prove highly profitable for an experienced Las Vegas operator like Stein.

In the mid-1970s, the illegal casinos were well organized and raked in huge profits. According to co-proprietor Patricia Moylan, the 33 Club, which opened its doors in 1968, employed 56 people and had turnover "five times greater than Tasmania's legal Wrest Point Casino . . . then earning the state $3 million-a-year profits."[21] Thanks to the Australian fondness for gambling and police turning a blind eye (usually for a fee), the casinos had become a normal part of life in New South Wales; thus, seeking to resolve the issue once and for all, Premier Neville Wran announced in June 1976 that his government planned to legalize casinos in the state. The intention was that legalization would regulate the industry, force out unscrupulous operators, and drive illegal enterprises out of business.[22] Certainly there were challenges in legalization for gambling czars like Freeman, but also opportunities if the transition was managed sensitively. As with the Double Bay meetings in 1972, a council was convened that included Sydney's most prominent illegal gambling identities at the Taiping Restaurant on Elizabeth Street on June 22, 1976, shortly after Wran's announcement. Freeman did not attend, but the meeting was led by his regular partner-in-crime, Smith. Unbeknownst to Smith, the Taiping meeting was captured on tape recording, and so we can be certain of the pitch he made that evening. Referring to the state's politicians as "the shiftiest bunch of fucking people that ever, ever lived," Smith proposed bribing members of parliament with "hard cash." His argument was that state parliamentarians would be responsible for appointing members to any casino board, which would, in turn, approve casino licenses—in Smith's view "you have got to have some control of who the board is and put men there that are sweet, not *might* be sweet." Notably, Smith told the group that this plan was actually the brainchild of "the little friend of mine," who believed that the casino operators could handle the threat of legalization "with our brainpower behind [us] and so on, but collectively, not as individuals."[23]

The "little bloke" was never named on the Taiping tapes, but most knew that Smith was talking about Freeman, one of the few conspicuous absences on the night. It is not surprising that Freeman might have been behind a push to bribe officials to stay in business, but his connections to Stein and (through him) Mafia-linked American casino operators puts another spin on events. It is known that Freeman was closely associated with Stein at the time of the Taiping conspiracy, but he was not the only one with links to the Caesars Palace empire: Reg Andrews, an illegal casino operator who was one of Testa's earlier Australian connections, would later serve as Caesars agent and "public relations officer" in the region, part of what was described by insiders as a "push into gambling in Asia and . . . extend[ing] into Australia."[24] There is no firm evidence that Caesars Palace was involved in the Taiping conspiracy in any way, but with Freeman as the protagonist of the plot and his links to Caesars executive Stein, as well as Caesars later efforts to enter the Australian market via Andrews, there is reason to speculate that at least certain elements (like Stein) were already eying opportunities for Caesars to enter a newly legal New South Wales casino industry. If so, it could be argued that Caesars was seen by some to have the potential to fill a gap left by Bally: a legitimate operation that could be used as a vehicle for American criminals to mount an assault on the Australian gambling scene.

Offering more proof of Stein's interest in the legal casino plot is Frank Webb, an old associate of Freeman. Webb said he joined Freeman and Freeman's doctor (later, drug trafficker), Dr. Nick Paltos, on a trip to the United States in March 1978. The nominal reason for the visit was so Freeman could take his son Grant to Disneyland, but the plan was also to meet with Stein and Testa while in the country, to discuss their interest in partnering with Freeman in pursuing a casino license when (eventually) the New South Wales premier made good on his commitment to legalization.[25] According to Webb, Freeman traveled separately from his 12-year-old son because (as in 1968) he was traveling on a false passport to avoid detection and did not want his son to be with him if he was caught. Instead, the boy was collected from the airport by Freeman's trusted friend, Stein. When Freeman arrived, Stein and the Australians all went to Las Vegas where they met with Testa. However, when it came time for Freeman to leave, he was detained at the airport in San Francisco, having been monitored by the FBI during his time in the country. Webb said he was sent to burn Freeman's fake passport to destroy any evidence of his illegal entry to the United States. Meanwhile, Testa swung into action, mustering an initial $240,000 to bribe officials and secure Freeman's release, with another $250,000 being organized just in case it was needed. In addition, Webb said Testa implied that he and his associates were "in the process of putting the squeeze on a judicial figure whom they knew to be gay."[26] Whether it was blackmail, bribe money or simple dumb luck, Freeman was released on bail and engaged the services of a top local lawyer to represent him. He ultimately dodged a criminal conviction and was simply deported back to Australia. He would not risk meeting Stein and Testa in the United States again, connecting with Stein in Tahiti the next year where the local authorities were less interested in the visitors' criminal background. Just as Freeman could not return to the United States, nor could Stein come back to Australia by this point. When his criminal connections came to the attention of the Australian federal agencies, he was refused any further visas to enter the country. Stein made attempts in 1983 to lobby newly elected Prime Minister Bob Hawke to have the ban rescinded, but his overtures were denied. To the best of our knowledge, he did not ever return.[27]

Legal reform was a sluggish process and, by the end of the 1970s, it was still business as usual in Sydney's illegal casinos. In November 1977, Wran ordered Police Commissioner Merv Wood to shut them down, which Wood resisted. Wood said when he was "told that more than 300 people were employed in casinos in Sydney and other parts of the state . . . [he was] rather shocked when it was pointed out to [him] that these people would be jobless a couple of weeks before Christmas."[28] He persuaded Wran to delay the crackdown until after Christmas in what was either a sign of altruistic magnanimity or, alternatively, a favor to illegal casino operators during one of their busiest periods. The casinos were eventually shut on December 31, 1977, though the major venues only stayed shut for a short time.

Another attempt was made to shut them down over a year later, in a blitz of raids carried out by Superintendent Merv Beck and the detectives of gambling unit 21 Division, who attracted the nickname "Beck's Raiders" for their enthusiastic efforts to end illegal casinos once and for all.[29] In 1979, over the course of ten months, Beck's Raiders "reportedly made 900 arrests for SP [bookmaking] offences and 3300 arrests for all offences" and, in doing so, drew the ire of senior police with a vested interest in protecting illegal gaming operators. Eventually, Beck was summoned into the office of his superior, Assistant Commissioner Bill Allen, and told "he had closed down all the casinos, and that he had done his job."[30] He was soon after promoted to superintendent rank and Allen took control of 21 Division—a serendipitous (or, likely, planned) change in leadership, considering later evidence of Allen's improper ties to the gambling milieu.[31]

At the same time that Sydney's criminals were contending with the ebbs and flows of gambling legalization, new markets were opening up that were of great interest to both those within the milieu and their American allies. Though McPherson often denied any involvement in drugs, there is some suggestion of his involvement with a man named Martin Olson, who acted as his agent in Manila where he allegedly "look[ed] after McPherson's prostitution business."[32] Beyond the sex trade, federal police also believed Olson was managing a drug connection out of Manila on McPherson's behalf. Intelligence in 1975 indicated that, once a month, a courier visited Olson to collect packages of white powder that were then delivered to McPherson in Australia. According to the feds, the courier was not always alone, sometimes traveling with McPherson's friend Freeman . . . or even Danny Stein.[33] Australian police had been told by confidential informants that in 1976 "the purpose of Stein's visit [to Australia] was to organise a network for the importation and distribution of heroin both here and in America."[34] This was never verified; however, the rumors that Stein's intention in Australia was to establish a narcotic trafficking network was not helped by his association with Murray Riley, who was becoming increasingly involved in the trade himself.

Stein was first linked to Riley during the Moffitt Commission, where it was reported that Stein was "entertainments manager" for the same Associated Motor Club being ransacked for profit by Riley and Dean.[35] After Moffitt, Riley turned his attention away from the club scene and became increasingly involved in the illegal casinos, becoming close to 33 Club proprietor Michael Moylan Jr. and his wife, Patricia. By 1975 the Moylans, who had inherited the club from father Michael Sr., had run the once prestigious gaming house into the ground and, needing money, began looking to the lucrative drug trade to make up for the losses. This was the beginnings of the "suitcase method," where contacts in Southeast Asia would pack drugs into false linings of suitcases and recruit couriers (usually women, as they were less suspicious) to bring the drugs back to Australia, where they would be collected by the Moylans.[36] Over the course of four months, from May to September 1975, the Moylan syndicate trafficked more than 300 kilograms of cannabis into Australia; they actually managed to get an entire ton of marijuana into Australia later that year, but were ripped off by a partner who told them it had been intercepted, keeping the profits for himself.[37] The Moylans brought Riley on board because of his heavyweight reputation and criminal connections, and so, when the Moylans fled Australia in late 1975, Riley took charge of the network that the husband and wife team had first started. Like the Moylans, Riley also aspired to enter the US market but, unlike the Moylans, he had the connections to make it happen.

Another person Riley met through the illegal casino scene was an American restaurateur named George "Duke" Countis. Apart from his legitimate hospitality business, Countis "owned" several card tables at a casino owned by Ronnie Lee and Reg Andrews, Testa's original contacts in Australia when he visited in 1965.[38] Countis, born August 23, 1915, in New York City, also had Mafia connections. He had worked as a bookmaker for Aladena "Jimmy the Weasel" Fratianno throughout the 1940s and 1950s and, later, plotted with Fratianno in a foiled 1965 attempt to take over a casino in Reno, Nevada.[39] Countis left for Australia shortly after, in 1967, and became part of a growing American ex-pat community that also included Bourbon and Beefsteak operator Bernie Houghton, former general (and CIA operative) Michael Hand, and former Mafia lawyer Harry Wainwright.[40] Wainwright, a New Orleans native, was under investigation (and, later, indicted) for skimming $1.7 million in profits from Mafia-controlled topless bars in San Francisco, but had conveniently fled to Australia in 1968 just before the grand jury could issue a subpoena.[41] Countis introduced Riley to Wainwright, and by 1976 the fugitive lawyer had joined Riley's growing drug smuggling operation as well. In the meantime, Riley traveled to San Francisco with

Countis, where he was put in contact with Fratianno—and the Sydney Connection was born.

Aladena "Jimmy the Weasel" Fratianno was born on November 14, 1913, in Naples, Italy. His family moved to the United States when Fratianno was just four months old, settling in Cleveland, Ohio. From an early age, Fratianno was destined for a life in the Mafia, becoming a low-level associate of Cleveland's Italian and Jewish organized crime syndicates and, later, robbing unsanctioned card games in the company of future Cleveland consigliere Anthony Delsanter and future Rochester Family boss Frank Valenti.[42] It is very possible that Fratianno ran across future Bally distributor (and Lansky associate) Dino Cellini during this period; Cellini, just a year younger than Fratianno, was performing a similar role for a wing of the Cleveland Family in Steubenville, Ohio, around the same time. After serving an eight-year stint in prison for robbery, Fratianno headed west for Los Angeles to try his luck. In prison, he had met a mafioso who in turn connected him with Johnny Roselli, a Chicago Outfit capo who looked after the family's interests in Los Angeles and Las Vegas.

Fratianno operated as a bookie alongside Mickey Cohen in Santa Monica but, when Roselli approached him to join a plot to oust his boss, he lived up to "The Weasel" moniker and turned on Cohen, working as a spy for Roselli and others. He even helped set Cohen up for an attempted hit, a response to Cohen's increasingly erratic behavior in the wake of his friend Siegel's 1947 murder.[43] In return for his loyalty, Fratianno was sponsored by Roselli for membership to the Los Angeles Family and became a "made man" in late 1947, later rising to capo in 1952.[44] Shortly after, Fratianno was sent to prison for six and a half years for attempted extortion—while he was locked up, LA boss Jack Dragna died and was replaced by Frank DeSimone, a Mafia lawyer who Fratianno blamed for not representing him well enough to help him beat the extortion wrap. As a result of this dissatisfaction with DeSimone, Fratianno transferred to the Chicago Outfit in 1960 when he was released from prison, though (like his mentor Roselli) was mostly active in Los Angeles and Las Vegas.[45]

As mentioned, Fratianno was involved with Countis in a plan to purchase a casino in Reno that was rejected by the Chicago Outfit in 1965, after which Countis relocated to Sydney.[46] Fratianno was also part of another gambling-related scheme involving Australia in 1967, in this case a "horse-racing machine" designed by an Australian engineer, which he believed could be the next wave of machine-facilitated betting. Using old horse-racing videos, a punter inserted a coin and laid a bet on whichever horse they thought would win, with a payout if they chose correctly.[47] Fratianno's attempts to get this ground-breaking machine into production placed him squarely in Bally's orbit. An FBI source at the time supplied intelligence that the machine would be "manufactured in Chicago and Chicago hoodlum money will be behind it," with the FBI report mentioning Bally as a likely candidate for the "Chicago manufacturer" mentioned.[48] This was seemingly supported by Fratianno himself in his memoirs (written with Ovid Demaris), where he talked about taking the idea to Chicago boss Sam Giancana, who said the idea "looks promising" and wanted to show it to "[his] man at Bally, Lou Lederer, to have a look at it."[49] The Australian engineer behind the machine was allegedly sent to Chicago to work with Bally for six months, but never returned as promised, putting an end to Fratianno's aspirations. Never deterred, Fratianno continued to search for opportunities to make money. In 1973, this search brought him back to the West Coast, and he set up in San Francisco, where he established a crew that often met at a pizza restaurant owned by Salvatore Amarena. An associate of the Tampa-based Trafficante Family, Amarena's restaurant became a central venue in San Francisco where Mafia figures could meet and do business—indeed, it was Amarena's restaurant where Fratianno met with the Australian end of the Sydney Connection on several occasions in the late 1970s.[50]

In the 1970s, the US Mafia was looking for more than just the cannabis that Riley had started trafficking with the Moylans. In 1972, the French Connection pipeline operated by the French Union Corse was busted, ending a longtime heroin pipeline for the Mafia.[51] Tampa boss Santo Trafficante Jr. had reportedly traveled to Southeast Asia to seek new opportunities to import narcotics, and as a trusted associate on the West Coast, Amarena was allegedly a significant cog in his trafficking operation.[52] The need for a reliable pipeline from Southeast Asia was a prime opportunity for Fratianno. Through Countis, he knew of an Australian ex-police officer who was running a successful smuggling syndicate from the region and could prove very useful to the hungry US market. Fratianno began meeting with Riley from at least 1975, and the Sydney Connection was born. Using his courier system, Riley could bring heroin from Southeast Asia into Australia and, from there, traffic it to the US West Coast where Mafia men like Fratianno and (possibly, as law enforcement suspected) Amarena could distribute it more widely.[53] Back in Australia, Riley brought San Francisco Mafia lawyer Wainwright on board to assist with the heroin smuggling venture; Wainwright, in turn, introduced Riley to American ex-pat Michael Hand, a former CIA operative and military general now serving as a named partner in the soon-to-be infamous Nugan Hand Bank.[54]

Hand arrived in Australia around the same time as Countis, in September 1967. In its early years, he had served in the Vietnam War and (according to reporter Jonathan Kwitny) returned to Southeast Asia in 1966 after leaving the military to work as a CIA operative training the Hmong guerrilla in Laos.[55] After coming to Sydney, Hand became a habitue of Houghton's Bourbon and Beefsteak in Kings Cross, and it was there he met Australia lawyer Frank Nugan after an introduction from none other than Countis.[56] In 1973, Hand and Nugan came together to open the Nugan Hand Bank. The bank grew rapidly and, thanks in part to the cache afforded to it by the retired US military officials that Hand attracted as employees of Nugan Hand, by 1977 had established an international presence across three continents.[57] Though never proven, the bank's links to the US intelligence community led to rumors that Nugan Hand was a CIA front operation, used to fund anti-communist revolutionaries and otherwise launder dirty money around the world.[58] There were also suggestions that, after Hand met Riley, Nugan Hand became complicit in the drug trade. At this point, Hand took Riley's suggestion to open branches in locations central to the Southeast Asian "Golden Triangle" heroin trade, like Chiang Mai and Bangkok, and began spending more time in Hong Kong to facilitate Nugan Hand's Asian operations personally.[59] Even more than the suggestion to open branches in Thailand, Riley's syndicate was also reputedly the trigger for one of Nugan Hand's most important laundering innovations. Prompted by a request for a fast transfer of money to Hong Kong by Wainwright, Nugan devised a system to avoid the mandatory reporting of large international money transfers where Nugan Hand could hold money in each international location, so that if a client from Sydney (for example) went to Chiang Mai and asked to withdraw a large sum, that money could be supplied from the Thai branch's reserves rather than being "sent" abroad, in a riff on the traditional *hawala* system.[60] The process was essential to Nugan Hand's secretive movement of illicit money around the world, both for drug traffickers like Riley and, allegedly, for the US government as well.

More than just a passive participant in the Sydney Connection, there are suggestions that Hand played a crucial role in some of the syndicate's most important plots, such as one involving Sydney socialite Bela Csidei. Born in Budapest on August 10, 1932, Csidei immigrated to Australia in the 1950s and linked up with a powerful clique of right-wing businessmen who had all relocated to Sydney and were collectively known as "the Hungarian Mafia."[61] The Hungarian Mafia was closely tied to the American ex-pat milieu as well, having funded Houghton's early business endeavors and employing Hand before he set up the Nugan Hand Bank. Csidei claimed that in 1976 he was approached by Hand on a flight from Hong Kong to Sydney, at which point Hand "proposed a serious criminal venture. . . . Wainwright had told him I was the only one who could solve their problem."[62] The "problem" was that the Sydney Connection needed an expansive patch of land on which to grow a strain of "superweed," supplied in seedling form by Fratianno in San Francisco; the strain was guaranteed to "blow your head off," but Fratianno could not find a safe place to plant large-scale crops in the United States, causing him to turn to trusted ally Riley instead.[63] Csidei agreed, and in June 1977 a four-acre plot of the superweed was planted at his property in the Northern Territory. Csidei claims he agreed to sell the land to Wainwright and did not know what he was planning to do with it, but this was dismissed by the court.[64]

When the crop still was not ready after several months, a cash-strapped Csidei allegedly went off the books and harvested 140 kilograms of the product to sell. His courier was caught by Queensland police and, after an intense interrogation, he pointed them back to the superweed's source. The property was raided and Csidei was arrested, later receiving a fifteen-month sentence, with the trial judge referring to him as a "silly and greedy man, not a criminal mastermind."[65] Others have questioned the extent of Csidei's role in the Sydney Connection. He routinely traveled to San Francisco with Riley to meet with Fratianno and admitted that he owed the American gangster $10,000, which he could not pay back without agreeing to provide a location for the superweed crop.[66] As for Hand, there are suggestions that Nugan Hand began actively financing Riley's heroin trafficking (to a limited extent) in 1976. Whereas usually an associate would deposit money at the Sydney branch for Riley to withdraw in Asia to purchase his consignment of drugs, a $70,000 withdrawal from Hand's Hong Kong branch in 1976 was *not* matched with a corresponding deposit in Sydney, indicating that the money was "on loan" from the bank to fund Riley's venture.[67] The truth will likely never be known, however; in 1980, Nugan died in an apparent suicide, and Hand fled Australia under a false identity, having first shredded all of the Nugan Hand Bank's files.[68]

Before his arrest and imprisonment, Csidei actually provided the link between the American Mafia and another of his powerful associates, serving as a crucial lynchpin in yet another Australian-Mafia collaboration. Csidei's affiliation with the Hungarian Mafia was primarily through his connection to Sir Peter Abeles, chairman of Thomas Nationwide Transport (TNT)—more than simply fellow émigrés, Csidei said that Abeles "treated him like a son."[69] Abeles was a classic migrant success story, fleeing the Communist advance in Hungary for Australia in 1949 and starting a logistics company with just two secondhand trucks that, in 1967, would merge with TNT to become a shipping empire.[70] By the mid-1970s, Abeles was in an ascendent position and looking to expand into the United States. However, TNT's expansion was curtailed by industrial action that threatened the move (and Abeles's potential profits). When TNT began operating in the New York area, it experienced a series of bombings, arson attacks, and strikes.[71] Enter Csidei, who was connected to West Coast Teamsters boss Rudy Tham through their mutual association with Fratianno, a close ally of Tham. On visits to San Francisco with Riley in 1976, Csidei had been photographed meeting with Tham and, after his mentor mentioned the problems he was having, an eager-to-please Csidei reached out to his American contacts for help. At a later trial, Fratianno testified that he was introduced to Abeles by Tham in 1977 and the pair met "three or four times."[72] After these reputed meetings with Abeles, Tham allegedly introduced the Australian shipping czar to "friends" from New York City who he thought might be able to assist: Venero "Benny Eggs" Mangano and Lawrence "Buddy" Garaventi.

Mangano was born into a Mafia family in 1921, a relative of former boss Vincent Mangano, who was the namesake of one of the original Five Families after the Castellammarese War. Venero Mangano joined a different family, eventually becoming an integral part of Vincent "The Chin" Gigante's Greenwich Village crew of the Genovese Family.[73] Gigante was notorious as the failed assassin of Frank Costello (on the orders of Vito Genovese himself) and, from 1981, would rise to lead the Genoveses with Mangano as his underboss.[74] This was all a few years away at the time Mangano offered to help Abeles; however, he still held considerable influence as a rising star of the New York Mafia. A deal was struck: Abeles agreed to purchase a local trucking business owned by the Genoveses for $700,000 and gave them 20 percent of his own American operation.[75] Garaventi was placed on a $50,000 a year "consultancy" for TNT, while Fratianno claimed Mangano had told him that he was paid $25,000 on at least one occasion to do "a favour for Peter Abeles at the docks."[76] Fratianno was adamant that Abeles's payments to the Genoveses as consultants were aboveboard and "he's not doin' anything wrong," but the connection between Abeles, Csidei, Fratianno, and the Genoveses was yet another example of the crossover between the Australian operators discussed here and the American Mafia.[77] After all, it was the same Genovese Family who held a major stake in Bally until at least the early 1970s, and featured prominently in the Moffitt Commission.[78]

In 1977 the downfall of the Sydney Connection was imminent, and the culprit was, in many ways, a faulty engine on a yacht called *Choyro Maru*. That year, around the same time that Csidei agreed for his land to be used to grow Mafia superweed, Riley traveled to Thailand to negotiate a major shipment of cannabis. The exact figure ranges from 1.5 tonnes (in one of Riley's many versions of the story) to 4.5 tonnes (in court proceedings).[79] Regardless, Riley was told by his Thai suppliers that they could not provide that much product on short notice and would have to grow it, setting a delivery date for some time the next year, at a price of $48,000 per ton plus $50,000 for "protection."[80] For transport, Riley reached out to a man named Graham Lyall Cann, an associate of the Mr. Asia heroin smuggling syndicate who owned a vessel called the *Choyro Maru*, based out of Singapore. Looking to make extra cash from the same voyage, Cann also struck a deal with a Sydneysider named Wayne Thelander, who was also on the search for someone to bring his own shipment of cannabis into Australia. When the shipment was later revealed, it remained unclear whether Riley and Thelander were aware they were sharing space on the *Choyro Maru*, but it is very possible as the two men moved in the same circles. Thelander was connected to Stan Smith via their shared employment at a company called Balmain Welding, later described by the Woodward Commission into drug trafficking as a probable front for criminal activity. Indeed, Woodward even speculated that the company's chief business doing welding work on shipping containers would be "a useful means of bringing illegal material [into Australia], namely drugs."[81] Though Smith was not linked to the Thelander importation at the time, it was around this period that he started to become increasingly involved in the cannabis trade as well.

In late March 1978, the plan swung into action with Cann first picking up a smaller shipment of cannabis on the western side of the Gulf of Thailand (considered by many to be Thelander's) and then sailing to Pattaya where he collected a much larger consignment (believed to be Riley's). Whether Riley and Thelander worked in conjunction with each other to begin with or not, the two groups were compelled to do so when the *Choyro Maru* began to experience engine failure. Forced to abandon the voyage, Cann dropped the drugs at Polkington Reef off the coast of

Papua New Guinea for later retrieval.[82] Coming together in crisis talks about how to collect the product, Riley and Thelander agreed to purchase a yacht called *Anoa* in the northern Queensland town of Cairns, which then sailed to Polkington Reef where the crew spent five hours loading the vessel with the bags of cannabis that were left there. Ultimately, the men loaded *Anoa* with just over half of the *Choyro Maru*'s shipment, 2.73 tonnes.[83] Neither Riley nor Thelander knew it, but the *Anoa* was being tracked from the outset "by no fewer than four law enforcement agencies," which were kept abreast of the yacht's movements by naval intelligence as it made its way down the Queensland coast.[84] When the *Anoa* eventually docked in the northern New South Wales town of Coffs Habour and began to off-load product into trucks under the watchful eye of Riley's associate Ken Derley on June 10, 1978, police pounced. The *Anoa* drugs were recovered by law enforcement, as were the remaining drugs left at Polkington Reef. It took six weeks to take all syndicate members into custody, including three weeks to track down Riley after he fled to South Australia after he was alerted to the bust in Coffs Harbour.[85]

Were *all* the syndicate members caught, however? The amount of cannabis recovered from the *Choyro Maru* shipment was considerable, and some researchers, like John Jiggens, suggest it represented too much to be sold entirely on the Australian market. Given Riley's connection with crime figures in the United States and concurrent scheme with Fratianno, Wainwright, and Csidei to grow marijuana for the American market, Jiggens (and others) speculate that the bulk of the *Choyro Maru* shipment was ultimately destined for the United States via the Sydney Connection.[86] Riley even admitted the drugs were eventually due to be transported to the United States, albeit as part of a dubious narrative that did not mention Fratianno and was a clear attempt to shift responsibility from himself. However, there were also suggestions of Mafia involvement in the *Choyro Maru* importation that did *not* have Fratianno as the ultimate beneficiary. In his royal commission, Woodward heard testimony that Danny Stein was a financier of Riley's portion of the *Choyro Maru* cannabis, negotiated with his former partner in the Associated Motor Club scam during his 1976 visit to Australia.[87] Woodward ultimately could not find evidence to substantiate the allegation, but conceded that "it may be that the Australian sales were to be made out of the shipment of 1.5 tonnes . . . and the shipment of 3.5 tonnes was to be distributed in America."[88] In a reflection of the lasting confusion over how much of the *Choyro Maru*'s haul belonged to Fratianno, here it appears Woodward was attributing the entire almost 5-ton shipment to Riley, with Thelander as a co-conspirator and not part of a separate trafficking group. The intended distribution point for the *Choyro Maru* cargo will never truly be known, nor will Fratianno or Stein's potential involvement, but the evidence suggests it cannot be ruled out and, if true, it reflects yet another case of local Australian links to the American Mafia continuing to expand in the 1970s.

Both Riley and Thelander were sentenced to ten years' imprisonment for their role in the *Anoa* importation—Riley was released after serving less than five years in May 1984, at which point he quickly returned to conspiring to import narcotics into Australia along with heroin trafficker Arthur "Neddy" Smith.[89] On this occasion, he managed to avoid prison. Riley's run of good luck continued until several years later, when he turned up half a world away and still up to his old tricks. For his part in the Mafia superweed crop, Csidei was sentenced to fifteen months in prison with a non-parole period of nine months, as he was considered by the trial judge as more patsy than mastermind.[90] Wainwright, the alleged "third man" in the scheme, avoided punishment entirely. On the American end of the Sydney Connection, life was not easy for Fratianno, either. In 1975, he transferred back to the Los Angeles Family he had abandoned fifteen years earlier as part of an arrangement where he would serve as acting boss in collaboration with Louis Tom Dragna, son of former boss Jack Dragna.[91]

The fallout was seismic: First, Fratianno was called on to arrange a hit on a close friend in the Family who was accused of being an informant (which he passively refused) and, when official boss Dominic Brooklier returned from prison in October 1976, Fratianno was demoted and Brooklier began telling other mafiosos that Fratianno had not been sanctioned to represent himself as acting boss in his absence.[92] Fratianno feared Brooklier was laying the foundations for a hit on him. Worse, at the funeral of his childhood friend Anthony Delsanter, he learned that the Cleveland Family had a mole in the FBI, who may have revealed that Fratianno had been informing to the agency since 1966.[93] In October 1977, the final blow came when Fratianno was implicated in organizing a hit on Cleveland-based Irish mobster Danny Greene. Choosing between life in prison for the Greene murder or certain death on the streets on Brooklier's orders, Fratianno agreed to become a government witness against the Mafia and entered the witness protection program, bringing an end to his criminal aspirations.[94] Fratianno has been described as the most connected and important Mafia supergrass of his time, surpassed only by the likes of Sammy "The Bull" Gravano more than a decade later.[95]

Aside from the collapse of Riley's Sydney Connection, other local criminals were also going through a crucible of sorts in the late 1970s. The once powerful triumvirate of McPherson, Smith, and Freeman each experienced their own personal challenges during this period, impacting their ability to carry out business as usual. McPherson was facing challenges to his former dominance on several fronts. Within the criminal set, his challenger was Lou "Mad Dog" Miller, an upstart described in police records as "a gunman, assailant, thief and procurer of prostitutes . . . an inveterate gambler who is hated by all hardened criminals."[96] Miller launched a frontal assault on the McPherson camp, hiring a gunman from Brisbane to assassinate one of McPherson's associates in a failed murder plot in 1975. In return, McPherson allegedly took out a contract on Miller and promptly (along with Smith) left Australia for Manila, where he would have a watertight alibi when Miller was killed. While Miller was not assassinated, he did get the message and voluntarily exited the power struggle.[97] His rival had bigger worries by that point, though. Upon arrival in Manila in June 1975, McPherson was arrested by Filipino police after Australian federal authorities had passed information to them (falsely, as McPherson tells it) that he was coming to the country to assassinate President Ferdinand Marcos. He dodged the firing squad but was deported, which put a strain on his burgeoning business interests in The Philippines.[98] Meanwhile, for Smith the problem was drugs—selling, not using. Having drifted somewhat apart from McPherson and Freeman, he forged a new relationship with international drug trafficker

Lawrence McLean that ultimately landed him 15 months in a Victorian jail in 1979 for possession of marijuana.[99]

Whereas McPherson and Smith were both finding their criminal activity curtailed by a more effective approach to policing, Freeman's woes were far more personal. When an up-and-coming Freeman associate named Michael Hurley was sent to prison for four years on stealing charges in 1977, he asked his mentor to look after his wife, Lena. Hurley certainly would not have expected the much older Freeman to engage his wife in a sexual relationship, but he did—worse, he even set Lena up as the madam in a new brothel operation that he had recently opened in Woolloomooloo.[100] The affair was an open secret, and one that Hurley could do nothing about from behind bars. Instead, he spoke to Lena's father, Jacky Muller, who was himself a much-feared Sydney gunman. Though never convicted, the story goes that Muller took action into his own hands on April 25, 1979, the night of the ANZAC Day public holiday. Freeman had been with his friend Nick Paltos for the day and, upon returning to his home later that evening, was grazed by a bullet as he attempted to unlock his front door. A .22-caliber bullet had struck him in the neck "and passed up through his mouth, grazing an optic nerve and exiting near the corner of his eye."[101] Though badly injured, Freeman had a lucky escape. Muller was less fortunate: In the early hours of June 7, 1979, the reputed shooter was himself shot dead execution style as he got into his car outside his home in Coogee.[102] While Freeman survived, and revenge was swiftly exacted (so it seems, though no one was ever convicted of the Muller murder), the attempted assassination had a lasting impact. Freeman became more reclusive after the near-death experience and, worse, developed a taste for the opioid drug pethidine that affected him until his death more than a decade later.[103]

Despite their aspirations in chasing an American dream, the Sydney milieu found themselves at a real low point as the 1970s drew to an end. Several were in prison, more than a few had been foiled by law enforcement, and some had even come perilously close to death. Hopes of a long-dreamed-of collaboration with the American Mafia seemed dashed, and the Sydney Connection had fallen apart due to a boat engine giving up somewhere in the Pacific Ocean. Meanwhile, Jack Rooklyn was having much better luck on the water. His yacht *Ballyhoo* won line honors in the Sydney to Hobart race on December 30, 1976, pulling into Hobart's Constitution Dock after three days, eight hours, and 630 miles.[104] *Ballyhoo* beat out *Apollo*, captained by Rooklyn's son, which came in second place. *Apollo* lost this time, but would go on to surpass *Ballyhoo*, winning the race in both 1978 and 1985.[105] While Rooklyn secured his place in Australian sporting history, his position with Bally Australia was far more tenuous. Just as 1976 ended in victory, the next year was destined to be a time of reckoning for Rooklyn, where his career would stumble and a new path would begin to take shape—one that led north, to the Sunshine State.

Figure 5.1. Jack Rooklyn: gambling mogul, champion yachtsman, and convicted criminal.

SOURCE: ABC AUSTRALIA.

Figure 5.2. Abe Saffron (sometimes called “Mr. Sin”) allegedly partnered with Rooklyn on several occasions.

SOURCE: NATIONAL ARCHIVES OF AUSTRALIA (ITEM 31636297).

Figure 5.3. Athol Moffitt, the judge who presided over the inquiry into Bally's Australian operation (1973–1974).

SOURCE: NATIONAL ARCHIVES OF AUSTRALIA (ITEM 31635966).

Figure 5.4. Terry Lewis, the corrupt Queensland Police Commissioner paid by Rooklyn (and others).

SOURCE: QUEENSLAND POLICE MUSEUM (CC BY 4.0).

Figure 5.5. Joh Bjelke-Petersen, Premier of Queensland (1968–1987).
SOURCE: NATIONAL ARCHIVES OF AUSTRALIA (ITEM 31870778).

Figure 5.6. The Sydney nightclub district Kings Cross (1970), where illegal casinos and the sex trade were rife.

SOURCE: NATIONAL ARCHIVES OF AUSTRALIA (ITEM 11484934).

6

Reinvention

THE BUZZ THAT CAME FROM *BALLYHOO*'S LINE HONORS VICTORY IN THE 1976 Sydney to Hobart race did not last long into the new year for the Rooklyn family. On New Year's Day 1977, Rooklyn's eighteen-year-old daughter was hospitalized with minor injuries in Sydney after a car accident that totaled the brand-new Alfa Romeo her father had given her for Christmas. The collision wasn't her fault—a fire truck "on its way to a small fire at the [Sydney] Opera House . . . passed through a red light at the intersection" and took her and the car with it as it did.[1] Nevertheless, the incident may have been a sign of things to come for the Rooklyns in 1977. By the end of the year, Jack Rooklyn's time as the managing director of Bally Australia would come to an end, thanks largely to the intervention of the Nevada Gaming Control Board. The dominoes that would lead to his ouster were already in place as 1977 began and, in some ways, had little to do with Rooklyn or the Moffitt Commission. In 1973, the Gaming Control Board began conducting an extensive investigation into Bally in response to the company's petition for a gaming license in the state, which would allow it to distribute its slot machines directly in America's single largest market.[2]

The gaming board had already taken exception to some of Bally's associates in Nevada. In 1971 gaming auditors conducted a surprise review of Mickey Wichinsky's affiliated Bally Sales Corporation, which was in 1972 purchased by the Bally organization as part of its push into direct distribution. Shortly after the Nevada Gaming Control Board commenced its 1973 investigation, Wichinsky was served with an order demanding he explain his "habitually consorting with, catering to and assisting persons of notorious and unsavory reputations."[3] While Wichinsky had sold his Bally Sales Corporation by this point, he continued to hold a stake in The Sands casino—the former employer of Danny Stein, and linked to the Meyer Lansky contingent. Despite the investigation finding that Wichinsky was in regular contact with Gerry Catena's son-in-law, he denied a relationship with Catena himself. He did, however, admit to being an associate of Dino Cellini, Lansky's agent who went to work for Bally in Europe. In the end, the gaming board's investigation lasted two years, spanned eleven countries, and cost an estimated $400,000.[4] In March 1975, the board decided to permit Bally to hold a gaming license under strict conditions. Among others, the board ordered that the company cease all business with Catena's front man Abe Green, former Louisiana distributor Louis Boasberg, and the head of Bally Continental, Alexander Wilms.[5]

With the probationary period on Bally's licensure coming to an end in 1977, yet another gaming board investigation was carried out to determine whether the company had adhered to the conditions of the 1975 decision. The board extended Bally's probationary period after hearing that it had failed to meet its requirements. Despite the order to end its dealings with Green, Bally continued to distribute its machines through a company owned by Green's son Irving that was "virtually indistinguishable" from the business it claimed to have broken ties with. Despite the order to end its dealings with Boasberg, Bally continued to sell its products through another company owned by Boasberg's children—again, "virtually indistinguishable" from the distribution business it had been banned from working with.[6] Bally *had* secured the resignation of Wilms, but with an important caveat. While he lost his operational position with Bally, the Wilms family remained a shareholder in the company. It was through Wilms that Rooklyn's name started to come to the gaming board's attention. In testimony to the board, Wilms admitted to a checkered past, including three black market trading convictions in Belgium and the employment of Cellini as a sales representative in Europe. Wilms also admitted to being the author of a company report "in which he suggested that bribery of government officials in various Southeast Asian countries should be accomplished through Jack Rooklyn . . . so that '[t]he Bally image would remain clean.'"[7] Although Wilms's suggestion of using Rooklyn as an agent of bribery clearly made him an inappropriate person to hold directorship in a gaming company, the idea itself was probably a logical one; Rooklyn had long-standing connections in Southeast Asia and, by his own admission, had (on occasion) offered personal benefits to officials in the region to enhance his business interests.[8]

Unfortunately for Bally, the Nevada gaming board did not see Wilms's recommendation in quite the same way. Apart from ordering that Wilms no longer be employed by Bally, it ordered that Bally either bring Rooklyn forward for licensing or secure his resignation from the company. The board believed that he was "involved in gaming activities in the Far East in violation of Nevada law"—a reasonable concern given his history in the region and the claims heard by Moffitt only a few years prior that Rooklyn and Saffron were looking to expand their operations into Indonesia.[9] While Rooklyn had survived Moffitt, the risk he posed to Bally's chances of securing a Nevada gaming license proved too much for the company to bear. The board's ultimatum that he be put forward for license or resign was issued in October 1977 and, by December 20, 1977, it was announced that he would be leaving his position as managing director of Bally Australia. His exit, negotiated with world marketing director Ross Scheer in Sydney, was something of a sweetheart deal: Rooklyn "bought back" the poker machine distribution business he sold to Bally in the early 1970s and secured the exclusive rights to sell Bally products throughout Australia.[10] In another connection that was not completely severed, Rooklyn's role as managing director was taken over by his longtime company secretary (and protégé) Jan Newell.[11] Initial reports had Rooklyn purchasing his distribution business back at around the same cost he sold it for in 1973, $3.4 million.[12] Later, Rooklyn's business associate Jack Herbert told the Fitzgerald Inquiry that "Rooklyn was paid $8.25 million by Bally to surrender the company's Australian franchise."[13] While this has not been verified, it is true that Bally would have been motivated to remove the problematic Rooklyn from its employment after the 1977 gaming board decision and, as such, a substantial payout is certainly not out of the realm of possibility.

Rooklyn may have technically been forced out of Bally, but the terms of his departure were reflective of the company adhering to the board's orders in the most tenuous of ways. Just as it had continued its relationships with Green and Boasberg's distribution businesses via proxies, Bally maintained its dealings with Rooklyn, albeit now at an arm's length. While his exit from Bally may have been a blow, Rooklyn seemingly had already been working in the background to diversify his Australian distribution portfolio. On April 3, 1974, in the midst of the Moffitt Commission hearings, the Queensland government agreed to issue permits for the sale and operation of in-line gaming machines in the state, under the proviso that "no betting on the result of the machine is permitted . . . [and] no prizes are to be given" in lieu of monetary rewards.[14] In essence, the in-line machines that were permitted in Queensland were just like the amusement games that both Rooklyn and Bally had originally made a name for themselves in, and so it is unsurprising that Queensland's decision to allow in-line machines attracted Rooklyn's attention. In 1984, while serving as Opposition police spokesperson, Labor politician Wayne Goss accused Rooklyn of infiltrating the in-line industry from the shadows at first, using a legitimate business called the United Coin Machine Co. "as a front to move into Queensland," and alleged that he was already lying in wait when the decision was made not to ban in-line machines. Goss claimed that, when that happened in 1974, "Jack Rooklyn and his group moved, in an overnight swoop, to change the locks on the machines, kick out the Queensland-based company, and take total control of the machines."[15] If true, it is possible that Rooklyn was already looking to his next move, in a different state, in the event that Moffitt's investigation went south. Queensland would have been an appealing choice. It was to Queensland that Rooklyn immigrated during World War II, and where he put himself on Bally's radar by managing the American Centre.[16]

Since Rooklyn's last jaunt to Queensland, the landscape had changed. Since 1968, the state had been under the rule of Premier Johannes "Joh" Bjelke-Petersen, an ultraconservative pastoralist from the rural town of Kingaroy, best known for boasting the title of Australia's "Peanut Capital."[17] The premier had grown up in a strict Lutheran household, and had cultivated a public reputation as a defender of traditional moral values since first being elected to public office in 1946 at age 35.[18] An abrasive character, it took Bjelke-Petersen thirteen years in state parliament before he was promoted to Cabinet but, by January 1968, he had risen to the position of Deputy Leader of the ruling Country Party. His ascension was completed with the untimely death of Premier Jack Pizzey from a heart attack in July of the same year. Even then, Bjelke-Petersen's rise was a matter of concern in the corridors of power, with some politicians concerned about his potential leadership seriously considering breaking with convention to support another candidate to replace Pizzey—it was only when Bjelke-Petersen and his supporters threatened to withdraw from the governing coalition, handing power to the opposition Labor Party, that the decision to name him premier was confirmed.[19] Contentious though it may have been, Bjelke-Petersen's rise to power appeared (on the surface, at least) to herald a renewed commitment by the government to defending the conservative moral order, enforced by a premier willing to use every means at his disposal to impose his traditionalist vision on the state.

One such tool favored by Bjelke-Petersen in the course of his almost 20-year tenure as premier was the Queensland Police Force (QPF), which attracted a reputation as Bjelke-Petersen's "loyal spear-carriers" as a result of their enthusiastic (often brutal) repression of left-wing protests at the premier's behest.[20] The irony is that, at the same time the QPF was accused of aggressively serving Bjelke-Petersen's arch-conservative agenda, it held a group of officers within its own ranks who would later come to prominence as some of Australia's most notorious corrupt police. At the time Bjelke-Petersen assumed the premier's role in 1968, the QPF had been led for a decade by Commissioner Frank Bischof, a man who had moved up the QPF hierarchy and taken power against the odds, just like his new boss. The son of a dairyman from rural Toowoomba, Bischof made a name for himself in the state's Criminal Investigation Branch (CIB) as a hotshot detective who rarely lost a case, with an almost perfect record of 32 convictions in 33 murder cases he worked.[21] Despite his stellar reputation as an investigator, Bischof was also heavily suspected of involvement in corruption—in particular, a protection racket that serviced SP bookies.[22] When he was promoted to police commissioner in January 1958, police and politicians alike raised the alarm and brought these concerns about his suitability to the government; however, the government stood by their appointment, and so began Bischof's reign.

With the spotlight on Bischof now that he was commissioner, he relied on allies in the QPF to represent his interests on the street. Over the years, a core group of three officers were alleged to have been close to Bischof, even described as his "bagmen" who were responsible for continuing his corrupt rackets when he was no longer personally able to do so.[23] The first of these men was alleged to be Tony Murphy, a hard-nosed detective from Queensland's southwest in the style of the commissioner himself. Like Bischof, Murphy also got results on the streets, and enjoyed a fearsome reputation in Brisbane underworld.[24] Murphy served under Bischof in the CIB before he became commissioner, and maintained a close personal and professional relationship with his old boss. Another member of the trio who served under Bischof in the CIB was Terry Lewis, a young officer who was eager to make his mark and please the venerated likes of then Detective Bischof. After taking office, Bischof handpicked Lewis to head his pet project, the Juvenile Aid Bureau (JAB), and, in doing so, put his protégé on the professional path to one day being named his successor.[25]

The final member of the group, Glen Hallahan, did not serve under Bischof in the CIB but rather came to his attention in spectacular fashion when he carried out what many in Queensland considered to be the arrest of the decade. In 1957 Hallahan was working as detective in Queensland mining town Mount Isa when he arrested Raymond John Bailey for the triple murder of mother and daughter Thyra and Wendy Bowman, as well as their friend Thomas Whelan, on the Sundown station in outback South Australia.[26] Under questioning, Bailey allegedly confessed and, as a result, was convicted and executed for the murders. Later, it was alleged by corruption whistle-blower (as well as Hallahan's lover and confidante) Shirley Brifman that Hallahan admitted to fabricating Bailey's confession and was plagued with guilt for sending a (potentially) innocent man to the gallows.[27] In any event, Hallahan's success in the Sundown murders case inevitably brought him to the attention of newly appointed

Commissioner Bischof, who organized his transfer to the Brisbane CIB where he would work alongside Murphy and Lewis, with the three officers referred to as "the Rat Pack."

In the Bischof era, the Rat Pack were at the center of the whispers swirling about corruption in the QPF. In 1959, shortly after Hallahan's arrival in Brisbane, he and Lewis were briefly demoted to uniform after being accused of standing over sex worker Leigh Hamilton for protection money. They were returned to their previous position, but only because of an alleged "tip-off" from Murphy and with the intervention of their patron, Bischof.[28] When allegations of police protection of illegal alcohol sales and sex work at the National Hotel resulted in a judicial inquiry in 1963, the Rat Pack were once again at the center of the allegations. Ultimately, the police were vindicated on all counts by Supreme Court judge Harry Talbot Gibbs—with some credit going to sex workers like Brifman, who told the inquiry she had not seen corruption while working out of the National Hotel. Later, when her relationships with police soured in the early 1970s, she admitted to lying at the behest of Hallahan and Murphy. Brifman's claims that she was incited to perjure herself led to charges against Murphy, which were only dropped when Brifman died of a drug overdose before the case could go to trial.[29]

The ethical (and legal) questions circulating around Bischof and the Rat Pack were not the only problematic areas for the Queensland police during this era. British émigré Jack Herbert joined the Licensing Branch in 1959, the same year that Hallahan and Lewis were demoted. When he arrived, he was almost immediately told over drinks with his new colleagues that it had been decided he was trustworthy enough to be brought "in on the Joke" that was going on in the office.[30] The Joke referred to a system of protecting SP bookies, separate to Bischof's own alleged racket. Herbert was told there was a list of protected bookies who were "paid up"—an officer "in on the Joke" was tasked with stopping any raids against bookies in the system or, if they could not, at the very least warning them in advance. In return, all officers in the Joke received £20 a month, a considerable top-up of Herbert's £90 salary.[31] When Herbert joined, the Joke focused on the protection of gambling interests—later, corrupt Licensing Branch officers would expand to providing a full-service package for Queensland's vice operators that included prostitution and, allegedly, the drug trade. When Herbert was initiated into the Joke, he could not possibly have known the impact this decision would have on his life. Almost thirty years later, Herbert would sit in the dock at the Fitzgerald Inquiry and reveal all he knew about the corrupt system and, in doing so, point the finger at the very people who used to share in his corrupt spoils, such as Police Commissioner Terry Lewis—and his co-conspirator, Jack Rooklyn.

All this was a long way into the future, however. In the early 1960s, Herbert was just another cog in the Joke's machine, one of several officers in the Licensing Branch offering corrupt protection to Queensland's vice purveyors. After five years in the branch, he took over as the chief organizer of the Joke in 1964, just after the National Hotel Inquiry concluded and at the peak of the Bischof era.[32] As organizer, Herbert's role was pivotal: He was responsible not just for distributing money to officers and ensuring bookies were paid up, but also for deciding which officers in Licensing could be trusted to bring into the scheme. One wrong decision could bring the Joke down, along with all the "Jokers" who were part of it. Though seemingly a stressful position to be in, Herbert later claimed otherwise, saying that in his time as the Joke's organizer not a single officer who he approached refused to take part. In 1966, Rat Packer Tony Murphy became one of Herbert's new recruits after transferring to Licensing—Herbert said that he was warned in advance not to "let a day go by" without bringing Murphy into the Joke, such was his influence with Bischof and his reputation in the QPF. Herbert claimed Murphy was more than willing to join the Joke, and even suggested bringing in Lewis as well, despite the latter not even working in Licensing. His rationale was that Lewis's closeness with Bischof meant he was a good person to keep on their side and, not wanting to refuse one of Bischof's protégés, Herbert said he agreed. If Herbert's testimony to Fitzgerald is to be believed, both Murphy and Lewis were active members of the Joke by 1966.[33]

In the late 1960s, with Bischof at the helm and a robust Joke in the Licensing Branch, it seemed that the corrupt factions of the QPF were on the ascendent. These rising fortunes were not to last, though. After several stints on sick leave in the years prior, Bischof finally resigned as police commissioner in February 1969.[34] The hunt for his replacement was on and, within government, the campaign for renewal and reform was growing. First, Police Minister Max Hodges called in the cavalry, bringing in well-respected South Australian police chief John McKinna to Queensland to conduct an audit on the QPF with the goal of getting to the bottom of what needed to change in a post-Bischof era. McKinna offered a number of recommendations, but, among them, he also put forward the name of a man he believed could implement the kind of change that Hodges was looking for: Raymond Wells Whitrod.[35] A former South Australian police detective, Whitrod had a strong resume. After helping establish the Australian Security Intelligence Organization (ASIO), a domestic spy agency, after World War II, Whitrod was chosen as the inaugural commissioner of the Commonwealth Police Force, now known as the Australian Federal Police. Around the time of Bischof's resignation, Whitrod took the job of Papua New Guinean police commissioner but, after persuasive entreaties from Hodges, agreed to give up this new role to come to Queensland and spearhead what was sure to be a challenging, but necessary, period of reform.[36]

Whitrod began his term as commissioner in September 1970. He admitted in his memoirs that, at the time, he had "little understanding of how entrenched corruption was" in Queensland, and the sheer scale of the job ahead of him.[37] It was a matter of minutes after touching down in Queensland that Whitrod began to understand. Ken Hoggett, the sergeant tasked with collecting the new boss from the airport, said in that first car ride, "I don't know how much you know about the [QPF], but it's pretty corrupt."[38] Before long, Whitrod learned about the Rat Pack and set about the task of marginalizing Bischof's protégés. One of his first initiatives was to establish the Crime Intelligence Unit (CIU), a permanent squad with a remit to investigate corrupt officers. The CIU's first major target was Hallahan, still up to his old tricks and standing over sex workers like Dorothy Knight for protection. Sick of paying Hallahan's extortionate "fee," Knight turned to the CIU and, on December 30, 1971, fit with a rudimentary electronic listening device, conducted a sting on Hallahan that saw him facing charges of official corruption.[39] The criminal charges against Hallahan were eventually dropped, as electronic recording was still a very new technique and its legality in Queensland was not clear. However, the sting nevertheless was a crushing blow to the once high-flying detective and, seeing that Whitrod would not stop pursuing him, Hallahan resigned from the QPF in October 1972.[40] The CIU almost claimed another Rat Pack scalp around the same time. Based on allegations from Shirley Brifman about Hallahan and Murphy's actions during the National Hotel Inquiry, Murphy was charged with perjury on February 4, 1972.[41] He escaped his date with court when Brifman died of a drug overdose, but was eventually transferred, in 1976, to rural western Queensland (along with Lewis) in a last-ditch attempt by Whitrod to keep the Bischof contingent away from the center of power in Brisbane.[42]

It was in the context of this scramble for control of the QPF that the state government considered whether or not to ban in-line amusement machines in the state in 1974. Under the moral regime of Bjelke-Petersen, as was the case in most of Australia, devices explicitly used for gambling purposes, like poker machines, remained banned. The in-line machines under consideration did not have the functional ability to offer payouts like poker machines could and, on the surface, appeared no different to the pinball games that were popular in amusement arcades, where young people paid to play but did not receive any reward in return.[43] The fear was, however, that in the wrong hands in-line machines *could* have the potential to act as gambling devices hiding in plain sight. While the machine itself could not "pay out" dividends, money or other rewards could still be paid manually by proprietors, just as had been the case in the early days of the poker machine industry before mechanization.[44] For this reason, the legalization of in-line machines came before the state's Justice Committee in 1974.

Leading the charge for legalization was a man familiar to police, Arthur Anthony "Tony" Robinson. Since the 1950s at least, he had been a player in the Brisbane nightclub scene, beginning with an unlicensed venue, the El Morocco, where musical superstars the Bee Gees began their career. Robinson's initial relationship with police was less than positive. He claimed that, after banning a New Zealand criminal from the El Morocco, he was driven "stone, motherless broke" by the Licensing

Branch, which raided the El Morocco and confiscated all of his alcohol. Robinson said he was later told that the criminal he had barred from his club had paid "old Frank [Bischof]" a bribe of £5,000 to shut him down.[45] Whatever the beginnings of the relationship, Robinson himself eventually came to an agreement with corrupt police, later opening a new venue called The Playboy Club at Petrie Bight that was allegedly permitted to trade liquor after hours, despite not even having a liquor license.

Anti-corruption campaigner Colin Bennett made these claims in state parliament in November 1968 after the brutal bashing-murder of Gary Venamore, who was killed after leaving The Playboy Club in the early hours of the morning, long after it was supposed to have closed. Bennett went further, claiming that "not only . . . has it [The Playboy Club] never been policed; I am claiming quite categorically that there are police in uniform drinking there at night-time."[46] The Playboy Club had shut down by the early 1970s, but by then Robinson had already turned his attention more closely to illegal gambling. Jack Herbert told the Fitzgerald Inquiry that part of the reason he initiated Murphy into the Joke so quickly in 1966 was that he had been told that Murphy and Lewis were already paying a Licensing Branch officer to protect one of Robinson's illegal baccarat schools in South Brisbane, and so (in some ways) Murphy was already part of the scheme.[47]

When Robinson lobbied for the legalization of in-line machines in 1974, he made direct approaches to a member of the Justice Committee who was also closely connected to the Rat Pack, Donald Frederick Lane. Before entering state parliament as the Liberal member for Merthyr in July 1971, Lane had served almost twenty years with the QPF alongside the likes of the Rat Pack and Jack Herbert. He was part of Murphy's team during the National Hotel Inquiry, working alongside him to discredit witnesses and vindicate Bischof and the Rat Pack.[48] He went on to join the state's Special Branch, where he made political connections that ultimately saw him preselected and elected to state parliament. Despite leaving the police, Lane remained close to his former friends in the force and served as an advocate for them in state Cabinet, where he had the ear of the premier. He was a staunch critic of Whitrod, who he regularly described as "that clown," and was allegedly part of a cabal working behind the scenes to see Whitrod fired and replaced with Lewis.[49] Given these links, it is unsurprising that Lane acted as Robinson's key contact in the Justice Committee throughout the campaign to legalize in-line machines . Though Lane himself was later accused of taking bribes, and convicted on misuse of ministerial expense charges, it would be far too simplistic to suggest that he alone was responsible for securing legalization in 1974—though he may have been influential beyond his status, Lane was still a junior parliamentarian at the time of the deliberations and, as such, the verdict to legalize went beyond his intervention. As Robinson himself later described it: "[Y]ou didn't have to be a Rhodes scholar" to see that the government clearly understood that in-line machines were more than just simple amusement games, as evidenced by the fact that permit fees for them were ten times that of pinball machines, which, in theory, were the same thing.[50]

Whitrod's anti-corruption team eventually came for Herbert in July 1974, when Arthur Pitts was named the new inspector of the Licensing Branch. Earlier that year, in April, a CIU report had found that up to 50 bookies were operating in Brisbane "with immunity because of collusion with the Licensing Branch."[51] It was this mess that Pitts was sent to clean up, and he did so with zealous vigor. Within months he established a system of conducting raids on bookies at short notice, preventing them from being tipped off, and arrested over a dozen major operators in the illegal industry.[52] Herbert and others in on the Joke were transferred out of Licensing in July 1974, around the same time Pitts arrived, with some officers like Herbert having 15 years of service in the branch. Not long after his transfer, Herbert resigned, claiming he was medically unfit for duty.[53] Nevertheless, he continued his involvement with corruption in the QPF, drawing on his years of experience to act as a middleman between vice traders and corrupt police. However, if the Joke were to survive, Pitts either had to be brought into the fold or he had to go. In a rare misjudgment, Herbert decided to try and bring the crusader in. But Pitts was ready and, expecting the call to come, had already set up recording equipment on his home telephone. When Herbert called and offered him $1,500 a month to protect a select group of bookies in December 1974, his offer was caught on tape and both Herbert and his partner Neal

Freier were charged with attempting to corrupt the head of the Licensing Branch.[54]

The fight was on for Herbert, but this time it was not just about saving the Joke—it was about saving himself from prison, as well. Fortunately, the old Joker still had friends on the force who were willing to help him strike back at Pitts. Just one month before Herbert and Freier's arrest, the Licensing Branch achieved a long-term goal when a team led by Pitts arrested suspected bookies Stanley Saunders and Brian Sieber on the Gold Coast, a beachside resort town on the Queensland–New South Wales border. Pitts and a small team of Licensers intercepted the duo's car on November 20, 1974, and charged them both with possessing instruments used to conduct illegal gambling.[55] The case against Saunders and Sieber seemed like a slam-dunk win for Licensing, but there was one small problem—in the course of his crusade to take down Queensland's bookies, Pitts broke the rules. After Herbert's December 1974 arrest, one of Pitts's team on the Gold Coast operation came to Herbert's home, bringing with him a blank warrant signed by Pitts and telling Herbert that the inspector "had not obtained a properly sworn out warrant" when he arrested Saunders and Sieber.[56] Though the Saunders and Sieber case was not directly connected to Herbert's own corruption charges, a plan started to take shape wherein this information could be turned to his advantage. Pitts had caught Herbert in a trap when he recorded his attempts to corrupt, but this time Herbert would turn the tables. He handed the Licensing Branch officer, Frank Davey, a small tape recorder and dispatched him back to work, this time to find as much evidence on Pitts's honesty as he could.[57]

Herbert's gambit paid off. Unknowingly being recorded by Davey, Pitts met with both his team and police prosecutor Alec Jeppesen to get their stories straight before the Saunders and Sieber trial. Pitts was caught on tape admitting having crossed the border into New South Wales (outside his jurisdiction) during the operation, and expressing frustration that other officers in the branch were not comfortable "dropping a brick"—a common colloquialism referring to the police planting or otherwise manufacturing evidence.[58] The first hints of Davey's deception came in Saunders and Sieber's trial, when Davey was called to the stand and revealed some of the impropriety that occurred around the bookies' arrest. The tapes were not played in court, but Davey's testimony was enough. In July 1975 the court determined that there was no case for Saunders to answer and, later, Sieber was found not guilty.[59] The collapse of the bookies' trial was just the tip of the iceberg, however. Davey's recordings were to play a significant role in Herbert's corruption trial, which began in the district court in May 1976.

Just as the prosecution played tapes of Herbert attempting to corrupt Pitts, the defense team was able to cast a shadow on the scruples of the prosecution with their own set of clandestine recordings. Thanks to "fabricated evidence, perjured corroborative evidence by co-operative police officers, the collaboration of a justice of the peace in falsification of evidence, and interference with the jury," Herbert's team was able to gain the advantage, and, in November 1976, Herbert was acquitted.[60] While the Joke's organizer walked free from court, the QPF turned its sights on the man who seemed to have fumbled the case so badly: Arthur Pitts. The once high-flying Licensing Branch inspector was demoted to working in the Stores Depot, away from the action.[61] Pitts's rise and fall is reflective of the distinctions between types of corruption in the QPF during the turbulent 1970s. Whitrod and his team, including Pitts, set out on a campaign to purge corrupt officers from the force. They kept a hawkish watch on police like Herbert, who they believed may have been receiving a brown bag of cash from illegal bookies to look the other way. In their righteous enthusiasm to claim victory over the Joke (and other corrupt groups), it seems that Pitts and his cohorts broke the cardinal rule—not descending to the level of the enemy—and acted corruptly themselves, albeit for a noble cause. The result was that a savvy operator like Herbert could slip the noose and live to scheme another day.

The forces of corruption in the QPF had much more to celebrate in November 1976 than Herbert's acquittal. In the two years that Herbert was fighting corruption charges, another battle was taking place within the force itself, between the reformers of the Whitrod regime and the still-powerful remnants of Bischof's era like Murphy and Lewis.[62] Whitrod had scored some major victories in his time. Despite not being able to sustain criminal charges against either, he had still managed to see the end of Hallahan and Herbert in the police force. He came close to doing the same to Murphy as well, but was foiled at the last minute by the untimely death of star witness Brifman. Lewis, from his secure position in the JAB, had proven somewhat more resistant, but even then Whitrod had successfully maneuvered to marginalize his opponent by creating a new branch of the QPF, the Education Department Liaison Unit (EDLU), to take much of the JAB's traditional power and responsibility from it.[63] Though he could not seem to get Murphy and Lewis out of the QPF, he did manage to get them out of Brisbane in 1976, transferring them to the western frontier of the state to languish as regional inspectors. While he had not scored a decisive victory, Whitrod could lay claim to having done the best he could to win the war against the old guard. It's possible that, with all of his focus on the problems within his force, Whitrod may have underestimated a challenge from the *outside*, emanating from the very center of power in Queensland: the premier's office.

The conflict between Bjelke-Petersen and Whitrod was not about protecting corrupt officers—it was about Whitrod's reluctance to cede operational control of the QPF to the premier. There were three events in 1976 that truly pushed Whitrod to resign. The first, on July 29, 1976, occurred when Traffic Branch inspector Mark Beattie was caught on camera striking a female protester with his baton in the midst of a demonstration over funding for university students. A firm opponent of all types of left-wing protest, Bjelke-Petersen advocated for police to use whatever force they deemed necessary to repress civil disorder. Whitrod, on the other hand, pledged to conduct a full internal investigation into Beattie's conduct. When Bjelke-Petersen intervened to stop Whitrod's investigation, the premier undercut the commissioner's authority and, according to critics, gave police "the green-light" to use excessive force against protesters in the future, safe in the knowledge that the premier would come to their rescue.[64]

Strike two was, again, about the premier's intervention in internal disciplinary matters. On August 29, 1976, the QPF conducted a raid on a hippie commune in far north Queensland called Cedar Bay. Intelligence suggested the commune hosted a substantial marijuana crop, but, when around 100 local police raided the property, only a small crop was located and just two residents faced charges.[65] In the meantime, police were accused of using extreme force and destruction of property—enough to warrant Whitrod sending his assistant commissioner to Cedar Bay to investigate, against the express wishes of Bjelke-Petersen. Finally, 10 days after Herbert's acquittal, Bjelke-Petersen struck the blow that ended Whitrod once and for all. On November 15, he announced the promotion of Terry Lewis to assistant commissioner, against Whitrod's recommendation and despite his repeated warnings about Lewis's alleged history of corruption.[66] For Whitrod, working so closely with Lewis was unsustainable and an affront to everything he had achieved in the QPF over the previous six years. He announced his resignation on the same day, citing the premier's intervention on the Lewis promotion as a major reason for his decision. With an empty vacancy in the commissioner's office to fill, Lewis's meteoric rise continued. Despite only just being promoted to assistant commissioner rank, Lewis was chosen to replace Whitrod and took on the mantle of QPF commissioner in late 1976.[67]

From the deep lows of the Whitrod era, corrupt elements of the police force were once again in the ascendant as 1977 dawned. Whitrod was finally gone, Pitts was discredited, Herbert was acquitted, and, most importantly, Lewis had reached the top of the QPF food chain and now had almost full control over the administration of law and order in Queensland. This changed landscape presented new opportunities for the state's vice purveyors, largely left out in the cold in the Whitrod era. It was not long before these illegal entrepreneurs began to emerge from the woodwork. The person they approached? Jack Herbert. Despite no longer serving as a police officer, Herbert still had all the right connections in all the wrong places, both in the state's underworld and in its police force. For two years, as charges hung over his head, Herbert remained unemployed. He "claimed poverty and was granted legal aid," but admitted to Fitzgerald that he had also collected a stockpile of money left for him by an illegal bookie, which he used to buy a house.[68] He said, at first, that he had no intention of returning to corruption, but "as it turned out, an opportunity did arise, and I took it." That opportunity came in the shape of two men, Geraldo Bellino and Tony Robinson. Bellino was a former adagio dancer who had worked for Robinson at one of his illegal nightclubs before branching out into Brisbane's illegal gambling scene. Bellino had known Herbert during his time in Licensing, and came to him for advice on how to "avoid being 'pinched' [arrested]."[69] What began as a request for guidance from Bellino eventually turned into an ongoing relationship in which Herbert acted as the chief "bagman" between Bellino's syndicate and a revived Joke.

Unlike Bellino, Robinson came calling with his own ideas of how Herbert may be able to put his experience and connections to good use in a life after policing. By the time Robinson made his approach to Herbert in 1977, he was the owner of Austral Amusements, a company specializing in the sale and distribution of in-line machines in Queensland. From 1974, when the Justice Committee agreed to issue permits to in-line machines, Robinson had been distributing Bally products in Queensland and, as such, was in frequent contact with Bally's regional managing director, Jack Rooklyn.[70] The Rooklyn and Robinson relationship made sense: While Rooklyn was occupied with his business in Sydney (as well as fighting to maintain his position in the Bally organization), Robinson had a long history in Brisbane's nightlife industry and enjoyed all the connections needed to operate in that realm. By late 1977, though, Rooklyn's position in New South Wales was more tenuous than ever. By October, the Nevada Gaming Control Board had issued its ultimatum that he be put forward for registration or resign, and in December he took a golden parachute from the company to walk away.[71] Part of Rooklyn's deal was that he assumed exclusive rights to distribute Bally products in Australia, meaning that Robinson's time as the company's Queensland point man would soon come to an end.

It is unlikely that Robinson knew Rooklyn was about to become his direct rival in the in-line trade when he suggested that Herbert work for Rooklyn's business Queensland Automatics in late 1977, as the deal regarding Rooklyn being given the exclusive rights to sell Bally machines in Australia was not made public until late December 1977. Even if Rooklyn himself knew this deal was on the table by the point he met with Herbert, Robinson was likely not privy to this information.[72] As such, when he introduced Herbert to Rooklyn at the iconic Lennons

Hotel, Robinson would not have been aware that he was handing over a critical resource to the competition. After their first meeting at Lennons, Herbert joined Queensland Automatics and, at the same time, resumed a relationship with Lane, whom Herbert had once partnered with as police officers in the 1960s. Lane was still on the Justice Committee, and Herbert said he knew that Robinson continued to pay him a kickback every month to use his influence to protect his in-line operation.[73] Lane denied this allegation under oath. Herbert also alleged that it was around this time that his communication with now Commissioner Terry Lewis began to increase in frequency. Lewis later asserted that he only had a passing relationship with Herbert (who he claimed was closer to mutual friend Tony Murphy), but Herbert said he and the commissioner met regularly at parties, and that Lewis even visited him at his home.[74] While he did not bring him in on the in-line protection racket until later in 1978, Herbert said he started planting the seed in Lewis's mind from the time of his first stint working for Rooklyn, and was effectively grooming the highest-ranking officer in Queensland to eventually secure his cooperation in protecting the interests of his employers.

Jack Rooklyn had started 1977 as a yachting champion and managing director of Bally Australia. He ended the year forced out of the company he helped build, almost back to where he started decades earlier as a simple distributor of Bally machines.[75] All was not lost, however; Bally was still a dominant player in the amusement machine business in Australia and, in securing the exclusive rights to distribute nationwide, Rooklyn was still in a powerful position. Better yet, his enlistment of Herbert to work with Queensland Automatics opened up new doors for the consummate hustler. Not only did Herbert have relationships with all of the main players in Queensland's illegal gambling scene, but he was also a former police officer with a direct line to active police in the state who were in a position to assist Rooklyn, like Lewis and his former co-conspirators from the Licensing Branch. Through Herbert, Rooklyn could stroll effortlessly into an already existing system of corruption that would allow him to rebuild from the challenges that had plagued him since the Moffitt Commission began in 1973. Rooklyn could not have foreseen a roadblock to his newfound ascendency, which emerged from the most unexpected of places. In order for his new plan to succeed, Rooklyn would have to do something he never thought he would have to do: scramble to make sure that poker machines remained illegal in Queensland.

7

Shut Down the Pokies

Changes were afoot in Queensland's in-line industry as 1978 dawned. Jack Rooklyn's departure from Bally Australia was announced in December of the previous year and, more importantly, so too was the gift of exclusive Australian rights offered to him by the Bally parent organization as an incentive to leave without a fuss.[1] The decision had implications not just for Rooklyn, but for his Queensland distributor Tony Robinson as well. While it did not happen overnight, Rooklyn had asserted his exclusive rights in Queensland by the time 1979 rolled around.[2] The shifting landscape of the in-line business was also reflected in the ambiguous loyalties of former Licensing Branch officer Jack Herbert, who in early 1978 left Rooklyn's Queensland Automatics after a brief period of employment to manage Robinson's business. Despite the potential for conflict between Rooklyn and Robinson during this period of reorganization, the pair remained cordial. The issue of distribution rights and Herbert's employment aside, Rooklyn had been around the game for a long time and was well aware that the secret to success in the vice trade is that there are always enough profits to go around. He also knew that conflict is never good for business, and cooperation between competing operations ensures that unnecessary attention does not impact on the trade. Indeed, after leaving Queensland Automatics, Herbert continued to represent Rooklyn's interests as well, facilitating meetings and helping negotiate corrupt protection deals between Rooklyn and his contacts in the police force.[3]

Without question, the most important contact that Herbert had access to was Queensland police commissioner Terry Lewis. The pair had resumed a social relationship in 1977 and, as Herbert later told the Fitzgerald Inquiry, it was on one such occasion that he mentioned to Lewis that member of parliament (and former police officer) Don Lane and head of the Licensing Commission Leo McQuillan were both receiving corrupt payments to protect in-line gambling in Queensland. According to Herbert, Lewis was "annoyed . . . [he] said that it was a police matter and had nothing to do with the Justice Department or Don Lane."[4] On the surface, it seems a clumsy move from Herbert to reveal his employer's corruption to no less than the highest-ranking police officer in the state but, as ever, there was an angle. Herbert admitted that he saw an opportunity to make extra money for himself in doing so. He was confident that Lewis would take the bait and attempt to use Herbert as an agent to extort money from Herbert's employer Robinson. When he did, Herbert would be able to take a cut of the action as a "finder's fee" of sorts.[5] If this was Herbert's plan, it worked. He arranged a meeting between Lewis and his old associate Robinson on a Brisbane street corner where a deal was struck. Robinson was furious, complaining that he was "paying Don Lane, paying Leo McQuillan, now [he had] to pay Terry Lewis."[6] Little did Robinson know that Herbert had manufactured the entire situation, seeking to line his own pockets at the expense of his boss.

Perhaps it was the agitation at having another person to pay for protection that prompted Robinson to reach out to Rooklyn, asking if he would also be interested in kicking in corrupt payments to Lewis. Herbert told the Fitzgerald Inquiry that Rooklyn "wasn't in the least upset about having to pay a police commissioner" and, as he had the bigger share of the in-line business in the state, even agreed to pay a larger share of Lewis's payments each month.[7] Herbert said that Robinson and Lewis reached an agreement where the commissioner would be paid $2,000 each month in bribes—Rooklyn would pay $1,500 and Robinson would pay the remaining $500.[8] While both Robinson and Lewis denied this arrangement to the Fitzgerald Inquiry, Rooklyn's accountant at Queensland Automatics, John Henry Garde, admitted paying Herbert each month for protection, though he denied knowing the ultimate beneficiary.[9] Lewis had already taken an interest in Rooklyn even before the corrupt payments were arranged with Robinson: Rooklyn's name and telephone number appears in Lewis's appointment book dated January 3, 1978.[10] The innocent explanation for this is that Lewis was keeping a close eye on the Sydney businessman, in the knowledge that the Rooklyn Trading Trust was the parent company behind Queensland Automatics. Technically, the Queensland government had the discretionary power to exclude Rooklyn from the local industry based on his poor character, with the findings of the Moffitt Commission (not to mention the Nevada Gaming Control Board) serving as a clear justification. At the Fitzgerald Inquiry, under-secretary of the Justice Department Col Pearson said that while the agency was aware that Rooklyn owned Queensland Automatics, it had ultimately decided not to exercise its discretion to exclude him from the in-line trade because they "came to the conclusion that this [the evidence against Rooklyn] was a report from the (royal) commission[,] not a decision from a court."[11] As with the 1974 decision to permit in-line gaming in Queensland, it no doubt helped Rooklyn's case to have an advocate like Don Lane on the committee, and a friend in the commissioner's office.

The first recorded meeting between Rooklyn and Lewis came on March 20, 1978, with Robinson escorting Rooklyn to visit Lewis at his office. Lewis's diary entry for that day noted that "Mr Rooklyn inquired re starting a 'Health Studio' on Gold Coast, informed him if prostitution involved prosecution would be certain."[12] The idea that Robinson and Rooklyn had come to the commissioner to inquire about opening a "Health Studio" is strange for a few reasons. While Rooklyn's sometime business partner Abraham Saffron was notorious for his involvement in the sex trade, Rooklyn's participation was typically restricted to the gambling side of the equation, not to mention that he was primarily focused on reasserting his position in the local in-line industry at the time of his meeting with Lewis. While it may be true that Rooklyn was seeking to enter into the sex trade as part of his new career path, the fact that he visited Lewis in company with Robinson so soon after the duo allegedly began paying the commissioner for protection indicates that one purpose of the meeting may have also been to discuss their corrupt arrangement.

Rooklyn appeared in Lewis's diary one more time in 1978, on November 28. Lewis notes that "Jack Rooklyn called inquiring if massage parlours [offering sexual services] were being legalised; I assured him they are not."[13] Again, Lewis raises the idea that Rooklyn was interested in prostitution, not illegal gambling.

There is no real suggestion that Rooklyn ever became involved in the Queensland sex trade, but it is possible that Lewis's diary entries were a remedial attempt to record the real purpose of their contacts without directly revealing the actual nature of their corrupt bargain. The first meeting where Rooklyn reputedly asked about opening a "Health Studio" came around the time he *actually* started regularly sending bribes to Lewis.[14] Similarly, the call from Rooklyn inquiring about whether Queensland was going to legalize massage parlors came at roughly the same time Rooklyn began to be concerned that the state was planning to legalize poker machines, threatening his in-line business.[15] It could well be that Lewis, in an attempt to hide the purpose of his contact with Rooklyn, was unwittingly giving a clue as to what was actually being discussed. The only people who really know this for certain are Lewis and Rooklyn (and Robinson, who was at the first meeting), but at the very least it is probable that the protection of in-line machines was a topic of conversation during these meetings.

With Lewis on board, Rooklyn set about expanding his Queensland business, which reputedly involved the same type of standover tactics referenced in the Moffitt Commission's final report when it discussed the attempts to strong-arm Bally products into New South Wales clubs. One incident was detailed in a statutory declaration from Desmond Victor Welk, a well-known amusement machine operator and distributor in Queensland's northwest. Welk alleged that in September 1978 he was approached by Queensland Automatics manager Barry MacNamara, who brought with him an offer from Rooklyn to purchase Welk's business. MacNamara told Welk, "Rooklyn wants to buy you out, and if you don't sell to us, you're history . . . we'll put a contract out on you and you'll end up in a 40-gallon drum out in the dam."[16] When Welk refused, he said the Queensland Automatics crew began targeting his operation. A number of Welk's machines in Mount Isa were sabotaged, and he even caught a serviceman from Queensland Automatics in the act of opening up Welk machines with the apparent intent to tamper with them. He was sent harassing, anonymous letters and, ultimately, in fear for his personal safety, he began wearing a bulletproof vest. The vest did not protect him entirely, though; after receiving a call late one night that one of his machines required servicing, Welk went to the club, where he was struck from behind by an unknown assailant. Unsurprisingly, the club had no knowledge of a call to Welk, indicating that he had been lured there so he could be attacked. Welk never reported any of these incidences to police at the time; he was "told by managers of various clubs that McNamara [*sic*], Rooklyn's Queensland representative, was being introduced round the clubs by a well-known Mt Isa [*sic*] police officer," and so he believed that any attempt to report the campaign of harassment would go unaddressed, or possibly put him at even further risk.[17] Considering that, by this point, Rooklyn had been paying the police commissioner for almost a year, Welk's concerns seem to be well justified.

At the same time that Rooklyn was making moves to consolidate his position in Queensland by fear and favor in 1978, the fortunes of his old comrade Saffron were waning. Even before Moffitt put his reputation under a microscope, Saffron had been attempting to diversify his interests into other states, including South Australia. In this, Rooklyn was an early partner. He and Saffron went in together on a deal to build a hotel in the seaside Adelaide suburb West Beach in 1970, with Rooklyn named as a co-director of the company pursuing the project, Burbridge Properties.[18] Saffron and Rooklyn's plans for the hotel collapsed when the South Australian Licensing Court refused their application in what would become the state's signature move against Saffron's attempted southern expansion.[19] The hostilities between Saffron and South Australian premier Don Dunstan were at fever pitch by March 1978, erupting in parliament when the state attorney-general, Peter Duncan, took aim at Saffron, calling him "one of the principal characters in organised crime in Australia" and publicly using a moniker Saffron openly hated: "Mr. Sin."[20]

Part of Duncan's public takedown of Saffron involved reference to his reputed involvement in the disappearance of heiress and social justice campaigner Juanita Nielsen in July 1975. Nielsen had been a staunch opponent of development in Victoria Street, Potts Point, just behind the strip of Darlinghurst Road where many of Saffron's properties were located. Saffron had interests in the proposed development, and was also connected to the primary developer, Frank Theeman.[21] Nielsen was last seen en route to Saffron-owned venue the Carousel Club on July 4, 1975. The Carousel Club's night manager, Eddie Trigg, and two other men were charged in late 1977, not with murdering Nielsen, but for conspiring to abduct her on behalf of unknown "people who wanted to talk to her."[22] While Saffron was never charged over the Nielsen disappearance, his peripheral involvement in the case cast a lingering cloud over his already tarnished reputation and, in turn, any ongoing attempts to expand his empire.

Though Saffron's expansion was faltering, he was not the only New South Wales underworld figure looking for success by muscling in on interstate rackets. The representative for Nevada-based gaming machine manufacturer Intermark Imagineering Inc. in New South Wales was former police officer Keith John Kelly, an associate of both Murray Riley and Tony Murphy.[23] One of his business partners was Paul Bruce Hardin—the son of an illegal bookmaker and business partner of George Freeman, Bruce Hardin. Kelly was playing both sides of the law in Queensland. While lobbying to have Intermark chosen as a supplier to the new (legal) Jupiters Casino on the Gold Coast, he was also selling equipment to illegal casino operator Geraldo Bellino, one of the men who sought protection from Herbert after his acquittal in 1976.[24] Another player in Queensland's underworld with links to Sydney was Paul Meade, connected to the Vanguard group based out of Sydney, but which also supplied in-line machines in Queensland. Like Robinson, Vanguard was also alleged to be paying bribes to Leo McQuillan from the Licensing Commission, and others involved in the in-line protection racket.[25] Former Licensing Branch officer Salvatore Di Carlo told the Fitzgerald Inquiry that Meade was part of a group of Brisbane identities connected to Lewis as well, and had no fear of the police. He recalled an incident during his time in Licensing when police attended one of Bellino's clubs that Meade was involved in running, The Beat on Ann Street. When the officers attempted to gain entry to the premises, they "were told to get lost or get a warrant"—a bold move, even in the Brisbane underworld.[26]

Meade's business interests expanded beyond the club scene and in-line machines. A tentpole of his operation were the "mock auctions" he conducted in Queen Street. The mock auction was a classic scam in which associates of the "auctioneer" purchased high-quality goods at bargain prices to lull the average buyer into a false sense of security, enough that they would then be sold inferior products at inflated values.[27] Meade's mock auctions were legendary, and he employed some of Brisbane's most notorious hardmen to work at them. One of those hardmen, Vincent O'Dempsey, had a reputation as a killer with the ability to make his victims disappear off the face of the earth. He and Meade shared a mutual friend in Sydney gangster Frederick "Paddles" Anderson, part of the milieu who attended the Double Bay meetings alongside the likes of Freeman and Lennie McPherson in the early 1970s.[28] Meade and O'Dempsey were also linked to the rogue gunman Stewart John Regan, murdered in 1974 after his renegade behavior found him on the wrong side of too many local criminals. O'Dempsey and Regan were kindred spirits who worked together in the Sydney standover trade, and, shortly before Regan's death, the two men invested in some property together, in partnership with Meade.[29] While Regan died young, O'Dempsey was a survivor. After decades dodging the law, it eventually caught up with him when he was arrested in 2014 for the January 1974 abduction and triple murder of Barbara McCulkin and her young daughters, Vicki and Leanne. The prosecution alleged that O'Dempsey committed these murders because he was concerned that Barbara, the wife of his criminal associate Billy McCulkin, was privy to information that could put him in the frame for the 1973 Whiskey Au Go Go arson, in which fifteen people lost their lives.[30]

The Sydney gangsters, Anderson and McPherson, also found themselves tied to the Whiskey Au Go Go fire. Not long before the club went up in flames, the two men visited the Whiskey in the company of Brian Aherne, owner of the Lands Office Hotel and a sometime associate of Meade's crew.[31] Anderson and McPherson never tried to extort the Whiskey, but the timing of their visit played into the narrative being pushed by Brisbane standover man John Andrew Stuart (who was convicted of conspiring to set the fire) that the arson was part of an attempt by Sydney gangsters to muscle in on Brisbane's underworld. While Stuart's claims about the Whiskey fire did not hold up, his argument that there was a push coming from Sydney to infiltrate the Brisbane club scene may not have been entirely without merit. Meade, at least, was working as an agent of Anderson and McPherson into the late 1970s. Wiretaps conducted as part of Operation Dazzler in June 1979 recorded a conversation in which Anderson complained that Meade was "behind in payments to himself and McPherson to operate gaming machines in Queensland."[32] In the tapes, Anderson told his criminal cohort Ronald Lopes Dias that Rooklyn had offered to pay him and McPherson "to remove Meade" from the Queensland gambling scene.[33] The move from Rooklyn makes sense: It was around this time that Queensland Automatics was engaged in aggressive expansion efforts, reflected in the attempted hostile takeover of Welk's business. Although Rooklyn accepted he would have to coexist with the likes of Robinson, it seems he saw Meade as vulnerable, enough that he felt it might be possible to use his southern connections to cut him out.

There were bigger problems facing Rooklyn in 1979 than Meade, however. Just as had been the case in New South Wales in the 1950s, there was a movement in Queensland pushing for the legalization of poker machines. Whereas in the 1950s legalization had proved a major boon to Rooklyn, now it presented a real threat to his operation. He had spent three years developing a business model in Queensland that was predicated on selling in-line machines in lieu of actual gambling devices. If poker machines were legalized, there would be no need for venues to purchase his in-line products—demand for his machines was driven by the fact that poker machines were illegal; if that changed, Rooklyn's buyers would simply take their business to other companies that could provide "the real thing." The poker machine industry was lobbying hard for legalization and, if Rooklyn were to protect his investment, he needed to use every connection at his disposal. For this, he turned to the same man who helped him negotiate his deal with Lewis in the first place: Jack Herbert. Herbert told the Fitzgerald Inquiry that Rooklyn asked him for help in convincing Lewis to use his influence to prevent poker machines being legalized.[34]

Herbert claims he organized three meetings between Lewis and Rooklyn to discuss these matters, held in private rooms at the Crest Hotel between late 1979 and 1980. The maitre d'hotel of the Crest, Serge Pregliasco, confirmed these meetings took place and said he served wine to Rooklyn, Lewis, and another unidentified man in the private room where they held their discussions. Pregliasco and Rooklyn knew each other from Sydney, where the former had worked as maitre d'hotel at the Chevron Hilton, the same hotel where Joseph Dan Testa stayed when visiting Australia.[35] Over the course of the Rooklyn/Lewis meetings, it was agreed that Rooklyn would pay $25,000 in return for Lewis organizing for an adverse report on the issue of poker machine legalization.[36] Once again, the deal was as beneficial to Herbert as it was to Lewis; part of the arrangement was for Lewis to keep $15,000 while Herbert would receive the other $10,000 as yet another broker's fee. In May 1980, as Rooklyn feared, the state government appointed a committee to explore legalization. As promised, Lewis forwarded a report to the police minister on July 11, arguing that the government should not introduce poker machines in Queensland. The committee agreed, and the status quo was maintained. Herbert said he attended a meeting at the Crest just before Christmas 1980 where Rooklyn fulfilled his end of the bargain and paid Lewis $25,000.[37] At the meeting, Rooklyn allegedly reminded Lewis not to go back on his decision to oppose poker machines, telling him not to "let the other side [the poker machine lobby] get to you." Herbert said Lewis affirmed his arrangement with Rooklyn, responding that he "never change[s] horse midstream."[38]

According to Herbert, the deal to save Rooklyn's in-line business was the cause for a degree of aggravation in his relationship with Lewis. At the final meeting, where Rooklyn gave Lewis the bribe, the commissioner handed Herbert his cut of $10,000, to be shared with two Queensland Automatics employees, MacNamara and Garde. However, when Herbert checked what Lewis had given him, he discovered the package was light; Lewis had shorted him by $1,000, only handing over $9,000 rather than $10,000 as agreed. In a telephone conversation recorded between

MacNamara and Herbert, MacNamara described Lewis's act as "a shitty trick . . . a very bad act."[39] Later, MacNamara said Garde "took it badly" when he heard about Lewis taking an extra $1,000 and suggested that Queensland Automatics should send $1,000 less in bribes to Lewis the next month, to recoup their losses. Herbert responded that Lewis "loves this stuff [bribe payments] now he's getting it, he got quite used to it. . . . I'd say he'd be a bit upset if I did it back to him."[40] Herbert and the Queensland Automatics crew were caught between a rock and a hard place with Lewis. While it was not good practice to let someone steal from you, Lewis was (after all) the police commissioner and, with a snap of his fingers, could bring the entire illegal house of cards down on Herbert and his colleagues. This time, at least, they would just have to take the hit and write off that missing $1,000 as the cost of doing business in Queensland.

In coercing Lewis to oppose the legalization of poker machines, Rooklyn struck a preemptive blow in the war to ensure that in-line machines reigned supreme in Queensland. However, there continued to be some parties who threatened to derail his plans—parties who were set to benefit greatly if machine-based gambling was introduced in the state. These individuals and organizations posed a real threat to Rooklyn. Just as he was willing to do whatever it took to get ahead, so too were they highly motivated (and incentivized) to exert pressure for the opposite decision on legalization. The company that posed the biggest threat to Rooklyn in Queensland was undoubtedly Ainsworth Consolidated Industries, an Australian poker machine manufacturer headed up by Leonard Ainsworth. Originally specializing in dental supplies and equipment, Ainsworth pivoted the direction of the business when he inherited it from his father, and began producing poker machines as a way of supplementing revenue. This sideline trade proved more lucrative than Ainsworth's core business and, in 1953, he started Aristocrat Leisure as a separate company dedicated to poker machine production.[41] Shortly thereafter, the New South Wales government decided to legalize poker machines, and so Ainsworth was well placed to grow his business even further, albeit in direct competition with more seasoned operators like the Americans from Bally and another Australian company, Nutt & Muddle.

The chaos within the industry in the 1970s actually served to improve Ainsworth's position. A report to the Queensland Criminal Justice Commission (CJC) notes that Ainsworth was "the chief beneficiary of the decline of Nutt & Muddle and the difficulties of Bally Australia following the Moffitt Royal Commission."[42] By the late 1970s, Ainsworth had secured as much as 75 percent of the New South Wales pokies business, then the only legal jurisdiction in the country. The fortunes of Nutt & Muddle had fallen so much that, by 1982, Ainsworth was in a position to buy the company outright, in a takeover attempt rejected by the federal Trade Practices Commission because it would result in Ainsworth having an almost complete monopoly of poker machine manufacturing in Australia.[43] Even after Ainsworth's ambition for Nutt & Muddle was denied, the CJC found that "subsequently there were attempts by less than reputable persons and organisations to purchase the company [Nutt & Muddle] . . . there were connections between these persons and the Ainsworth group."[44] One notable attempt was spearheaded by English operator W. R. Ruffler, who came to Australia to acquire Nutt & Muddle. His local business was registered to the Texas Tavern in Kings Cross, owned by the principal of Meade's employer, Vanguard. More curiously, Ruffler stayed with Ainsworth while negotiating the deal for Nutt & Muddle, and also used a lawyer associated with Ainsworth as part of the process. The deal with Ruffler did not go through either, and Nutt & Muddle was ultimately purchased by a company with no links to Ainsworth.[45] Nevertheless, at the time Rooklyn was fighting to prevent poker machines being legalized in Queensland, Ainsworth was looking to expand his reach. This put Rooklyn's interests at odds with Ainsworth's, and explains his caution to Lewis at their Crest Hotel meeting not to "let the other side" get to him.[46]

Lewis's connection to Rooklyn featured during his testimony at the Williams Royal Commission in 1980, where the police commissioner found himself backed into a corner. In 1977, Queensland Supreme Court judge Edward Williams was appointed to preside over a nationwide inquiry into the state of drug trafficking in Australia. Though it encompassed the entire country, the Rat Pack were nonetheless at the center of the Williams Commission thanks in part to the revelations of John Edward Milligan, a former court clerk and criminal associate of Stewart John Regan who by 1979 had moved into the profitable business of heroin trafficking. When the law caught up to him and Milligan was arrested in Sydney, he began to talk almost immediately, alleging that his partner in the narcotics operation was none other than former Queensland detective Glen Hallahan. Perhaps aware of Hallahan's reputation, federal narcotics officers took Milligan's claims seriously and, within hours of his arrest, raided Hallahan's farm near rural Gympie. While they found nothing to support Hallahan's connection with heroin trafficking, Milligan continued to insist before the Williams Commission that Hallahan was part of a "three-man team in controlling aspects of crime in Queensland. . . . Hallahan was identified as the person who did the dirty work."[47] While Milligan later retracted this claim, his allegations put the Rat Pack squarely in the firing line. Though Hallahan was the person Milligan said he dealt with most, the other two members of the triumvirate he mentioned were Murphy and Lewis.

As the Williams Commission stretched on, Lewis came under fire from Federal Narcotics Bureau chief Harvey Bates, who complained to his minister, Wal Fife, in September 1979 that the QPF was taking steps to undermine the commission through personal connections to Williams, who was known to the Rat Pack from his time as a barrister in Brisbane.[48] Bates warned that the police identified by Milligan—the Rat Pack—had "extensive contacts in most areas of law enforcement through which they can manipulate or control investigative activities."[49] If Bates feared that the Williams Commission was going to turn out poorly for his agency, his concern was well founded. Ultimately, Williams recommended that the Narcotics Bureau be disbanded entirely.[50] Before that, however, Lewis would have his day before Williams on February 4, 1980. Among other questions, Lewis was directly asked whether he knew, or had a relationship with, Jack Rooklyn. Despite being in active negotiations over the poker machine report at the time, Lewis categorically denied any and all dealings with Rooklyn. He told Williams that he had "heard the name Jack Rooklyns [*sic*], who I am told has been said to be the person behind the introduction of poker machines . . . I have never had anything to do with him in any way."[51] Not only was this untrue, it was demonstrably so. Lewis's own diaries explicitly show him meeting with and taking phone calls from Rooklyn throughout 1978, and the behind-the-scenes meetings taking place at the Crest were around the same time Lewis issued his denials at the Williams Commission. Most ironic is Lewis's vague recollection that Rooklyn was "the person behind the introduction of poker machines"—all the while knowing full well that Rooklyn was actually offering $25,000 for Lewis to *stop* the introduction of poker machines entirely.

When Herbert told MacNamara that Lewis had gotten a taste of the profit to be made from taking bribes, he was not lying. Lewis included 16 unique "codes" in his 1980 pocket diary, each referring either to a predetermined meeting place or a person. He used these codes in his telephone conversations with Herbert, to avoid the risk of being clandestinely recorded and revealing too much about his connections to organized crime. Herbert later helped the Fitzgerald Inquiry unravel Lewis's coding system. The first five codes on the list referred to places like the Crest Hotel, locations where he would meet Herbert to exchange illegal bribes. The rest were people who were involved in the racket—Lewis and Herbert would use the corresponding number when talking about each person. For example, "Jack R." (Jack Rooklyn) was listed as number 9 on the list, and so whenever Rooklyn was discussed, the number 9 was referenced.[52] Others on the list from the gaming trade included number 10, "Tony R." (Tony Robinson), and number 11, "Paul M." (Paul Meade). There were other police on the list, too. Numbers 14 through 16 were "Noel" (allegedly, Licensing Branch boss Noel Dwyer), "Syd" (allegedly, CIB boss Syd Atkinson), and "Brian" (allegedly, Assistant Commissioner Brian Hayes).[53] Years later, Dwyer admitted to corruption after being offered an indemnity from prosecution by Fitzgerald—the other two police officers (Atkinson and Hayes) remained staunch, not making any admissions of corruption, though further testimony to the Fitzgerald Inquiry also seemed to support the position that they were the individuals the list was referring to.

It is clear that corruption was far more extensive than just Lewis's arrangement with the likes of Rooklyn and Robinson. Negotiating Rooklyn and Lewis's deal regarding the adverse poker machine report was far from the only hustle that Herbert was involved with in 1980. He was also back to work with the Licensing Branch, albeit not as a police officer. Now that Whitrod and his reformers were out, there was an opportunity for the Joke in the Licensing Branch to be reborn, with Herbert perfectly positioned to act as liaison between illegal vice traders and corrupt police given his lengthy experience in the first Joke. However, an impediment existed in the form of Alec Jeppesen, who became the Licensing Branch's new inspector on January 31, 1977, not long after Lewis succeeded Whitrod as QPF commissioner.[54] The problem with Jeppesen was not that he was incorruptible—indeed, he was one of those accused of conspiring with Pitts to commit perjury during the Saunders and Sieber case. Nevertheless, Jeppesen was still one of Whitrod's acolytes and (despite some irregularities in his professional practice) firmly opposed to mercenary corruption among the Licensers. Like Pitts before him, Jeppesen swiftly got to work leading the Licensing Branch in raids against bookies across southeast Queensland. As a precaution, Jeppesen handled the majority of informants relating to illegal bookmaking personally, as a way to limit the spread of information in a branch that he believed was still compromised by corrupt police.[55] While the decision made sense given the context he was operating in, Jeppesen's unilateral control over informant handling ultimately proved his downfall when the time came to remove him from his post, clearing the way for a more amenable Licensing Branch inspector to take his place.

The first move against Jeppesen came on September 8, 1978, when Lewis wrote to Cabinet with a recommendation that he be transferred out of Licensing. He justified his argument with reference to the then-recent Lucas Report, which suggested that officers serve no more than two years in the branch to avoid the potential of being corrupted.[56] Convinced that Jeppesen was achieving results in his current post, Cabinet rejected Lewis's suggestion. The next maneuver was far more successful. On November 24, 1978, one of Jeppesen's apparent allies at the Licensing Branch, Brian Marlin, asked for a meeting with Lewis during which he alleged that Jeppesen was not only leaking inside information to Opposition politicians, but also inventing fake "informants" and then claiming the moiety payments due to them for himself.[57] Given the secrecy with which he managed informants, there were few who could unequivocally prove that Jeppesen's informants were real. Marlin's allegations were the ammunition that Lewis needed to trigger an investigation into Jeppesen, and he did so on December 12, 1978. He commissioned allies Atkinson and Hayes to do the job, the same senior officers later believed to be referenced in the commissioner's coded "list." When their investigation concluded, Atkinson and Hayes asserted that the allegations against Jeppesen were true, but (to protect the anonymity of real informants) charges should not be laid. Whatever the case, the findings were enough to tarnish Jeppesen's reputation in Cabinet and, on February 13, 1979, it agreed to his transfer.[58] It is not clear if the claims against Jeppesen were legitimate, or fabricated as a way to remove him from his position, but it is important to note that one of the chief anonymous witnesses against the Licensing Branch inspector was a person who was also an informant of Atkinson, and had a personal relationship with the very person to which he gave evidence against Jeppesen.[59] No matter if the claims were true or not, the outcome was the same: Jeppesen was out, and there was a vacancy in the Licensing Branch.

Before he made a decision on Jeppesen's replacement, Lewis sought out expert guidance. He approached Herbert to ask him for recommendations and, in turn, the disgraced Licensing Branch officer floated the name Ross Rigney. Lewis may well have simply been canvassing a range of opinions and asked Herbert based on his service in Licensing, but, given the duo were actively involved in corruption together by 1979, there is a strong possibility that his discussion with Herbert was more about putting someone in place who would work with them in Licensing rather than someone who (like Jeppesen) aggressively pursued illegal bookies.[60] If this was the case, though, recommending Rigney was a misstep. When Herbert approached him about "getting something going" shortly after his appointment, Rigney shot him down.[61] Herbert's records of bribes received and paid (which were provided to the Fitzgerald Inquiry) supported Rigney's honesty, registering no payments during his time as inspector.[62] Perhaps unsurprisingly, Rigney's time in Licensing did not last long and he was transferred from the branch in December 1979, after just 10 months in the job. He was replaced in January 1980 by Noel Dwyer, an old associate of Lewis. Herbert tested Dwyer's openness to corruption early, contacting him to suggest that there may be some benefit to Dwyer if he decided not to go through with a prosecution against bookie Terrence McMahon that had commenced before his arrival at Licensing. When Dwyer agreed and the charges were abandoned, the new inspector enthusiastically accepted a corrupt payment via Herbert—from then on, the second Joke was on.[63]

While the second Joke was being set up, Rooklyn was in the midst of organizing with Lewis to stop poker machines being legalized in Queensland. That plan proved to be a winner, thanks to a $25,000 "donation" to the commissioner, but there were other losses for Rooklyn in 1980 that served to dim some of the elation derived from his successful defense of the in-line industry. Until 1980, he had seemed an almost unstoppable force in Australian yachting, taking line honors in both *Apollo* and *Ballyhoo* at the Sydney to Hobart race and seeing success in several other major events. The streak of good luck ended in early April 1980 during the Brisbane to Gladstone race—the same event he first competed in, over three decades earlier in 1949, with *White Wings*.[64] Despite being a favorite to win the event from the outset, the Rooklyn-skippered *Apollo* was run aground by heavy seas at a reef off Lady Elliott Island, just 50 miles from the finish line.[65] It was immediately apparent that the damage was too great, and there was no saving *Apollo*. The crew were forced to wade to safety and, over the next four days, stripped the yacht of all the gear that was still usable; Rooklyn himself took the mast and flagpole back to his Sydney home as a memento of the once great vessel.[66] Never one to wallow in defeat, Rooklyn almost immediately announced the building of a new *Apollo*, which, in 1985, would ultimately deliver him a third (and final) line honors in the Sydney to Hobart race.[67]

Just as *Apollo* came to a dramatic end in 1980, so too did the life of person whose story had long been entwined with Rooklyn's own: Joseph Dan Testa. Returning home to Chicago after the Moffitt Commission, having been labeled a Mafia associate and criminal, Testa soon discovered that among the criminal milieu loyalties could shift in an instant, with deadly repercussions. In the mid-1970s, Testa allegedly found himself on the wrong side of several members of the Chicago Outfit who believed that he owed them money that was originally loaned to another person who had "gone to prison and died."[68] When these would-be collectors upped the ante by commencing a bombing campaign of his homes and businesses, Testa went to a person he knew had the authority to stop them in their tracks: "retired" Chicago Outfit boss Tony Accardo. According to Testa's friend (and former Willow Springs police chief) Michael Corbitt, Testa "golfed with [Accardo] . . . we took him fishing, we took his wife and him fishing in Florida, we took him and other associates fishing to Bimini [in The Bahamas]."[69] Meeting with Accardo at 3 a.m. at a restaurant in Elmwood Park, Testa hoped his friendship with the old Capone ally would be enough to get the violent campaign of harassment to stop, but he was greatly mistaken—Corbitt said he was present when Accardo told Testa: "[Y]ou're my friend. . . . I've known you for a lot of years, and you don't owe me nothing. . . . But apparently you owe somebody something and it's out of my control." Accardo then told Testa he had two options: "[Y]ou pay them or you chop [kill] them."[70]

Rather than heeding Accardo's advice, Testa opted for a third choice. He left the United States, traveling to Egypt and through Europe before eventually returning to his Florida home in June 1981. When he returned, he called Corbitt and asked him to come down from Chicago for a welcome home party, but Corbitt told him that he could not make it. The next day Testa's car was blown up using a remote-detonated explosive device after he finished playing a round of golf at Tamarac Country Club in Fort Lauderdale.[71] The explosion on June 27, 1981, was so great that Testa's right leg was completely severed from his body. Though no one was ever charged over Testa's murder, the alleged bombmaker was identified to the FBI by renowned jewelry thief Robert Siegel in the mid-1990s.[72] Testa's total wealth at the time of his death was listed as around $51 million. Among his heirs were two former police officers: Corbitt and retired Chicago Police commander John Hinchy, who was visiting Testa at the time of his death and received around 5 percent of the total value of his estate.[73] Less than a decade earlier, Testa had been heralded as the vanguard of the American Mafia's infiltration of the Australian underworld. He was targeted in the Moffitt Commission but, unlike Rooklyn, Testa was seemingly never able to rebuild, forced to flee Chicago and ultimately having his life end in violent fashion. It was an inglorious end, but not unexpected for a person whose name was so often linked to some of the most notorious killers in American organized crime.

Around the same time that Testa met his demise, Rooklyn was again involved in a scandal that revived suspicions about the connection between Australian and American organized crime. While the debate over whether to introduce poker machines in Queensland was seemingly settled in the negative, the status quo in New South Wales was far more advanced; in the early 1980s, discussions were taking place not *if* casino gambling should be legalized, but *how* it should be introduced. With New South Wales looking set to open up an entirely new industry, the scramble to dominate the new market was on in earnest, with some of the global casino industry's biggest players joining the fight for poll position. One of the interested parties was Caesars Palace, employer of Las Vegas–based Sydney milieu associate Danny Stein. However, the links between Caesars and the criminal operators already running (illegal) gambling in Sydney went beyond informal friendships—the company's "public relations officer" in Australia was none other than Reg Andrews, an illegal casino operator who, along with partner Ronnie Lee, was one of Testa's first connections in Australia going back to the mid-1960s.[74] In November 1981, Andrews was caught up in an Australian Federal Police (AFP) operation targeting Caesars Palace senior vice president Murray Gennis, then in Australia (at least nominally) to drum up new clients for the Las Vegas casino. In pursuit of this, Gennis and Andrews hosted a soiree at the Sydney Hilton on November 1, 1981, attended by a who's who of the city's most prolific gamblers. Though attendees said there was "nothing sinister or nefarious" about the event, it was nevertheless placed under surveillance by the AFP. Later, as Gennis went to leave Australia, he and Andrews (who was with him at the time) were arrested at Sydney Airport on charges of trying to leave the country with five suitcases "stuffed with $120,750—most of it in Australia $50 bills."[75]

Despite claiming he was doing his bosses a favor by collecting gambling debts, there were suspicions whether Gennis was acting as a "bagman" for organized crime interests in Las Vegas working in partnership with their contemporaries down under. Ultimately, both Gennis and Andrews pleaded guilty and were fined $30,000.[76]

The Gennis affair highlights concerns around the persistent attempts of US-based groups to muscle in on a New South Wales gambling scene on the cusp of legalization. However, it also reflects the abiding connection between parts of the Sydney milieu and Las Vegas casino interests. The same connection was at the heart of another scandal involving Caesars Palace in 1981—this time, though, the controversy had Rooklyn's name all over it. Assistant Commissioner Bill Allen was the person with overall control over the squads responsible for gaming and licensing in New South Wales, including the Special Licensing Squad, which was under the command of Sergeant Warren Molloy. Approaching his new job with gusto, Molloy took a square aim at Abe Saffron's business interests in Kings Cross, causing consternation for Saffron and pushing the wily operator to reach out to Molloy's boss, Allen, to complain that Molloy was "antagonistic towards him."[77] According to police records, Saffron visited Allen at police headquarters six times over the course of the year, and, shortly after his first visit, Allen approached Molloy in April 1981 to offer him $500 to leave Saffron alone. Not corrupt, but in fear of the repercussions of saying no to Allen, Molloy accepted the money and set it aside while he figured out what to do about it.[78]

Fortunately, Allen was also under scrutiny from other directions. Saffron's once staunch ally Jim Anderson was at war with his old boss and, as part of his reprisal plan, began informing to the National Crime Authority (NCA). It was Anderson who attended Gennis's Hilton party and tipped the police off about the money he was carrying, and it was allegedly Anderson who also told the NCA that Allen had taken an all-expenses-paid trip to the United States in June/July 1981.[79] The airline tickets were paid for by the Queanbeyan Leagues Club, which was an applicant for a casino license, and his hotel bills in San Francisco were paid by high-profile bookmaker Bill Waterhouse.[80] Allen's activity in Las Vegas was perhaps most concerning; staying at Caesars Palace, his registration was marked "on the account of Jack Rooklyn," and the bill was paid by the Bally organization. Allen even "happened to meet Jack Rooklyn" while staying at Caesars Palace—an unlikely coincidence at the best of times, but even more so with Rooklyn allegedly footing part of Allen's bill.[81] It took a few months, but in September 1981 the AFP alerted the New South Wales police commissioner about Allen's activity overseas and the force launched an inquiry into his conduct. Now against the ropes, Molloy saw the opportunity to strike and told Internal Affairs about Allen's bribery on Saffron's behalf. Ultimately, Allen was demoted to sergeant and forced into retirement. The man once in line to take the commissioner's job and (seemingly) restore a corrupt order to the New South Wales police was foiled, the victim of a bitter snitch and a comped bill in the name of "Rooklyn."

While Rooklyn was on the rise once again in Queensland, by the early 1980s the mere invocation of his name elsewhere in Australia was enough to cast suspicion on anyone associated with him. Not only did his involvement in the Allen incident contribute to the assistant commissioner's career being scuttled, his attempted partnership with Saffron in South Australia was highlighted in parliament as another sign that Mr. Sin was up to no good in the state. More crucially, his past with Bally continued to come back to bite his former employers. Victoria commissioned Murray Wilcox QC in 1983 to determine if poker machines should be legalized in the state, as they were in their northern neighbor New South Wales. Appearing before Wilcox, Rooklyn's former secretary and then Bally Australia director Jan Newell agreed that there was corruption in the New South Wales pokies trade but that Bally had no part in it, and that was why its market share in the state was so small.[82] Despite Newell's attempt to cast Bally Australia as the victim of corruption, Wilcox was unconvinced and wanted whatever proof Bally could provide that "the leopard had changed its spots" in relation to improper or corrupt practices. In asking for his proof, he invoked the name of Jack Rooklyn and referred back to the findings of the Moffitt Commission, questioning why Rooklyn still had links with the company at all, even as a distributor. In the end, Wilcox did not recommend legalization of the poker machine industry and asserted that "there is not merely a risk of increased crime. Under any scenario crime will increase" if Victoria legalized the trade.[83]

Despite connections with his brand causing severe problems for his associates elsewhere, Rooklyn was still going strong in Queensland. Aside from being the site of *Apollo*'s 1980 demise, the state had been good to Rooklyn, thanks in large part to Jack Herbert and the relationship he had helped Rooklyn cultivate with Police Commissioner Terry Lewis. What Rooklyn was likely hoping to achieve by grooming Assistant Commissioner Bill Allen in New South Wales came to fruition in Queensland, where he enjoyed a direct line of communication with the police chief that gave him the power to not just avoid prosecution, but actively shape the nature of law and order in the state. In paying Lewis to ensure poker machines stayed illegal, Rooklyn demonstrated the power he had to effectively change the playing field to suit his own interests. The relationship with Lewis was costly in financial terms, but priceless in so many other ways. So long as Lewis remained in place, Rooklyn's star was certain to rise in Queensland. There seemed to be no stopping Lewis. In 1979 he was made an officer of the Order of the British Empire and later, in 1986, became the first serving Australian police officer to be knighted.[84] On the surface it appeared that Lewis and, with him, Rooklyn and the Joke could look forward to a long run of success in the late 1980s. What they could not have known at the time was that, behind the scenes, pieces were moving into place that would bring the entire system crashing down.

8

Moonlight

If there was a disruption in the corruption in the Queensland Police Force (QPF) in the 1970s, it was well and truly over by time the new decade dawned. Using his prerogative as commissioner, Terry Lewis began to fill the upper ranks of the force with allies like Brian Hayes and Syd Atkinson.[1] Another friend who benefited from Lewis's largesse was fellow Rat Pack member Tony Murphy, who, like Lewis himself, was a chief target of Whitrod's anti-corruption crusade. Transferred to regional western Queensland at the same time Whitrod similarly reassigned Lewis to rural Charleville, the new boss brought Murphy back to Brisbane in February 1977 to serve first as head of the police anti-corruption unit, the Crime Intelligence Unit (CIU). Soon after Murphy was promoted to Criminal Investigation Branch (CIB) superintendent and, later, rose to the rank of assistant commissioner. It was during his time leading the CIB in the late 1970s that Murphy allegedly made an open play for control of the corrupt rackets in the capital's entertainment (and vice) district, Fortitude Valley. Former Licensing Branch officer Domenico Cacciola recalls "two of Murphy's heavies" coming to him after he was reassigned to Fortitude Valley, at a time when Murphy was serving as CIB superintendent. Cacciola said that these men "reminded [him] on more than one occasion that they ran the Valley and to stay out of their way."[2] While Murphy did rise to assistant commissioner, his career was not destined to go any further. In 1982, public broadcaster the ABC televised allegations identifying Murphy and Lewis as corrupt members of a "Rat Pack" within the QPF. Claiming repeated accusations of corruption had irreparably damaged his chances for further promotion, Murphy finally relented and took an earlier than expected retirement.[3]

Murphy survived for a decade longer than his Rat Pack colleague Glen Hallahan, but his 1982 resignation left Lewis as the last remaining member of Bischof's former protégés in the QPF. With Lewis at the helm, corruption began to rise once again in the areas of the QPF where it had previously taken root, like the Licensing Branch. Not only that, it evolved. The vice trade in Queensland had grown since the Bischof era and, now, there were greater profits to be made by police protecting prostitution and illegal casinos rather than the traditional neighborhood bookmaker. The system that emerged under the renewed "Second Joke" set up by Jack Herbert and Licensing Branch inspector Noel Dwyer was less fragmented than the original Joke, with most vice controlled by one of two distinct groups operating with the sanction of corrupt police. The first of these groups, sometimes referred to as "The Syndicate," had interests in a range of areas, from the brothels managed by Geoff Crocker to illegal gaming managed by Syndicate members like Vic Conte and Geraldo Bellino (Bellino had first approached Herbert about police protection in the mid-1970s, just after his acquittal on corruption charges).[4] The other major enterprise protected under the Second Joke was operated by Sydney criminals Anne-Marie Tilley and Hector Hapeta, who relocated to Brisbane in 1978 and began a sex empire that lasted for almost a decade.[5]

After Tilley was caught up in a police raid on one of her and Hapeta's premises in April 1981, resulting in a short prison term for the aspiring prostitution czarina, she negotiated an agreement directly with Licensing boss Dwyer. The next year Dwyer retired, and, with the memory of the Pitts/Rigney/Jeppesen era still fresh, it was essential that his replacement also be "in on the Joke." The Jokers needed not look far for the perfect person. Dwyer's second-in-command, Graeme Parker, was a longtime associate of Herbert going back to their time serving in Licensing together in the early 1960s. Parker was also close to Dwyer, and an early (and easy) recruit to the Second Joke after it was reestablished when Dwyer first took control of the Licensing Branch. Under Parker, the Joke was in safe hands and continued to flourish, thanks to the experienced management of trusted bagman Jack Herbert.[6] Though he was working for Tony Robinson during much of the time the Second Joke was being reborn, Herbert also continued to assist Rooklyn where possible. It was in this period that he helped Rooklyn organize a negative report on poker machines from Lewis, and, in early 1981, he even returned to work for Rooklyn's Queensland Automatics for several months.[7] The web of corruption in Queensland was complex, but no matter whether we are talking about the prostitution managed by the Tilley/Hapeta organization, the illegal casinos of The Syndicate, or the in-line machines operated by Rooklyn, there is a single consistent feature—Herbert, an ever-present character with knowledge of the entire system, seeing all the angles from his position at the center of it all.

With Herbert's help, Rooklyn had managed to stave off moves to legalize poker machines in 1980 that would have demolished his business in Queensland with a simple pen stroke. He won that battle; however, the war was far from over. Just as it was worth a lot of money to Rooklyn to ensure pokies remained illegal, securing the opposite decision would be equally lucrative for companies like Ainsworth Consolidated, which was eagerly seeking to expand its reach from Australia's only legal market for the machines—New South Wales. Len Ainsworth and his team were not alone in their campaign for legalization in places like South Australia, Victoria, and Queensland in the early 1980s. Professional lobbyist Edward Phillip Vibert was cofounder of the Australian Club Development Association (ACDA), an industry body dedicated at least in part to promoting the introduction of gaming machines in states where they were illegal.[8] In theory the law has no issues with people who have convergent interests like Ainsworth and Vibert working together to achieve a mutual goal, but the relationship between Vibert and the Ainsworth group seemed, at least to some in law enforcement, to go beyond this. Set up in 1978 partly in response to the Moffitt Commission's recommendations, New South Wales Police unit Task Force Two had a remit to investigate crimes in the club scene. Suspicious of Vibert's lobbying tactics, Task Force Two came to believe that the ACDA was a "deception" and, in reality, Vibert was posing as an independent lobbyist while at the same time acting as an agent of Ainsworth, seeking to promote his patron's interests and, in turn, his own.[9] Subsequently, Task Force Two charged both Ainsworth and Vibert with several offenses connected with a conspiracy to "monopolise" the poker machine trade by forcing out competitors, including rival Bally Australia, which was languishing after the Moffitt inquiry and departure of Rooklyn as managing director.[10] Ainsworth allegedly sought to use Vibert to strike the final death blow, with the consultant accused of paying secret commissions to clubs to ensure Ainsworth was the preferred supplier of pokies in New South Wales.

Though an interesting aside when it comes to the story of poker machines that interconnects with Rooklyn's own personal narrative, the connection between the Ainsworth/Vibert case and Queensland goes even further. On March 6, 1982, Task Force Two raided Vibert's office and found evidence of correspondence between the ACDA and Queensland's Opposition Labor Party relating to donations that, under the circumstances, required further investigation. Around a month later, the New South Wales Police contacted Lewis to notify him about Task Force Two's findings. In his diary entry for April 5, 1982, Lewis notes "A/Comm R. DAY [NSW Assistant Commissioner Bob Day], then Det/Insp Cliff MCHARDY, NSW, phoned re Task Force 2 investigation . . . Messr's VIBERT and AINSWORTH have paid secret commissions to politicians in Qld and Vic."[11] He goes on to record that he referred the matter to Tony Murphy, who was now assistant commissioner, as well as told Detective Inspectors Don Bradbury and Bernard Ingham to go to Sydney to investigate further. Much later, in 1990, an investigation into the matter, conducted by the Queensland Criminal Justice Commission, claimed that Bradbury and Ingham "may have compromised the investigation" based on several factors, including their connections to corrupt police and the events that transpired when they went to Sydney at Lewis's direction.[12]

Bradbury and Ingham were trusted agents of the Lewis contingent in 1982 and, around the same time they were dispatched to deal with the fallout of the Task Force Two raids, were already working for the commissioner on other important projects. Documents tendered to the Fitzgerald Inquiry showed that on March 31, 1982, just days before

Lewis assigned them to the Ainsworth/Vibert investigation, Bradbury and Ingham had completed a report on "alleged malpractice at the Licensing Branch 1979–80" that, in part, vindicated Lewis's decision to appoint corrupt allies like Dwyer and Parker to lead the branch.[13] Further, Bradbury had actually served in the Licensing Branch from 1968 to 1970 alongside the likes of Murphy and Herbert, at a time when the first Joke was in its golden age and, in Herbert's words, corruption among Licensers was rife.[14] Herbert even implicated Bradbury in helping cover up his own misconduct. He told the Fitzgerald Inquiry that Bradbury was one of eight officers who "falsely swore that [Herbert's accomplice Neal] Freier told them in advance he was thinking of offering Inspector [Arthur] Pitts a bribe to test his honesty" and, thereby, supported Herbert and Freier's story that things were not as they seemed when they were caught on tape attempting to corrupt Pitts.[15] In hindsight, this prompts questions over the appropriateness of selecting Bradbury for the task of investigating corruption in Licensing. While he was never proven to have been involved in corruption during his tenure in Licensing, Bradbury's repeated selection by Murphy and Lewis to lead important investigations suggests that (at the very least) the duo trusted him. While perhaps a sign of respect for Bradbury and Ingham's capabilities as investigators, this story has already shown that being an officer who enjoyed the trust of the police commissioner was not always a good thing in the QPF of the 1980s.

Later, in June 1982, Bradbury and Ingham were also dispatched by Assistant Commissioner Murphy to look into the publication of a pamphlet called *The Woolloongabba Worrier*. The unofficial newspaper was a real headache for the Lewis administration. Written and published by police officer (and Lewis enemy) Bob Campbell, *The Woolloongabba Worrier* routinely attacked the commissioner and his allies in the QPF. It was also Campbell who leaked evidence to the political Opposition that Lewis had personally intervened to make a drunk-driving charge against influential businessmen Ted Lyons disappear in December 1981; later, Campbell was one of the whistle-blowers who was interviewed on the 1982 ABC news program that led to Murphy's resignation.[16] That Bradbury and Ingham were entrusted with such sensitive tasks as investigating the Licensing Branch and *The Woolloongabba Worrier* suggests that Lewis and others believed they could be counted on to support Lewis's interests, begging the question of what was so sensitive about the Ainsworth/Vibert case that they would be sent interstate to look into it for their bosses in Queensland—especially when considering the special interest Lewis no doubt would have taken on matters related to corruption and poker machines, given his still-recent illegal interference in the gaming industry.

Bradbury and Ingham moved quickly. Within a day of Lewis being informed about the evidence found during Task Force Two's raid on Vibert's office, they were already in Sydney to commence their inquiries. On the same day, April 6, 1982, Lewis's diary records a suspicious contact related to the Ainsworth/Vibert case; he notes that Herbert reached out, calling to make a "request re knowledge of Vibert and Ainsworth re New South Wales police inquiry."[17] Whatever the truth of the allegations was, the scandal had understandably captured the attention of the Queensland in-line machine operators that Herbert worked with. When Bradbury and Ingham arrived in Sydney, they requested permission from their New South Wales counterparts to conduct a further search of both the ACDA office and Ainsworth's business premises, seeking to obtain more evidence of the alleged political bribery in Queensland. The search was set for April 21, 1982, but, at the last moment, something happened that compromised the entire operation. When Bradbury and Ingham arrived, in company with detectives from Task Force Two, "it was apparent that Ainsworth executives had forewarning of the raid and that they were aware there would be Queensland detectives present" to investigate the bribery allegations.[18] In the view of the New South Wales Police, someone had tipped Ainsworth off. While a subsequent investigation could not determine the source of that leak, police zeroed in on one of two possibilities. The first was that a senior New South Wales Police officer with knowledge of the impending raid had passed the information to an Ainsworth executive at a social lunch they both attended. The second was that the leak came from Bradbury and Ingham themselves. On the day of the raid, the Queensland detectives stopped off to visit the Texas Tavern in Kings Cross for lunch. There they dined with none other than

Paul Meade, the Queensland organized crime figure who allegedly ran in-line machines for Lennie McPherson and Paddles Anderson, and who was associated with the Ainsworth group through his business relationship with Vanguard owner Harry Calleia—who also, coincidentally, owned the Texas Tavern.[19]

Unsurprisingly, the Ainsworth search failed to yield the kind of "smoking gun" documentation required to prove the company was involved (or complicit) in bribing Queensland Labor politicians. Ainsworth emphatically denied "any suggestion that he had solicited the assistance of [Labor leader Ed] Casey in relation to the introduction of poker machines in Queensland" and said that, if it did happen, it was solely instigated by Vibert without his knowledge.[20] Documents showed that Vibert had indeed donated sums of money to Queensland Labor around the time of Casey's 1980 announcement that Labor would support the legalization of poker machines; however, there was still not enough evidence to tie the donation directly to the change in party policy. After the failed raid, Bradbury and Ingham continued to conduct a relatively lax investigation into the bribery claims in which they did not even interview Vibert or the alleged recipient of the secret commission, Ed Casey. When Lewis eventually forwarded Bradbury and Ingham's final report to the Queensland Solicitor-General to recommend if charges could be laid against anyone involved, the Solicitor-General described the case file as "inconclusive" and said "it is pointless to indulge in any speculation on what criminal charges might be open. Clearly there is no evidence at all in relation to any claim of bribery."[21] With the Solicitor-General's response on August 12, 1982, the case against Ainsworth, Vibert, and Casey was closed. Ainsworth and Vibert still faced charges of deception and conspiracy in New South Wales, but most of these were also dropped in 1983 based on lack of evidence. Vibert was convicted of conspiring to pay secret commissions to a rural New South Wales club to stock certain products, but was later acquitted on appeal.[22]

As the Criminal Justice Commission (CJC) investigation of the poker machine industry noted in 1990, the investigation into the bribery claims against Ainsworth and Vibert by the Queensland detectives was a key reason why the case was never brought before court. There were few proactive attempts made by Bradbury and Ingham to conduct interviews or gather information. The one example of true proactivity, the search of Ainsworth's premises, was even compromised by the leak in the investigation, which meant police were never likely to find what they needed to bring charges, if such evidence did exist. The New South Wales Police suspected (as did the CJC later) that Bradbury and Ingham may have been responsible for tipping off Ainsworth, possibly using Meade as an intermediary given his connection to the New South Wales poker machine scene.[23] But why? If Bradbury and Ingham were Lewis's chosen "fixers" at this time, what reason would they have to help someone like Ainsworth, who was actively working *against* Lewis's friend Rooklyn's mission to keep poker machines illegal in Queensland? It is possible they alerted Meade inadvertently, letting slip about the raid without realizing his connection to Ainsworth's group. It is also possible that tipping off Ainsworth would protect Meade's own interests—after all, "Paul M." was still named on Lewis's list of people involved in his corruption racket as late as 1981, so there may have been some pressure to scuttle an investigation that might put his own businesses at risk. The tip-off also may not have been about Ainsworth or Meade at all, but about currying political favor with Labor leader Ed Casey. In 1982, Labor staffer Malcolm McMillan said Tony Murphy came to him to ask if it may be possible for Murphy himself to run for office as a Labor candidate after he resigned from the police force.[24] While this electoral run never happened, it is possible that helping Casey out was an attempt to create a *quid pro quo* that could catapult Murphy into parliament, much like his former colleague Don Lane on the other side of the political aisle. Or, also likely, Bradbury and Ingham did not have anything to do with a tip-off to Ainsworth. This was, after all, Sydney in the 1980s. The strong possibility of home-grown corruption is certainly not out of the question.

In the end, we do not know what truly happened in Bradbury and Ingham's 1982 investigation, other than the outcome: While Ainsworth and Vibert walked away without serious consequence, their reputations and that of the poker machine industry were dragged through the mud, setting back their ambitions to move into other states considerably—a state of affairs that clearly benefited Rooklyn's in-line business in

Queensland. Not only did the allegations against the Ainsworth group damage their aspirations for legalization, they also served as a political weapon with which to bludgeon the Opposition whenever it turned its attention to the industry—and Jack Rooklyn—once more. For example, in March 1984, Labor police spokesperson Wayne Goss launched a scathing salvo against Rooklyn in state parliament, where he tabled documents alleging Rooklyn's Queensland Automatics operated like an organized crime syndicate, using violent tactics to gain control of the Queensland gaming machine market. In one statement Goss tabled, from Sunshine Coast machine distributor Brian Vidulich, it was asserted that Rooklyn's local manager Barry MacNamara had told Vidulich that Rooklyn had "fixed it with the local police" to allow Queensland Automatics to operate, and if Vidulich tried to resist Queensland Automatics dominance, he "would end up in the prawning nets."[25]

Despite the damning public allegations of police corruption and death threats, Goss's attacks on Rooklyn did not go anywhere, largely because of the impression that they were part of a tit for tat between Labor and the government. In response to Goss's allegations, government politicians suggested that Goss and the Labor Party "should look to its own area of concern" in its connections with Ainsworth and Vibert, but that doing so "would not suit the motives of the Labor Party."[26] For his own part, Rooklyn also responded to Goss's allegations, calling them "absolute nonsense" and describing Goss as "a fledgling politician who sees this [attacking Rooklyn] as a good opportunity to make a name for himself."[27] While Goss was taking a stand, his bold actions were failing to gain traction. The public was less concerned with what Goss had to say about Rooklyn than about the accusations of political bribery, unaware that Rooklyn himself had paid $25,000 to the police commissioner to get his way on the issue of legalization, handing over a paper bag of cash in the Crest Hotel at around the same time the questionable donations to Labor were being paid out.

Rooklyn had little to fear about a Labor renaissance delivering legalization in Queensland. The Bjelke-Petersen government was stronger than ever and, at the 1983 state election, ascended to new heights. Previously, Bjelke-Petersen presided over a coalition government made up of the state's two conservative political parties, the National Party (which Bjelke-Petersen belonged to) and the Liberal Party (his junior coalition partners). This traditional status quo changed in 1983, when the National Party came close to winning enough seats across the state to ditch the Liberals and govern in its own right.[28] The National Party found itself two seats short of an absolute majority, and so Bjelke-Petersen publicly offered Liberal politicians the opportunity to defect, join the Nationals, and allow them to form government. Two Liberal MPs took Bjelke-Petersen up on his offer, one of whom was former police officer Don Lane, a man always looking for the best angle to get ahead.[29] Lane's defection helped deliver Bjelke-Petersen greater power than ever before and secured his position as a rising star in Queensland politics. At the same time, it is alleged that Lane continued to foster his corrupt relationships with people like Herbert and Rooklyn, looking to use his growing power to assist his old friends in their illicit endeavors wherever possible—for a fee. Lane denied this, but financial records presented to the Fitzgerald Inquiry suggested significant amounts of unexplained income—perhaps vindicating Herbert's allegation that he regularly paid Lane bribes on behalf of illegal operators.[30]

In the mid-1980s it seemed that fortunes were on the ascendant across corrupt Queensland. The Bjelke-Petersen government was stronger than ever, and its strength meant that the premier's patronage of Lewis was secure. Lewis was even knighted in 1986 on the recommendation of Bjelke-Petersen, the first serving police officer in Australia ever to receive the honor.[31] On the home front, the corrupt system of the Second Joke was also firmly reestablished, overseen in the Licensing Branch by Graeme Parker and managed deftly by Herbert to the great benefit of both Queensland's vice trade and the police officers (like Lewis) who benefited from it. As for Rooklyn, the threat of pokies legalization seemed to have passed. The Labor Party had been decimated, the threat of Ainsworth's intervention seemed to be over, and the pay-to-play system established by the police seemed set to go on uninterrupted. If these individuals were confident in their continued success, they may not have noticed the beginning of the end when zealous young *Courier-Mail* journalist Phil Dickie began to investigate the ownership of Brisbane venues where sex was sold and illegal gambling conducted. Dickie's articles started to be published in December 1986. He named names: Dickie identified 21 brothels operating in the Brisbane metropolitan area alone as belonging to protected participants in the Joke like Geoff Crocker, Hector Hapeta, and Anne-Marie Tilley.[32] He also turned the spotlight on illegal casinos, publishing the names of operators attached to The Syndicate like Geraldo Bellino and Vic Conte and, more importantly, pointing the finger at a corrupt Licensing Branch as the reason why so many vice traders were allowed to do business in plain sight, without repercussion.[33]

Dickie's work was important in that it lifted the veil over organized crime in Queensland, in a newspaper widely read throughout the state. All of a sudden, the idea that vice was rampant in Queensland and, perhaps, protected by corrupt police was splashed all over the *Courier-Mail*. It set the scene for the reckoning that was still to come in 1987, starting the chain of dominos that ultimately led to the Fitzgerald Inquiry. It was not until May 1987 that these dominos truly began to fall at a rapid pace, however. Chris Masters was a reporter for ABC's current affairs program *Four Corners*, and had experience in producing complex stories about crime and corruption in Australia. On one such story about the Calabrian Mafia, televised in June 1986, Masters had worked with an informant named Peter Vassallo who worked with the Australian Bureau of Criminal Intelligence in the nation's capital, Canberra.[34] After the report aired, Vassallo came to Masters again offering an even bigger story—a huge claim, given Masters had just worked on a report that implicated the Australian Mafia in a plot to kill anti-drugs campaigner Donald Mackay in 1977. Vassallo told Masters that he had an old friend who was a serving police officer in Queensland, and who was ready to speak out about the corruption in the QPF. Masters was initially reluctant, having seen the failure that previous investigative reports into corruption in Queensland had experienced when it came to prompting actual reform. Nonetheless, trusting Vassallo's instincts, Masters agreed to meet with him and his Queensland cop friend at a pub on September 27, 1986, just to hear what he had to say and decide for himself if the story was worth pursuing.[35]

Vassallo's friend was Jim Slade, a decade-long veteran of the QPF who worked undercover jobs for the Bureau of Criminal Intelligence (BCI), where he had trained under the tutelage of Tony Murphy. More recently Slade had been dispatched on operations targeting drug trafficking in Queensland's tropical north, going deep undercover to understand the key players and methods for moving narcotics into Australia. He said he kept coming up against a familiar name from his time serving in Brisbane: Bellino. Despite being aware of the rumors that the Bellinos were protected in the QPF, he reported the intelligence about their alleged involvement in trafficking to his superiors on November 21, 1984.[36] He told Masters that shortly after, he was approached by his boss at the BCI, Alan Barnes, who offered him "a bit of extra money" from "Gerry" (presumed to be Geraldo Bellino)—Barnes said the money was filtered through a group of officers who "met at Jack Herbert's place" and, thus, were likely part of the Second Joke.[37] Slade was offered $100 a month for "helping" Bellino, which he initially accepted. He later took his allegations to another superior, Col Thompson, but became frustrated when no real action was taken as a result. Barnes was transferred to rural Longreach, and Slade himself was shifted out of the BCI to Beenleigh Police Station, which was notorious as a dumping ground for problematic officers, away from the main action taking place in Brisbane. It was this failure to act on Barnes's attempted corruption that prompted Slade to act and, through Vassallo, reach out to Masters to blow the lid off the webs of graft at play in the QPF.

When the *Four Corners* report on corruption in Queensland aired on May 11, 1987, it was not just Slade's allegations that formed the basis of the story. In "The Moonlight State" (as the episode was titled), Masters conducted a deep dive into how vice operated in the state in a narrative that was built on evidence from a range of sources, including former and serving police, sex workers, escort service managers, and others.[38] Combined, the stories they each told painted the picture of a state where all kinds of vice—drugs, sex, gambling—were available from one of two preferred suppliers, with "The Moonlight State" openly naming these criminal operators as The Syndicate and the Tilley/Hapeta group, just as Dickie had been doing for months. But Masters steered clear of suggesting that either of these organizations actually *controlled* organized crime in Queensland; that, he said, was the role of the QPF. Masters described a "Queensland system" in which certain officers (many of a senior rank) acknowledged that vice could never be completely stamped out and, instead, sought to control it, deciding which groups were allowed to operate and under what circumstances. It was effectively a policy of containment that, according to the people Masters spoke to, was designed to keep peace on the streets.[39] Central to the system was that vice operators did not just pay corrupt police in a monetary sense, but also paid deference to the badge and the rules set out for them, such as how many brothels they could own or how many sex workers they could employ at any one time. Masters mostly steered away from stating the names of police he believed to be corrupt outright. On the program, he clearly states that he does not accuse Lewis of corruption directly, but that the commissioner nevertheless bears ultimate responsibility for police misconduct that happened on his watch. The program also raised the specter of Jack Herbert and tied him directly to The Syndicate, citing the bagman's 1985 purchase of a house from Gerry Bellino and Vic Conte as evidence of a relationship between police and the Brisbane milieu. While Masters again did not allege explicitly that this home sale was part of a corrupt trade-off, his report left viewers with the implication that somehow, despite leaving the QPF many years earlier, Herbert was still heavily involved in any corruption that was still occurring into the mid-1980s.[40]

Masters had initially feared that "The Moonlight State" would not have an impact on a state notoriously resistant to introspection and reform when it came to its police and public institutions. He may have been right, under normal circumstances, but on this point the timing of the report was crucial. When ABC aired Masters's report, the premier was distracted with a quixotic tilt at becoming the Australian prime minister. Through his "Joh for PM" campaign, Bjelke-Petersen believed he could be voted into the highest elected office in the country without even serving first as a member of the federal parliament.[41] The power grab was ultimately unsuccessful, but held Bjelke-Petersen's attention just as "The Moonlight State" hit the airwaves. Adding to this, the premier was out of the country when it aired, leaving Police Minister Bill Gunn in charge. Where Bjelke-Petersen may have dismissed the report's claims with a characteristic hubris, Gunn did not. On May 12, 1987—just a few hours after "The Moonlight State" aired—Gunn used his temporary authority to commission a formal inquiry into the allegations raised by Masters.[42]

The genie was out of the bottle, and there were many in the state who felt the impending investigation might pose a serious risk to them, if action were not taken to manage its fallout. First, the goal was to ensure that a "friendly" commissioner was appointed—someone like Lewis's old friend Eric Pratt, the judge who presided over the Police Complaints Tribunal and was famously resistant to negative findings against QPF officers. That plan was nipped in the bud thanks to the intervention of Director of Public Prosecutions, Des Sturgess, who was aware that appointing Pratt as commissioner risked a complete whitewash.[43] Instead, he suggested an outsider for the role. Barrister Tony Fitzgerald had previous experience as a federal court judge and, importantly, few connections among the police and political circles that would inevitably come under scrutiny during the corruption inquiry. Sturgess took his concerns about Pratt to Chief Justice Dormer Andrews, who, in agreement, sent Gunn a letter advising against Pratt's appointment. When Pratt's name was raised in Cabinet, Gunn produced the letter and put an end to the campaign to name Pratt to lead the commission. Without other options to suggest, Pratt's supporters floundered, whereas Gunn (armed with a recommendation from Sturgess) proposed Fitzgerald, who was duly appointed.[44] The first scramble to control the commission had failed. The Fitzgerald Inquiry was born.

When Fitzgerald was appointed, panic began to set in. Cabinet ally Don Lane advised Lewis to go personally to Bjelke-Petersen and plant seeds in his head that Fitzgerald was a poor choice for the role. Lewis did as Lane suggested, traveling to the premier's rural homestead in Kingaroy and spinning a story about rumors that Fitzgerald had voted for Labor and would be out to get the sitting government. Again, distracted with his Joh for PM campaign, and perhaps underestimating the threat the commission posed, Bjelke-Petersen dismissed Lewis's concerns.[45] Now inevitable that the Licensing Branch was bound to come under serious public scrutiny, the corrupt officers who were part of the Joke began to circle the wagons in an effort to protect themselves. Preparing to make a quick exit if need be, Herbert sold his home to friends "for less than its full value" less than a week after the Fitzgerald Inquiry was announced.[46] On June 13, 1987, ahead of the first public hearings, Herbert flew to Hamilton Island off the northern Queensland coast. Coincidentally or otherwise, he ran into Rooklyn on the island. With the matter of the Fitzgerald Inquiry naturally coming up in conversation, Herbert said Rooklyn, perhaps recalling his own experience with the Moffitt Commission, "advised him [Herbert] to leave Australia."[47] Herbert took Rooklyn's advice to heart: He cut his island stay short, returned to Brisbane to arrange for the continuation of graft collections in his absence, and, on June 20, promptly left Australia for parts unknown.[48] At the same time, his co-conspirators in Licensing were also making their own contingency plans, and "numerous meetings" were held to discuss how to proceed without Herbert as the bagman, under the watchful eye of Fitzgerald. Senior Sergeant Noel Kelly took charge, advising Tilley on how to keep her brothels running despite the close scrutiny and taking the role of "collector of prostitution graft."[49] Even as the pressure started to grow, the Jokers were still hell-bent on ensuring that the corrupt racket they presided over would not come to an end.

Fitzgerald's much anticipated proceedings began in Courtroom 29 of the Brisbane court complex on July 27, 1987. Lewis, the first witness to give testimony, dropped an early bombshell to the commission, setting the tone for what was to come. Though denying that police were protecting the sex trade in return for bribes, he claimed to have received verbal instructions from five successive police ministers *and* the premier to give "low priority" to policing of brothels.[50] As the *Courier-Mail* reported, Lewis appeared set to "serve rather than receive . . . what he obviously hopes will be aces into the government court."[51] Already, the commissioner was turning on his former masters in parliament, looking to abdicate responsibility for the rampant vice trade. Lewis was followed into the witness box by a variety of senior police and vice figures, including Hapeta and the Bellinos. During these lines of questioning, one of Rooklyn's old friends even made a cameo appearance. The lawyer for the ABC,

Bob Mulholland, questioned Hapeta as to whether he had business dealings with Abraham Saffron and, in particular, whether Saffron was the supplier for Hapeta and Tilley's chain of sex shops. Hapeta denied an association with Saffron and, incensed, Saffron called the *Courier-Mail* to reject the suggestion he even knew Hapeta, despite the latter's past as an associate of the Sydney milieu.[52] For the most part, both police and vice operators toed the line and refused to give away much in their testimony, but by late August the first crack appeared—and it was a major one.

As one of the key bagmen and "handlers" for the Hapeta/Tilley group, Sergeant Harry Burgess was looking for a way out. He was on the frontlines of corruption as an organizer and collector of corrupt payments and, in both Dickie's articles and Masters's report, whistle-blowers had told stories that, while not naming Burgess explicitly, outlined events where he had played a leading role.[53] His name had also started to recur in the early testimony at the Fitzgerald Inquiry, and it was only a matter of time before some of the mud being thrown around started to stick. Burgess wanted to get ahead of the problem and so, on August 28, 1987, he admitted corruption in return for conditional immunity from prosecution.[54] Three days later, Burgess took the stand to tell all he knew about the Joke and others involved in it, including his one-time boss and now recently minted assistant commissioner, Graeme Parker. He confessed to receiving around $27,000 in bribes over his career, implicating not just Parker but also Herbert and others. According to later testimony from Parker, he and Lewis met in person several times after Burgess's explosive testimony to workshop ways to undermine his evidence, and slip free of the noose their former ally had thrown around them.[55] Despite working with Lewis, Parker was also considering his own position. Only a few weeks after Burgess's testimony implicated him, Parker resigned from the QPF and the next day, September 17, 1987, it was formally announced that he would admit corruption and tell all as an indemnified witness.[56] Four days later, perhaps given forewarning of the content of Parker's admissions, Gunn ordered Lewis to temporarily stand down as police commissioner. Taking the stand for a grueling six-day interrogation in November 1987, Parker admitted to receiving $130,000 in bribes in his career and named both Lewis and Cabinet minister Lane as others involved in the same corrupt racket.[57]

Another person mentioned by Parker was the still-missing Jack Herbert. Rooklyn's advice during their chance encounter on Hamilton Island was fortuitous, as the bagman had slipped away just before the wheels started to fall off the Joke. During his testimony, Burgess had said Herbert called him around the time he left to say he was going "to see mummy"—a statement Burgess took to mean that Herbert had left for his home country, England.[58] With his wife, Peggy, Herbert had been living in a one-bedroom flat in Kingston-upon-Thames, just southwest of London, since around the time Burgess testified before Fitzgerald. The Herberts had been there for six months by February 1988, watching the developments from Brisbane from afar. Indeed, on the cold morning of February 9, Jack and Peggy were up early with plans to travel to Australia House in central London to read the newspapers from back home, to help them prepare to rebut Burgess and Parker's allegations. They were getting ready to leave when a team of police burst through the door and took them both into custody on charges of perverting the course of justice.[59] Initially, Herbert thought he had run out of options. With big names in the corruption racket like Burgess, Parker, and Dwyer "flipping" in return for immunity, the inquiry (and public) would be looking for a scapegoat to prosecute, and the fact that Herbert had been caught rather than coming to Fitzgerald voluntarily was not in his favor. Nevertheless, he had an ace up his sleeve—his intimate knowledge of corruption—and so, even though he felt it may be too late, Herbert asked his solicitor to check with the commission to see if indemnity was still an option on the table.[60] Not only was it still on the table, but the inquiry was eager to secure Herbert as its next supergrass. Just a few days later, inquiry lawyer Bob Needham met with Herbert at Kingston police station with a document for Herbert to sign giving him immunity in return for his testimony. Herbert signed and, on March 17, 1988, he returned to Australia ready to join the cavalcade of corrupt officers who had turned witness against the Joke.[61]

For six months, Jack and Peggy Herbert were moved around southeast Queensland to various safe houses while being debriefed by

Fitzgerald Inquiry lawyers and preparing their testimony. Finally, on August 31, 1988, Herbert's day in court arrived. Later, he recalled seeing Terry Lewis in the courtroom as he took the stand, and wondering what was going through the commissioner's head. In Herbert's words: "Terry Lewis was as guilty as I was and we both knew it. But Terry always thought he was too clever to be caught. That was the difference between us. I knew when the game was up but Terry never did."[62]

Herbert pulled no punches on the witness stand. Unquestionably the most significant thing he could offer the commission, beyond what Burgess and Parker already had, was his firsthand knowledge of Lewis's involvement in corruption. He spoke of having paid Lewis bribes out of the Joke since the 1960s, and described the code system he and Lewis used to organize the meetings where corrupt monies changed hands. On his second day of testifying, Herbert raised the specter of Rooklyn; he told Fitzgerald that he helped facilitate a $25,000 bribe from Rooklyn to Lewis in return for the adverse poker machine report in 1980.[63] These revelations went beyond anything the Fitzgerald Inquiry had heard before, and put Lewis, still adamantly denying all allegations of corruption, firmly in the hot seat. The day after Herbert's testimony began, around the same time he was again in court talking about the Rooklyn bribe, Lewis received a letter from Gunn advising him that he was now formally suspended—without pay.[64] The suspension became permanent on April 19, 1989, after further damning allegations at the inquiry led to Governor Wally Campbell formally declaring the position of police commissioner vacant.[65]

Over the course of 13 days and 56 hours of testimony, Jack Herbert did not reserve his accusations for the commissioner. For example, he also took aim at Cabinet minister Don Lane, whom he described as a corruption "pipeline." He said Lane had been paid bribes since at least Herbert's time working for Tony Robinson, and capitalized on his political position to funnel information to corrupt police, helping them stave off scrutiny and protect the corrupt network.[66] In another case, Herbert's claims even brought former boss Tony Robinson to tears. On September 19, 1988, Robinson personally cross-examined Herbert for around 80 minutes in response to Herbert's accusations that he had paid Lane on behalf of Robinson while employed by Robinson's in-line business, Austral Amusements. As the witness stuck to his story, Robinson told him not to lie and that "for the lies you've told in here I hope you rot in hell."[67] Robinson told the commission that he had never paid bribes to Lane, but that Herbert wanted to "crucify" him because he had secretly taped a conversation between Herbert and Rooklyn in which Herbert had initially raised the prospect of bribing Lewis over the poker machine report. Robinson said he had recorded the discussion to leave with his solicitor as a means of protection, in the event that Herbert ever sought to "knock him off."[68] For his own part, Herbert remained firm that Robinson paid Lane (among others) as part of the corruption related to in-line gaming, as did Rooklyn.

It seemed like Herbert's appearance was the crescendo of the Fitzgerald Inquiry and could not be beaten, but there was one more star witness yet to come: the former state premier, Joh Bjelke-Petersen. After almost 20 years, Bjelke-Petersen's reign came to an end in late 1987 in stunning fashion. With the Fitzgerald Inquiry putting him under pressure from within his own party, Bjelke-Petersen attempted to defend against a leadership challenge by firing five "rogue" ministers. Seeing the premier as mad with power, even Governor Campbell refused his demand to sack the ministers.[69] The party room decided it was time to make a change and, on November 26, 1987, Bjelke-Petersen was officially voted out as Nationals leader and, not long after, resigned as state premier.[70] When he faced Fitzgerald, Bjelke-Petersen was questioned not just about his oversight of the QPF, but also political bribery—in "The Moonlight State" it had been alleged by a member of The Syndicate that organized crime figures paid large "donations" to the National Party in hopes of receiving favorable treatment.[71] The premier agreed that anonymous donors "regularly" left sums of money in his office; however, it was not bribery as he never sought out the source of the cash and, thus, could not return any benefit to the donor.[72] Bjelke-Petersen's performance before Fitzgerald was seen as arrogant and defensive, characteristic of the man who had notoriously declared "I am the National Party" when advised he should not fire his Cabinet.[73] Once the all-powerful patron of the Lewis administration, Bjelke-Petersen now found himself without the protection afforded to him by the office of the premier and, in just a few short years, his hubristic appearance at Fitzgerald would come back to haunt him.

Bjelke-Petersen was one of the last witnesses to take the stand in Courtroom 29, and, soon after, Fitzgerald adjourned the hearings to spend several months preparing his final report. In the end, what many initially thought would be yet another short, inconsequential investigation instead convened for 238 days of public hearings in which it untangled the web of organized crime and corruption in Queensland to an extent never seen before in Australia—perhaps even *anywhere* before in the world.[74] As the state waited patiently to see what Fitzgerald's final report would say, the repercussions of the commission's revelations were already playing out. Named repeatedly as a conduit for corruption, and with the premier he had switched political allegiances for now kicked out of office, Lane found himself left with few options. He had lost his Cabinet post after Bjelke-Petersen's exit (and, importantly, Parker's testimony implicating him in corruption); however, he did not resign from parliament until January 30, 1989—by then, Lane was staring down criminal charges of misappropriating ministerial expenses after making admissions to Fitzgerald.[75] He was not the only one to lose his job ahead of the Fitzgerald Report being released. Lewis's suspension became permanent on April 19, 1989, and, in a letter from Premier Mike Ahern, he was notified that his term as police commissioner had officially been terminated.[76] The new government did not need to wait for Fitzgerald. It had seen enough to pass judgment. Ultimately, the Fitzgerald Report was released to the public on July 3, 1989. It was scathing of Lewis's administration and, in particular, of a culture of corruption in the QPF that became the norm over Lewis's decade as its leader.

It was only a matter of weeks before the first wave of criminal charges began to be issued based on Fitzgerald's findings. Lewis was among twenty people summonsed on July 26, 1989, and the commissioner was informed that it was expected he would be charged with 16 counts of official corruption and two additional charges of perjury.[77] Lewis was not alone, as there were other big names among this set of charges: Hector Hapeta and Anne-Marie Tilley, Vic Conte and Gerry Bellino from The Syndicate, several police officers who did not take indemnities, and Queensland Automatics employees John Garde and Barry MacNamara.[78] However, the most recognizable name—aside from the police commissioner, of course—was Jack Rooklyn. Fitzgerald had achieved something Moffitt and the others who followed his path could not. The cigar-chomping gambling mogul and champion yachtsman would face court, charged with corruption related to the regular "protection" payments Queensland Automatics paid to Lewis, as well as the $25,000 bribe paid to Lewis in 1980 in return for him agreeing to oppose the legalization of poker machines.[79] The chief witness against Rooklyn was Herbert, who, as per his indemnity agreement, would be doing the rounds of Brisbane's courts to repeat all he knew about the illegal conduct of Rooklyn, Lewis, and others.[80] The sheer amount of high-profile cases brought about as a result of the Fitzgerald Inquiry caused a slight backlog, and Rooklyn's case did not come up for committal until early 1990. At the committal on March 30, 1990, Rooklyn entered a plea of not guilty. Never one to give up while there was still an angle to play, Rooklyn intended to see the case through, all the way to trial.[81]

Conclusion

Cashing Out

Before Rooklyn was to have his day in court, the state's focus was on making its case against one of his alleged partners in crime: the former police commissioner, Terry Lewis. Unlike some of his fellow defendants, Lewis had confidently waived his right to a committal hearing after being charged, preferring instead to move immediately to have the allegations against him tested in court.[1] Since then, he had been living in a sort of legal limbo as his lawyers and the prosecution fought over what evidence could be heard in the trial. In the end, the long-awaited Lewis trial did not properly begin until March 18, 1991, around twenty months after he was first charged.[2] From the outset, the court was told that Lewis's trial would be a Fitzgerald Inquiry reunion, of sorts. The prosecution outlined a list of up to 110 witnesses who would testify, including former members of the Joke like Harry Burgess and Noel Kelly. The star witness was set to be Jack Herbert, an important figure who could provide a direct link between Lewis and corruption—after all, Herbert said he was the one who handed the commissioner his corrupt profits on a regular basis.[3]

As in the Fitzgerald Inquiry two years earlier, Herbert spent an extended amount of time (12 days here) on the stand giving evidence about the corruption he was intimately acquainted with. Lewis's lawyers took aim at his credibility, painting him as a mercenary liar who was dancing to the prosecution's tune to protect his indemnity and cover his own back. During one back-and-forth with Lewis's lawyer John Jerrard, the defense reminded Herbert of the lies he admitted to telling in court throughout his career and asked why his swearing an oath of honesty in

Lewis's trial would be any different. Admitting to a history of perjury, Herbert could only offer that "in the position I am in now, I'm telling the truth" by way of response.[4] In summing up, even the trial judge made a point of cautioning the jury to take Herbert's evidence with a grain of salt. While prosecutor Bob Mulholland reminded them in his concluding statement that "the truth has a strength of its own no matter from what sullied source [e.g., Herbert] it emanates," Judge Anthony Healy "strongly urged a cautious or sceptical approach to the Crown case."[5] He said it would be "dangerous to convict the accused on the evidence of Jack Herbert" when taking into account his proven lack of trustworthiness, and that Herbert had "the strongest motive imaginable for fabricating a story to implicate the accused."[6] Despite Healy's warnings, after five days of deliberating the jury returned a verdict, convicting Lewis on all counts. Within minutes, Healy sentenced Lewis to the maximum term of 14 years in prison, saying, "Well Sir Terence, the verdicts speak for themselves."[7] Within 90 minutes, the former commissioner was being processed at Boggo Road jail and, finally, the Fitzgerald Inquiry had claimed its biggest scalp. While Lewis would appeal his conviction, arguing that adverse media coverage meant the trial was never going to be fair from the outset, his efforts were in vain. Lewis served around four years before being released to community detention and, perhaps worse for a man whose social status mattered so much, was stripped of his knighthood by Queen Elizabeth II.[8]

With the Lewis case almost wrapped up, state prosecutors were turning their attention to others caught up in the post-Fitzgerald frenzy of criminal charges, including Rooklyn and his Queensland Automatics accountant, John Garde. Rooklyn's trial had not been underway long when it was abruptly aborted in August 1991—with Lewis's verdict coming in, local newspapers had been reporting his crimes, including several that were also the subject of Rooklyn's own court proceedings. The flurry of articles put a halt on Rooklyn and Garde's trial, infuriating the prosecution. Indeed, Queensland attorney-general Dean Wells pursued a contempt of court case against the *Sunday Sun* over an article he argued had risked unfairly prejudicing jurors and, as a result, compromising the Rooklyn/Garde case. Though agreeing the *Sunday Sun* article was "not fair," the Queensland Supreme Court failed to come to a finding of contempt, determining that any "prejudicial impact on their [Rooklyn and Garde] fair trial was an incidental by-product of the discussion of a matter of public importance."[9] The verdict that the trial was not unduly prejudiced came in January 1992, with the trial set to resume in April. One may assume that the corruption case would have occupied Rooklyn's every waking moment in the interim, but the accused had other problems to contend with. Two months after his trial was put on hold in August 1991, Rooklyn underwent a single heart bypass surgery as a result of ongoing health complications.[10] No doubt the stress of potential conviction contributed to the 84-year-old's declining health, but whatever the case, the Rooklyn who returned in April 1992 for his second trial was described by onlookers as "a shadow of his former verbose self."[11]

Rooklyn's health problems shone through at his second trial. At one point during proceedings, he even collapsed in court, "slumping in his chair."[12] Nevertheless, already delayed by earlier media reports, the case went on. The district court was told that, in 1978, Rooklyn had organized with Herbert (who was once again providing key evidence) to pay $2,000 a month in return for Herbert's contacts protecting his illegal in-line gambling business. It also heard, based on Herbert's testimony, that Rooklyn had stumped up a further $25,000 bribe on top of his monthly payments to secure Lewis's cooperation in producing the infamous 1980 report advising against legalizing poker machines. Overall, the prosecution did the math and claimed that Rooklyn had paid at least $189,000 in bribes to Herbert and Lewis in the almost decade he operated in Queensland.[13] So much of the evidence against Rooklyn came from Herbert, as it had with Lewis. Without Herbert's cooperation, both cases likely would not have moved forward successfully. Indeed, a former prisoner who was incarcerated with brothel czar Hector Hapeta was reputedly told that the matter of killing Herbert before his appearance at the Fitzgerald Inquiry was mooted by Hapeta and other organized crime figures as a way of putting the brakes on his inevitably explosive testimony. However, Hapeta said that "no one had the intestinal fortitude to do it [kill Herbert]. They relied on Jack Rooklyn. They thought Rooklyn would do the job."[14] If true, the concerned Brisbane milieu was mistaken, perhaps (wrongly) taking Rooklyn's reputation as an American Mafia associate as an indication that he would ensure Herbert met the same grim fate of other "rats." In any case, by the end of the Rooklyn/Garde trial, the evidence provided by Herbert had once again hit its mark and painted a damning portrait of Rooklyn as a man who was not only involved in corruption, but actively *relished* it.

In his summing up, Judge Brian Boulton instructed the jury of seven men and five women not to allow emotions to cloud their judgment on Rooklyn's guilt. For much of the trial, Rooklyn had appeared a sickly man, but Boulton cautioned that the jury "should, as far as humanly possible, remove considerations of sympathy or of prejudice."[15] Unlike Healy's caution about believing Herbert's evidence in the Lewis case, it seems the members of Rooklyn's jury were more receptive to Boulton's instructions. Ultimately, Rooklyn's decades-long run of good luck ran out in Brisbane District Court on Friday, May 22, 1992, where, after 30 hours of deliberations, the jurors returned their verdict: guilty on all counts.[16] When court resumed on Monday, May 25, 1992, Boulton was ready to issue Rooklyn's sentence. Though the prosecution had requested jail time, commensurate with what Lewis had received the year prior, Boulton rejected a custodial sentence due to Rooklyn's advanced age and ill health. He said he "accept[ed] medical evidence that to send you to jail would be to risk your life. . . . I would say if you were younger and in better health, beyond a shadow of a doubt you would have gone to jail for a number of years."[17] Instead, the court punished Rooklyn with a series of fines: $250,000 for his conviction over the monthly payments to Herbert, and $100,000 for the bribe to Lewis in return for the 1980 poker machines report, for a total of $350,000 in penalties.[18] Boulton rejected the argument that Rooklyn had no choice but to cooperate with the powerful Lewis and his bagman, Herbert. Rather, in the judge's view, he was a wealthy and influential businessman who could have taken a stand against the corruption if he so chose, but instead "allowed himself to be cajoled into sustained criminal activity, for which he had expressed no moral concern."[19] The characterization that Rooklyn had been "cajoled" into paying bribes to police must have raised some eyebrows among his former associates, particularly those in New South Wales whose memories still went back as far as the Moffitt Commission.

He may have avoided jail, but the specter of his corruption conviction followed Rooklyn for what remained of his life. Unlike with Moffitt, where Rooklyn was able to run far enough from the bad press to reinvent himself, he was an elderly man by the time he was convicted in Queensland, making it tough to recover and rebuild as he had before. His conviction meant he was forced to sell off his gambling interests and other businesses in Asia, forcing his once booming international empire into decline. Never properly recovering from his bout of ill health in 1992, Rooklyn died at his Vaucluse home in Sydney on July 10, 1996.[20] Just two days before, his old cohort Lewis, recently released from prison on community detention, had returned to the public eye in stunning fashion. He had participated in an interview with a Brisbane journalist, arranged by Tony Murphy, where he protested that his conviction was based on a "set up" perpetuated by the likes of Herbert, at the behest of enemies in the government—he was, from his own perspective, a political prisoner.[21] In the furor around Lewis's claims, it may have been easy for Queenslanders to miss Rooklyn's comparably quiet exit from the mortal stage. Even so, his death was marked by some willing to look past his convictions and recognize his contribution to Australian society. In recognition of his prowess on the water, the organizers of the annual Sydney to Hobart race announced that it would award the "Jack Rooklyn Memorial Trophy" to the first yacht to sprint out of Sydney Heads each year.[22] No matter the fall from grace of the late 1980s and early 1990s, at least in the yachting community the Rooklyn legacy seemingly remained intact.

Lewis continued to fight for his ownlegacy for years after leaving prison, still adamantly insisting that the evidence given about his corruption was part of a dishonest plot against him. Quite to his displeasure, the accusations of corruption against him were not rescinded, but renewed. Shortly after his release from prison, the *Courier-Mail* commenced publishing a series of articles alleging, among other things, that Lewis had kept "dirt files" on prominent individuals accused of child sexual abuse—reportedly to use for blackmail as much as to protect the accused.[23] Lewis denied these accusations, but nevertheless found himself once again in a familiar situation: As before, the bombshell media reporting led to a public commission being called in 1997, the Kimmins Inquiry. Ultimately, Kimmins rejected the idea that Lewis was extorting child sex offenders. Even so, the experience of yet another corruption inquiry was the last thing Lewis needed as he continued to try to clear his name and salvage a reputation that, in reality, was destroyed long ago.[24] Lewis was eventually released from community detention in a Brisbane halfway house and permitted to return to his family home on May 11, 1998—coincidentally (and ironically) eleven years to the day since "The Moonlight State" set his demise into motion.[25] Rather than withdrawing quietly into obscurity, Lewis continued to profess his innocence and, to the bitter end, fight to clear his name in the court of public opinion, albeit with little success.

Escaping the QPF before the storm of Fitzgerald, the other members of Lewis's Rat Pack were far more content than the former commissioner to drop out of the public eye. After leaving the police force in 1972, in the aftermath of the Dorothy Knight corruption sting, Glen Hallahan left Brisbane altogether, first buying and operating a small post office and, later, purchasing a farm north on the Sunshine Coast.[26] Despite his apparent adoption of a quiet rural life, rumors persisted that Hallahan continued to dabble in the criminal world. It was around this time that drug trafficker John Milligan told federal police (though later recanted) that he worked in partnership with the disgraced police officer on narcotics importations. Milligan also said Hallahan was part of a three-person group—the Rat Pack—that controlled organized crime in Queensland.[27] Hallahan went on to work as an insurance investigator in the 1990s before passing away after a long health battle in the midst of Lewis's trial on June 17, 1991, aged 59.[28] The final member of the trio, Tony Murphy, was assisted by the Lewis connection after his own 1982 retirement from the QPF. In 1983, Lewis appealed to his (and the premier's) friend Ted Lyons, head of state-run betting agency, the Totalisator Administration Board (TAB), to offer Murphy the license to run a TAB office on Stradbroke Island, off the southeast Queensland coast.[29] Despite being named repeatedly in testimony, Murphy was never called to testify before Fitzgerald—even so, he regularly attended the public hearings to observe from the back of the room and, after Lewis's conviction, wrote to his old mate in prison with both gossip from the police community and ideas of how to strike back at their shared enemies.[30] In 1994, he won a defamation case against the *Sun* newspaper group over an article published in 1988 that implied he was involved in organizing the deadly 1973 Whiskey Au Go Go nightclub fire.[31] Murphy died on December 21, 2010, aged 83. Having dodged most of the fallout of the Fitzgerald Inquiry, Murphy nonetheless remained under a cloud, fatefully linked to Lewis and Hallahan as part of the notorious Rat Pack.

Another person whose life and legacy would forever be inextricably linked to Lewis (and, indeed, Rooklyn) was Jack Herbert. After he completed his obligations as the state's star prosecution witness in the post-Fitzgerald corruption trials, Herbert and his wife Peggy retired to the Gold Coast. Like any typical retiree, Herbert spent his days by the ocean reading, drinking tea, and (occasionally) popping into the new, legal Jupiters Casino.[32] He died of brain cancer in April 2004, aged 79.[33] To the end, Lewis's feud with Herbert continued. Former police officer Ron Edington claimed that, hearing of Herbert's terminal illness, Lewis asked him to pass on a request to Herbert two months before his death, imploring him to compile a statement, to be released after he passed away, admitting to lying and absolving Lewis of blame. Herbert, reputedly furious, refused. Lewis, for his own part, denies making this bold request.[34]

Where Herbert escaped prison, others shared Lewis's fate after the Fitzgerald Inquiry, including the once ascendent Cabinet minister Don Lane. Lane was sent to prison even before Lewis, in 1990. He was not sentenced for his alleged involvement with Rooklyn or police corruption, but for the misuse of ministerial expenses, which he admitted to during the Fitzgerald proceedings.[35] Like Hallahan, Lane died young at 59, succumbing to a heart attack on his rural Warwick property on March 11, 1995.[36] Then there was Joh Bjelke-Petersen. The ignominy of being ousted as premier was not the last straw for Lewis's old ally; in 1991, he faced a criminal trial for perjury during his Fitzgerald Inquiry testimony, where he denied personally receiving corrupt "donations" from property developers. When it came time for the jury to consider its verdict, they could not come to an agreement and Bjelke-Petersen walked free. It was later revealed that the jury foreman, Luke Shaw, was a member of the Young National Party and part of the "Friends of Joh" campaign—he was also the holdout who refused to convict, allowing the premier to slip the net.[37] In spite of the suggestions of impropriety around his trial, Bjelke-Petersen was not retried and lived out the remainder of his life at his Kingaroy property. He died in April 2005, aged 94, and was awarded a state funeral in recognition of his contributions to the state of Queensland.[38]

While Rooklyn's story came to an end in Queensland, his old peers in Sydney continued to operate into the 1990s. Abe Saffron experienced a string of problems in the 1980s, many of which emanated from Juanita Nielsen's disappearance in July 1975. At the 1983 inquest into Nielsen's presumed murder, former Saffron deputy (and prolific police informant) Jim Anderson admitted that, when working for Saffron, he kept two sets of accounting records in order to hide illegal profits, a routine Saffron practice.[39] Anderson's revelations set the police on the new course, employing the "Capone approach" to taking down the once untouchable organized crime figure, and, in November 1987, he was found guilty of tax evasion and served 17 months in prison.[40] Famously litigious, Saffron threatened defamation suits against any publication connecting him with organized crime or using the moniker he hated so much, "Mr. Sin." He died on September 15, 2006, aged 86.[41]

Even after Saffron's death, accusations of his involvement in major criminal activity continued—including at least one instance reputedly involving Rooklyn. In March 2021 an ABC television documentary revived the idea that Saffron was responsible for the 1978 Luna Park Ghost Train Fire—previously blamed on an electrical fault, the fire at the amusement park claimed the lives of seven people, including six children.[42] The program made the case that Saffron, desperate to gain the lucrative rights to the Luna Park site, had commissioned persons unknown to set a fire that would cause enough damage to force redevelopment. Police who attended the scene of the fire included Bill Allen and Doug Knight, both officers implicated in corruption with Saffron and Rooklyn. Indeed, the ABC report even featured interviews with a witness who suggested Rooklyn had prior knowledge that the Luna Park fire was going to occur, connecting him to Saffron's alleged takeover scam. While these allegations against Saffron or Rooklyn have not been proven, it is true that a company connected to the Saffron family *did* gain the rights to the site after the fire and, further, Saffron was able to install at least 100 of his own gaming machines at Luna Park under this new management.[43]

Where Saffron struggled with the law in the 1980s, the decade was tough in a different way for Sydney's would-be mafiosos of the 1970s—George Freeman, Stan Smith, and Lennie McPherson. The boom in drug trafficking, especially heroin, sent Sydney's underworld into open warfare in 1984. The primary combatants were generally aligned with one of two groups: on one side, a contingent led by drug trafficker (and Murray Riley associate) Arthur "Neddy" Smith, Graham "Abo" Henry, and Christopher "Rent-a-Kill" Flannery; on the other, another narcotics consortium led by Barry McCann that allegedly consisted of players like Tom Domican, Kevin Theobald, and Victor Camilleri.[44] The warring parties engaged in a tit-for-tat conflict that resulted in a series of public shootings and the murder of several criminals aligned to one faction or the other.[45] In testimony to the Independent Commission Against Corruption (ICAC), Neddy Smith alleged that corrupt police like Roger Rogerson were also part of this gangland war, with Rogerson and other police allied with him choosing to partner with Smith's group.[46]

With the underworld in upheaval, there was little money to be made for old-school crims like Freeman, Smith, and McPherson. So, in 1985, the still-respected trio determined to use their influence to intervene and end the war once and for all. In cooperation with corrupt police like Rogerson, McPherson helped organize summits at the home of his associate Louis Bayeh to discuss a resolution. McPherson was in a perfect position to do this, as his long history in the Sydney criminal milieu meant he had strong connections on both sides of the conflict.[47] Together, the cabal was able to ease tensions and bring the gangland war to a conclusion, but not without at least one more apparent casualty. Flannery, one of Neddy Smith's crew, was considered by all (including his own allies) to be a loose cannon that would never stop his campaign of retribution against the other side. For peace to reign, Flannery would have to go. On May 9, 1985, the man dubbed "Rent-a-Kill" received a summons to attend a meeting with Freeman, his occasional employer. He was never seen again. Rumors in regard to his disappearance (and presumed murder) abound, but there is a general belief that he was killed because he was impossible to control, and without removing him from the playing field, the Sydney milieu could never return to their core business—making money.[48]

Despite their reputations still giving them influence in Sydney's underworld, the trio of Freeman, Smith, and McPherson never truly recaptured the heights of their power in the 1970s. After recovering from the 1979 shooting that almost claimed his life, Freeman returned to his gambling businesses, receiving convictions in 1983 and 1985 for illegal betting.[49] In all likelihood, these minor charges were just the tip of the iceberg, as Freeman's name continued to recur in royal commissions into organized crime in New South Wales for the remainder of the decade. Like so many of his era, Freeman died young—albeit not at the receiving end of a bullet. He died at age 55, on March 20, 1990, the result of an asthma attack. In addition, Freeman had developed a persistent addiction to the painkiller pethidine after his shooting over a decade earlier, and some suggest this factor added to his early death, if not being the direct cause.[50] McPherson was the next of the trio to meet his fate. As with Freeman, McPherson continued to be involved in organized crime after his role in ending the 1984–1985 gangland wars. Just as Freeman focused on his first love, gambling, McPherson returned to what he knew best: standover. Accused of muscling in on the construction industry in the early 1990s, McPherson was eventually convicted of commissioning the assault of a Sydney businessman in 1994 and sentenced to four years in prison. He died of a sudden heart attack at Cessnock Correction Centre on August 28, 1996.[51] Stan "The Man" Smith outlived his contemporaries by a significant stretch, dying on January 13, 2010. This can, perhaps, be attributed to a change of heart Smith experienced late in life. Though still listed as a prime target for police in the mid-1980s, Smith reputedly "found religion" in 2003 and began using his skills to manage legitimate enterprises.[52]

When last we checked in on Murray Riley, the former police officer turned narcotics baron had been released from prison in 1984 after serving time for the failed *Anoa* importation and, promptly, went back into business trafficking drugs with Neddy Smith, around the time the gangland wars were heating up.[53] The duo conspired to fly 50 kilograms of heroin into Australia via Papua New Guinea not long after Riley's release from prison, and from there they continued their working relationship for some period of time before Smith became too much of a liability. Smith was sent to prison himself in the late 1980s, convicted of killing brothel operator Harvey Jones and the unconnected road rage murder of tow truck driver Ronnie Flavell.[54] Meanwhile, Riley was embarking on a new and elaborate scam. He flew to the United Kingdom and opened a bank account on the Isle of Man, where he attempted to convince the manager that conglomerate British Aerospace would soon be depositing a substantial sum of money in the account as part of a "secret government operation to assist with the release of hostages in the Middle East."[55] It was Riley's plan to intercept British Aerospace's cash, but he was foiled and sentenced to five years imprisonment in 1991. Within a few months, he was out—but not through the leniency of the British government. Moved to a minimum security "prison farm" a matter of months after his sentence began, Riley simply walked out without the guards even noticing (in some versions of the story, his unlawful departure was not even reported for several weeks).[56] He was recaptured the following year, but had spent his time wisely, allegedly making contacts with the Provisional Irish Republican Army (PIRA). After again being assigned to a minimum-security facility in Kent, Riley escaped for a second time, reputedly going to work for the PIRA in a counterfeiting operation.[57] Later, he traveled to Hong Kong where he was met by girlfriend Carol Dean, once married to Wally Dean—best remembered as Riley's co-accused at the Moffitt inquiry.[58] He eventually did return to Australia, living under the radar and on the run for the rest of his life. He died in 2020, aged 94.[59]

At the time of his conviction in the *Anoa* case, it was rumored that Riley's importation was financed by one of the American Mafia figures who were often connected with the Sydney criminal milieu in the 1970s: Jimmy Fratianno and Danny Stein. It was not long after the *Anoa* incident that Fratianno turned government witness after being implicated in the bombing murder of Cleveland gangster Danny Greene and, reputedly, having a contract put out on his own life by his own Los Angeles Family.[60] As part of Fratianno's deal, he pleaded guilty to five counts of murder and served 21 months in prison. In return, his supergrass testimony resulted in racketeering convictions against five high-level Mafia figures and the promise of a lifetime in witness protection.[61] Fratianno was kicked out of witness protection in 1987 when a government audit revealed that the United States had spent more than $1 million on protecting the Fratianno family over 10 years. Still in hiding, Jimmy Fratianno died on June 29, 1993, aged 79.[62] For Stein, the former associate of Bugsy Siegel from the early Las Vegas era, life was a lot quieter than it was for Fratianno. Though he maintained ties with local crime figures like Freeman, the Australian government's decision to ban him from coming to the country put a damper on Stein's business interests in the country.[63] He settled in California, where he lived until his death on June 3, 2004, just shy of his 88th birthday. Stein was remembered as a "pioneer" of the Las Vegas casino world, someone who "believed in the old ways of Las Vegas, taking care of the customers."[64] There was some suggestion in the late 1970s that Stein, as a representative of Caesars Palace, was working with Sydney's illegal casino bosses to gain a foothold in the soon-to-be-legal casino market in New South Wales. For a number of reasons, not the least a series of lengthy delays in legalization, this never came to pass. The Darling Harbour Casino Act eventually passed in 1986; however, even then, a legal casino did not open until almost a decade later, in 1995.[65]

It was also the campaign to establish a casino that brought an end to a controversial and iconic period for the Bally empire. Once the savior of a flailing business, Bally president William O'Donnell was forced out in 1979 when the New Jersey Division of Gaming Enforcement declared him an unfit person to operate a casino because of his connections to organized crime.[66] Despite his protestations that it was *him* who had purged Bally of secret shareholders like Genovese underboss Gerry Catena, casino regulators in both New Jersey and Nevada remained unconvinced that Bally was a completely legitimate operation under O'Donnell's leadership.[67] Following O'Donnell's departure, the door was open for Bally to make an aggressive expansion and, in the 1980s, it acquired an entirely new portfolio of businesses including the Six Flags amusement park chain and several casinos in Las Vegas, going so far as to purchase the MGM Grand casino on the Las Vegas Strip and rename it "Bally's Las Vegas."[68] The shifting business model was such that, by 1994, Bally Manufacturing no longer existed—the company officially changed its name to "Bally Entertainment" to reflect the fact that it no longer produced gaming machines, but was now exclusively focused on its casino trade.[69] Soon after, in 1996, Bally was sold to the Hilton Hotels Corporation for a reported $2 billion.[70] Since then, the brand has changed ownership on several occasions, notably to both Harrah's and Caesars Entertainment. Despite this, the Bally name continues to shine in fluorescent neon lights over the Las Vegas Strip—a perpetual reminder of a company that, for all its faults, helped turn on the bright lights of that magical city in the desert.

The story of Bally is inextricably intertwined with the tale of Jack Rooklyn, a man who built his reputation in Australia as the quintessential cigar-chomping poker machine mogul with connections to American Mafia—a connection that was, almost exclusively, based on the proven links between Bally and organized crime. For so long, Rooklyn has been treated as a peripheral character in this narrative, lurking on the edges of the Moffitt Commission and, later, the Fitzgerald Inquiry without ever attracting full focus, which has been more focused on the colorful characters of the local milieu like Lennie McPherson, Murray Riley, or Jack Herbert. Instead, Rooklyn has been characterized in broad terms as a nefarious corrupter of police, associated with thugs willing to break the law to advance his interests. What has been missing is a more complete understanding of who Rooklyn actually was, and the events that led a Jewish immigrant boy growing up in the Hunter region north of Sydney to become so closely tied to an Italian American crime group based thousands of miles and an ocean away. While men like McPherson dreamed of carrying a tommy gun and being mentioned in the same breath as his idol, Al Capone, Rooklyn could do little to escape the mafioso label, especially after the Moffitt Commission laid the tattered history of his parent company Bally out in public for the entire world to see.

Back in the 1930s, few would have imagined that Rooklyn—the brother of magicians and vaudeville performers—would one day be a central focus in not one, but *two* of the most significant investigations into organized crime in Australian history. At first, Rooklyn seemed destined to follow his brothers into the entertainment business and, in a sense, he did. His prowess as a businessperson and his connections in the amusement trade put him in prime position to be chosen to run the recreational facility for US troops in Brisbane during World War II and, from there, his empire only grew. Rooklyn was far more than a Mafia-linked poker machine distributor. After learning from the likes of the great British entertainment czar Billy Butlin, he made a fortune bringing his products to Southeast Asia. He was no fringe player, but important, and capable, enough for Bally to buy his operation out and name him managing director of Bally Australia. He was also a big enough name for the Nevada gaming regulators to take note in the late 1970s, forcing his exit from the company that had facilitated his rise in the industry. For some, being dropped by Bally may have been the end, but not Rooklyn. Ever an adaptable operator, Rooklyn took his exit from Bally in stride and, heading north, reinvented his business model. With the assistance of connections like Jack Herbert and Terry Lewis, Rooklyn was able to rise again. But, like Icarus, one can only spend so long at the top of their game before the wings fall off, and they come crashing back to earth with a thud. Such was Rooklyn's fate, burned by a desperate whistle-blower backed into a corner, with no choice but to name names in return for his own freedom.

The Rooklyn story (and the other stories connected with it) spans at least four continents over an almost 90-year period—from Capone's Chicago, where Bally was born, to Lansky's Cuba, where the Mafia's gambling dreams were quashed in revolution. From the London of the Swinging Sixties, where Cellini held court at the Colony Club, to the bright lights of Siegel's Las Vegas, the city that would demonstrate what legal gambling could achieve. From Rooklyn's Singapore, where a fortune was made in a country rebuilding from the horrors of war, to Riley's Golden Triangle, where tonnes of marijuana were loaded onto boats destined for Australia and, possibly, beyond. From Freeman's illegal casinos in inner-city Sydney, to McPherson's local clubs in the suburbs, where he instilled fear and demanded loyalty with his thuggish standover tactics. From Lewis's furtive meetings in Brisbane hotel rooms, where the police commissioner accepted bribes, to Herbert's witness box at the Fitzgerald Inquiry, where an entire system of graft came crashing down. Rooklyn's story is important, but so too is the way it intersects with those mentioned, and many more. Together they paint the picture of an Australia that, far from being isolated from the world around it, was strongly linked with international organized crime in a range of ways. More than the story of one man, or several, it is a snapshot of an era in which Australia changed, growing from a relatively naïve (even, innocent) nation to one in which legal gambling was a possibility, the sex and drug trade thrived, and, ultimately, corruption and organized crime were simply facts of life.

NOTES

INTRODUCTION

1. "Summonses for Lewis, Rooklyn and 18 others," *Canberra Times*, July 27, 1989, 1; "Rooklyn guilty of corruption," *Canberra Times*, May 23, 1992, 1; Matt Condon, "Rooklyn's final curtain," *Sydney Morning Herald*, May 24, 1992, 15.

2. Chris Masters, "The Moonlight State [video]," *Four Corners*, May 11, 1987, Australian Broadcasting Corporation.

3. Gerald E. Fitzgerald, *Report of a Commission of Inquiry Pursuant to Orders in Council* (Brisbane, QLD: Commission of Inquiry into Possible Misconduct and Associated Police Misconduct, 1989), 3.

4. "Summonses for Lewis, Rooklyn," 1.

5. Charles Pickett, "Rooklyn, Israel (Jack) (1908–1996)," *Australian Dictionary of Biography* (Canberra, ACT: Australian National University, 2021), https://adb.anu.edu.au/biography/rooklyn-israel-jack-30530/text37850.

6. Athol Moffitt, *Report of the Honourable Mr Justice Moffitt Appointed to Inquire in Respect of Certain Matters Relating to Allegations of Organised Crime in Clubs* (Sydney, NSW: Government Printer, 1974), ii.

7. Ibid., 134.

8. Rosalind Smith, "Dark Places: True Crime Writing in Australia," *Journal of the Association for the Study of Australia Literature*, 8, 2008, 17.

9. Ibid.

10. Richard White, *Inventing Australia* (Abingdon, UK: Routledge, 2020), 1; Smith, "Dark Places," 17–18.

11. Scott Prasser, "The fate of inquiries: Will Fitzgerald be different?" in Scott Prasser, Rae Wear, and John Nethercote (eds.), *Corruption and Reform: The Fitzgerald Vision* (St Lucia, QLD: University of Queensland Press, 1990), 118.

12. John Scott, "'True Blue' Crimes and Other Infamous Aussie Yarns," *Journal of Commonwealth and Postcolonial Studies*, 17 (2), 2011, 112.

13. The Howard years mentioned here refers to the tenure of conservative John Howard as prime minister of Australia from 1996 to 2007—the second-longest serving term as prime minister after Robert Menzies. Melissa Gregg and Jason Wilson, "*Underbelly*, true crime and the cultural economy of infamy," *Continuum: Journal of Media & Cultural Studies*, 24 (3), 2010, 411.

14. Peter Coaldrake and John Wanna, "'Not like the good old days': The political impact of the Fitzgerald Inquiry into police corruption in Queensland," *Australian Quarterly*, 60 (4), 1988, 404.

15. See: Tony Reeves, *Mr Big: Lennie McPherson and His Life of Crime* (Crows Nest, NSW: Allen and Unwin, 2005); Tony Reeves, *The Real George Freeman* (Melbourne, VIC: Hybrid Publishers, 2013); *Underbelly: A Tale of Two Cities* (Nine Network Australia, 2009); *Underbelly: The Golden Mile* (Nine Network Australia, 2010).

16. Reeves, *Mr Big*, 181. For mischaracterization as American, see Jonathan Kwitny, *The Crimes of Patriots: A True Tale of Dope, Dirty Money, and the CIA* (New York City, NY: W. W. Norton, 1987), 231.

17. "Chicago chatter," *The Cash Box*, August 20, 1945, 10; "Coin Operated Radios Coming; An Australian Enterprise," *The Straits Times*, June 8, 1954, 12; Pickett, "Rooklyn, Israel (Jack)."

18. Jack Rooklyn, interview [audio], October 15, 1984, National Library of Australia, http://nla.gov.au/nla.obj-216953128.

19. Fitzgerald, *Report of a Commission*, 61; "Rooklyn guilty of corruption," 1.

20. Samuel Milner, *Victory in Papua* (Washington, DC: US Department of the Army, 1957), 48.

21. Moffitt, *Report of the Honourable Mr Justice Moffitt*, 134; Fitzgerald, *Report of a Commission*, 61.

22. *Bally's Park Place, Inc., In the Matter of the Application for a Casino License and the Application of Bally's Manufacturing Corporation for a Casino Service Industry License* [1978] 10 NJAR 356, 17–18.

23. Gregory H. Smith, letter, September 1, 1982, quoted in William V. Roth, *State Lotteries: An Overview* (Washington, DC: US Government Printing Service, 1984), 217.

24. *Bally's Park Place, Inc.*, 19–20; Ovid Demaris, *The Last Mafioso: The Treacherous World of Jimmy Fratianno* (New York City, NY: Bantam Books, 1981), 233.

25. John Lawrence Jiggens, "Marijuana Australia: Cannabis Use, Popular Culture, and the Americanisation of Drugs Policy in Australia, 1938–1988" (PhD thesis, Queensland University of Technology, 2004), 230–32.

26. Graham Huggan, "Cultural memory in postcolonial fiction: The uses and abuses of Ned Kelly," *Australian Literary Studies*, 20 (3), 2002, 142–43; Paul Bleakley, "A new front in the history wars? Responding to Rubenhold's feminist revision of the Ripper," *Criminology and Criminal Justice*, doi: 0.1177/1748895821992460, 1–2.

27. Gregg and Wilson, "*Underbelly*, true crime and the cultural economy of infamy," 411–12.

28. Lois Presser and Sveinung Sandberg, "Narrative Criminology as Critical Criminology," *Critical Criminology*, 27, 2019, 131–32.

29. Kester Aspden and Keith J. Hayward, "Narrative Criminology and Cultural Criminology: Shared Biographies, Different Lives," in Lois Presser and Sveinung Sandberg (eds.), *Narrative Criminology: Understanding Stories of Crime* (New York City, NY: New York University Press, 2015), 235.

30. See full explanation in Paul Bleakley, *Under a Bad Sun: Police, Politics and Corruption in Australia* (East Lansing, MI: Michigan State University Press, 2021).

31. Sveinung Sandberg, "What can 'lies' tell us about life? Notes towards a Framework of Narrative Criminology," in Heith Copes (ed.), *Advancing Qualitative Methods in Criminology and Criminal Justice* (London, UK: Routledge, 2019), 44.

32. Paul Bleakley and Thomas J. Kehoe, "Historical Criminology as a Field for Interdisciplinary Research and Trans-Disciplinary Discourse," in Thomas J. Kehoe and Jeffrey E. Pfeifer (eds.), *History and Crime: A Transdisciplinary Approach* (Bingley, UK: Emerald, 2021), 125.

33. Henry Yeomans, David Churchill, and Iain Channing, "Conversations in a Crowded Room: An Assessment of the Contribution of Historical Research to Criminology," *Howard Journal*, 59 (3), 2020, 254.

34. Rooklyn, interview [audio].

35. Demaris, *The Last Mafioso*.

36. Christian Marfels, *Bally: The World's Game Maker* (Las Vegas, NV: UNLV International Gaming Institute, 2001), 2–7.

1

1. Christian Marfels, *Bally: The World's Game Maker* (Las Vegas, NV: UNLV International Gaming Institute, 2001), 2.

2. Alexander Smith, *They Create Worlds: The Story of the People and Companies That Shaped the Video Game Industry, Vol I: 1971–1982* [online] (Boca Raton, FL: CRC Press, 2020).

3. Rufus King, "Pinball Problem in Illinois—An Overdue Solution," *Journal of Criminal Law and Criminology*, 57 (1), 1966, 19.

4. Rick Kogan, "Historic Chicago Taverns: How about another round?" *Chicago Tribune*, August 27, 2015, https://www.chicagotribune.com/entertainment/museums/ct-chicago-tavern-history-2-story.html.

5. Richard M. Bueschel, *Encyclopedia of Pinball, Vol. 1* (LaGrangeville, NY: The Pinball Resource, 1996), 22.

6. Marfels, *Bally*, 6–7.

7. Arvind Rangaswamy, Raymond R. Burke, and Terence A. Oliva, "Brand equity and the extendibility of brand names," *International Journal of Research in Marketing*, 10 (1), 1993, 61–62.

8. Marfels, *Bally*, 7–8; Troy Cooper, "'You can fool some of the people some of the time': Perspective by incongruity in *Ballyhoo* magazine, 1931–1932" (PhD thesis, University of Illinois Urbana-Champaign, 2014), 2.

9. *Bally's Park Place, Inc., In the Matter of the Application for a Casino License and the Application of Bally's Manufacturing Corporation for a Casino Service Industry License* [1978] 10 NJAR 356, 17.

10. Smith, *They Create Worlds*.

11. Ibid.

12. Ibid.

13. Marshall A. Fey, "Charles Fey and San Francisco's Liberty Bell Slot Machine," *California Historical Quarterly*, 54 (1), 1975, 57–58.

14. "New law bans slot machines," *San Francisco Call*, April 6, 1909, 33; Roger Dunstan, *Gambling in California* (Sacramento, CA: California Research Bureau, California State Library, 1997), 6.

15. Edward Behr, *Prohibition: Thirteen Years That Changed America* (New York City, NY: Arcade, 1996), 81.

16. Ibid., 177.

17. Ovid Demaris, *The Last Mafioso: The Treacherous World of Jimmy Fratianno* (New York City, NY: Bantam Books, 1981), 228.

18. Smith, *They Create Worlds*.

19. Marfels, *Bally*, 2.

20. Smith, *They Create Worlds*.

21. Marfels, *Bally*, 3.

22. Ibid., 3–4.

23. Tim O'Reiley, "Legalizing casino gambling helped revive Nevada 80 years ago," *Las Vegas Review Journal*, March 27, 2011, https://www.reviewjournal.com/business/casinos-gaming/legalizing-casino-gambling-helped-revive-nevada-80-years-ago/.

24. Shannon Bybee, "History, Development, and Legislation of Las Vegas Casino Gaming," in Cathy Ho Hsu (ed.), *Legalized Casino Gaming in the United States: The Economic and Social Impact* (Binghamton, NY: Haworth Press, 2013), 4–6.

25. Jeff Burbank, *Las Vegas Babylon: The True Tales of Glitter, Glamour, and Greed* (Lanham, MD: M. Evans, 2008), 37–38.

26. William R. Wilkerson, *The Man Who Invented Las Vegas* (Bellingham, WA: Ciro's Books, 2000), 62.

27. Conny B. McCormack, "Certificate of Death: Benjamin Siegel," *County of Los Angeles*, July 1, 1947, 1.

28. James M. O'Kane, *The Crooked Ladder: Gangsters, Ethnicity and the American Dream* (New Brunswick, NJ: Transaction Publishers, 2009), 69.

29. Ed Koch and Mary Manning, "Mob Ties," *Las Vegas Sun*, May 15, 2008, https://m.lasvegassun.com/news/2008/may/15/mob-ties/.

30. William Brashler, "Big Tuna," *Chicago Tribune*, November 18, 1984, 17.

31. Koch and Manning, "Mob Ties."

32. "Phoenix couple murdered: Greenbaums gang victims?" *Arizona Republic*, December 4, 1958, 1.

33. John Kass, "Unlike his many victims, hitman dies a quiet death," *Chicago Tribune*, September 12, 2003, https://www.chicagotribune.com.news.ct-xpm-2003–09–12–0309120427-story.html.

34. Marfels, *Bally*, 13–14.

35. "Pinball Machines Loses in Supreme Court Tilt," *New York Times*, June 18, 1957, 21.

36. "Ban on Shipping Slot Machines Hits City Firms," *Chicago Tribune*, January 3, 1951, 7.

37. Smith, *They Create Worlds*.

38. "Ban on Shipping," 7.

39. Oren Harris, *Hearings Before the Committee on Interstate and Foreign Commerce, House of Representatives, Eighty-Seventh Congress* (Washington, DC: Committee on Interstate and Foreign Commerce, 1962), 130.

40. Heidi McNeil Staudenmaier and Andrew D. Lynch, "The Class II Gaming Debate: The Johnson Act vs. The Indian Gaming Regulatory Act," *Gaming Law Review*, 8 (4), 2004, 228–29.

41. T. J. English, *Havana Nocturne: How the Mob Owned Cuba and Then Lost It to the Revolution* (New York City, NY: William Morrow, 2008), 15–16.

42. Peter Schneider, "Havana, Cuba: Contraband Capitalism and Criminal Organization in North America," *Italian American Review*, 6 (1), 2016, 21–22.

43. English, *Havana Nocturne*, 318.

44. "Batista and Regime Flee Cuba; Castro Moving to Take Power; Mobs Riot and Loot in Havana," *New York Times*, January 2, 1959, 1; Phillip Crawford Jr., "Meyer Lansky in His Own Words," *Medium*, July 22, 2020, https://medium.com/@phillipcrawfordjr/meyer-lansky-in-his-own-words-a096367afc4b.

45. Shekhar Bhatia, "Exclusive: Give us back the empire built on mob blood money: Mobster Meyer Lansky's family tell of fight to get his Havana hotel and casino back from Castro's clutches after Obama's end to embargo," *Daily Mail*, December 23, 2015, https://www.dailymail.co.uk/news/article-3369434/Give-empire-built-blood-money-Notorious-Mafia-figure-s-family-tell-fight-Havana-hotel-casino-Castro-s-clutches-Obama-s-end-embargo.html.

46. Howard J. Osborn, "Family Jewels," Central Intelligence Agency, May 16, 1973, 1–5.

47. "Obituaries," *Chicago Tribune*, February 27, 1958, 52; Smith, *They Create Worlds.*

48. *Bally's Park Place, Inc.*, 9.

49. Ibid., 15.

50. Marfels, *Bally*, 26–28.

51. Ibid., 29.

52. *Bally's Park Place, Inc.*, 15–16.

53. King, "Pinball Problem," 22–23.

54. *Bally's Park Place, Inc.*, 16; Nelson Johnson, *Boardwalk Empire: The Birth, High Times and the Corruption of Atlantic City* (London, UK: Ebury Press, 2011), 215.

55. *Bally's Park Place, Inc.*, 16.

56. Johnson, *Boardwalk Empire*, 215.

57. Estes Kefauver, *The Kefauver Committee Report on Organized Crime* (New York City, NY: Didier, 1951), 105; Arthur L. Reuter, *Report on the Activities and Associations of Persons Identified as Present at the Residence of Joseph Barbara, Sr., at Apalachin, New York, on November 14, 1957, and the Reasons for Their Presence: Appendix C* (Albany, NY: State of New York Executive Department, 1958), 12.

58. Reuter, *Report on the Activities*, 12–13.

59. Ibid., 12.

60. William Donati, *Lucky Luciano: The Rise and Fall of a Mob Boss* (Jefferson, NC: McFarland and Company, 2010), 31.

61. G. Robert Blakey, *Organized Crime in the United States: A Review of the Public Record* (Notre Dame, IN: Notre Dame-Temple Organized Crime Research Program, 1982), 120–21.

62. Donati, *Lucky Luciano*, 201.

63. Jeffrey Sussman, *Big Apple Gangsters: The Rise and Decline of the Mob in New York* (Lanham, MD: Rowman & Littlefield, 2020), 38.

64. English, *Havana Nocturne*, 28.

65. Joe Bonanno and Sergio Lalli, *A Man of Honor: The Autobiography of Joseph Bonanno* (New York City, NY: St. Martin's, 1983), 172.

66. Emanuel Perlmutter, "Syndicate Cities Listed by Valachi," *New York Times*, October 10, 1963, 44.

67. Blakey, *Organized Crime in the United States*, 104–5.

68. Ibid., 108–9.

69. Kefauver, *The Kefauver Committee*, 101; Reuter, *Report on the Activities*, 13.

70. Carl Sifakis, *The Mafia Encyclopedia*, 3rd ed. (New York City, NY: Facts on File, 2005), 186.

71. Charles Grutzner, "Jailing of Catena, Genovese's Successor, Is Viewed as Weakening Mafia 'Family,'" *New York Times*, October 11, 1970, 78; Blakey, *Organized Crime in the United States*, 119.

72. *Bally's Park Place, Inc.*, 18.

73. Ken Miller, "How Bally Manufacturing Cleaned Up Its Act," *Reno Gazette-Journal*, March 30, 1986, 20.

74. *Bally's Park Place, Inc.*, 18; Miller, "How Bally Manufacturing Cleaned Up," 20.

75. *Bally's Park Place, Inc.*, 17.

76. Ibid., 16–17.

77. Ibid., 17.

78. *Catena v Seidl* (1975) 68 NJ 224, 343 A.2d 744.

79. Douglas Thompson, *Shadowland: How the Mafia Bet Britain in a Global Gamble* [ebook] (Edinburgh, UK: Mainstream Publishing, 2011).

80. Federal Bureau of Investigation (New York Office), "American Gambling Activities in Cuba," interoffice memo, June 16, 1958, 5.

81. *Bally's Park Place, Inc.*, 19–20.

82. Ibid., 20.

83. Gregory H. Smith, letter, September 1, 1982, quoted in William V. Roth, *State Lotteries: An Overview* (Washington, DC: US Government Printing Service, 1984), 215.

84. *Bally's Park Place, Inc.*, 20.

85. "Lansky indicted in U.S. tax plot," *New York Times*, June 7, 1972, 21.

86. *Bally's Park Place, Inc.*, 20.

87. "Informer names crime kingpins," *Daily Banner* (Greencastle, IN), October 2, 1963, 2.

88. Miller, "How Bally Manufacturing Cleaned Up," 20.

89. *Bally's Park Place, Inc.*, 21–23.

90. "Ex-Officer, Pinball Men Sentenced," *Town Talk* (Alexandria, LA), January 24, 1974, 28; *Bally's Park Place, Inc.*, 26.

91. Ronald Goldfarb, "What the Mob Knew About JFK's Murder," *Washington Post*, March 14, 1993, https://www.washingtonpost.com/archive/opinions/1993/03/14/what-the-mob-knew-about-jfks-murder/9803e911-f52f-4944–88f1-c26863e35867/.

92. Jack Brooks, "Forced to Lie by U.S. Government; Investigator Says He Framed Garrison," *Vancouver Sun*, May 23, 1972, 1.

93. *Bally's Park Place, Inc.*, 20–21.

94. Smith in Roth, *State Lotteries*, 216–17.

95. Ibid., 215–16.

96. Ibid., 216.

97. *Bally's Park Place, Inc.*, 44–45, 50–51.

98. Ibid., 3.

99. Ibid., 1.

100. John Mintz, "Gambling Industry Agog," *Washington Post*, January 4, 1981, https://www.washingtonpost.com/archive/business/1981/01/04/gambling-industry-agog/75df27d1-4714–4e75-8ba5–9b458afe7822/.

101. Smith in Roth, *State Lotteries*, 217.

2

1. Charles Pickett, "Rooklyn, Israel (Jack) (1908–1996)," *Australian Dictionary of Biography* (Canberra, ACT: Australian National University, 2021), https://adb.anu.edu.au/biography/rooklyn-israel-jack-30530/text37850.

2. Derek Beattie, *Blackburn: The Development of a Lancashire Cotton Town* (Keele, UK: Keele University Press, 1992), 17.

3. "Jewish Massacre Denounced," *New York Times*, April 28, 1903, 6.

4. Rhoda G. Lewin, "Stereotype and reality in the Jewish immigrant experience in Minneapolis," *Minnesota History*, 46 (7), 1979, 259.

5. Jack Rooklyn, interview [audio], October 15, 1984, National Library of Australia, http://nla.gov.au/nla.obj-216953128.

6. Picket, "Rooklyn, Israel (Jack)."

7. Andrew Taylor, *20th Century Blackburn* (Barnsley, UK: Wharncliffe Books, 2000), 11.

8. Ibid., 24.

9. Rooklyn, interview [audio]; Pickett, "Rooklyn, Israel (Jack)."

10. Pickett, "Rooklyn, Israel (Jack)."

11. Evan Whitton, "Allan, Norman Thomas (1909–1977)," *Australian Dictionary of Biography* (Canberra, ACT: Australian National University, 1993), https://adb.anu.edu.au/biography/allan-norman-thomas-9333.

12. Rooklyn, interview [audio].

13. Ibid.

14. "The Fire at Brooklyn's; Inquiry Held; An Open Verdict," *Singleton Argus*, March 12, 1927, 8.

15. Ibid.

16. "Singleton Fire; An Open Verdict," *Maitland Daily Mercury*, March 10, 1927, 5.

17. Charles Pickett, "Rooklyn, Maurice (1905–1992)," *Australian Dictionary of Biography* (Canberra, ACT: Australian National University, 2021), https://adb.anu.edu.au/biography/rooklyn-maurice-31260.

18. Maurice Rooklyn, *Spherical Sorcery and Recollections of a Pro* (Sydney, NSW: Emmar Investments, 1973).

19. Ibid.

20. Ibid.

21. Pickett, "Rooklyn, Maurice."

22. "Ike Beck's Vaudeville," *Cessnock Eagle and South Maitland Recorder*, October 28, 1932, 2; Pickett, "Rooklyn, Maurice."

23. "Marriages celebrated during the year," *Hebrew Standard of Australasia*, September 10, 1926, 12; Pickett, "Rooklyn, Maurice."

24. Rooklyn, interview [audio].

25. Ibid.; Matt Condon, "Rooklyn's final curtain," *Sydney Morning Herald*, May 24, 1992, 15.

26. Rooklyn, interview [audio].

27. "Case listed for to-day," *Daily Telegraph*, September 24, 1931, 10.

28. "Quarter Sessions," *Sydney Morning Herald*, September 26, 1931, 10.

29. Ibid.

30. "Maccabean Institute; Last Sunday's Concert," *Hebrew Standard of Australasia*, September 15, 1933, 9.

31. Monica Crouch, "Harry Rickards: The Napoleon of Vaudeville," *Australasian Drama Studies*, 0 (73), 1990, 73.

32. Pickett, "Rooklyn, Israel (Jack)."

33. Pickett, "Rooklyn, Maurice."

34. Bob Cameron, "Magician Keeps Vow of Silence," *Sun Herald* (Sydney), March 24, 1974, 19.

35. "'Human Target' Explains It," *Labor Daily*, March 10, 1934, 5.

36. "'Human Target' Trick Goes Wrong; Performer Shot in Head," *The Argus*, May 7, 1934, 9.

37. Pickett, "Rooklyn, Maurice."

38. Condon, "Rooklyn's final curtain," 15.

39. Rooklyn, interview [audio].

40. Ibid.

41. "Amusement Machine Bargains," *The Mercury* (Hobart), November 26, 1938, 8.

42. Rooklyn, interview [audio].

43. Ibid.

44. John O'Hara, *A Mug's Game: A History of Gaming and Betting in Australia* (Sydney, NSW: NSW University Press, 1988), 198–99.

45. "Fruit Machine Inquiry; Why Licences Were Granted by Lang Government; Ex-Minister Gives Evidence," *Australian Worker*, September 28, 1932, 8.

46. "Fruit Machines to Be Banned; Minister's Decision," *Tweed Daily*, May 21, 1932, 4.

47. Geoffrey Thomas Caldwell, "Leisure co-operatives: the institutionalisation of gambling and the growth of large leisure organisations in New South Wales" (PhD thesis, Canberra, ACT: Australian National University, 1972), 97.
48. Michael Duffy and Nick Horden, *World War Noir* [ebook] (Sydney, NSW: NewSouth Publishing, 2019).
49. Mark Johnston, *The Australian Army in World War II* (Oxford, UK: Osprey Publishing, 2013), 8.
50. Claire Phelan and Janet Adamski, "From Mystery to Memory: The Loss of HMAS *Sydney*," *Journal of Maritime Archaeology*, 15, 2020, 283.
51. Scott D. Sagan, "The Origins of the Pacific War," *Journal of Interdisciplinary History*, 18 (4), 1988, 893.
52. Rooklyn, interview [audio].
53. Duffy and Horden, *World War Noir*.
54. "Registered firms," *Dun's Gazette for New South Wales*, January 23, 1942, 4.
55. Nicholas Anderson, *To Kokoda* (Sydney, NSW: Big Sky Publishing, 2014), 27–39.
56. Rooklyn, interview [audio].
57. Samuel Milner, *Victory in Papua* (Washington, DC: US Department of the Army, 1957), 48.
58. "United States forces in Queensland, 1941–45," *National Archives of Australia*, http://www.naa.gov.au/collection/fact-sheets/fs234.aspx.
59. John Hammond Moore, *Over-Sexed, Over-Paid and Over-Here: Americans in Australia, 1942–1945* (Brisbane, QLD: University of Queensland Press, 1981), 100.
60. Rooklyn, interview [audio].
61. "Bowls Alleys at USA Club," *The Telegraph* (Brisbane), September 15, 1943, 3.
62. "1 Man Killed, 8 Injured in City," *The Courier-Mail*, November 27, 1942, 3.
63. "Big American Centre Open," *The Courier-Mail*, July 5, 1943, 3; "Upkeep of Lavish American Centre Was £2,000 Weekly," *The Courier-Mail*, January 3, 1945, 3.
64. "Upkeep of Lavish American Centre," 3.
65. "Boy Killed By Slot Machine," *Daily Telegraph*, April 3, 1943, 5.
66. William Mackay, *Annual Report of the New South Wales Police Force* (Sydney, NSW: Police Department, 1943), 11.
67. Duffy and Horden, *World War Noir*.
68. Hyman Rooklyn, building survey card, April 24, 1944, City of Sydney Archives IDA-00509426, 1.
69. "Records of General Headquarters Southwest Pacific Area (GHQ SWPA)," *National Archives* (USA), https://www.archives.gov/research/guide-fed-records/groups/331.html.
70. "American Centre in Brisbane to Close Down," *The Telegraph* (Brisbane), December 27, 1944, 3.
71. "Offer to Take Over American Centre Rejected," *Morning Bulletin* (Rockhampton), January 17, 1945, 3.
72. "Chicago chatter," *The Cash Box*, August 20, 1945, 10.
73. "For Sale," *Sydney Morning Herald*, December 16, 1946, 11.
74. "For Sale," *Sydney Morning Herald*, April 19, 1948, 6.

75. Pickett, "Rooklyn, Israel (Jack)."

76. Rooklyn, interview [audio].

77. Billy Butlin, *The Billy Butlin Story: A Showman to the End* (London, UK: Robson Books, 1993).

78. Ibid.

79. Rooklyn, interview [audio].

80. Jennifer O'Brien, "New golden age for the holiday camp," *The Times*, May 26, 2017, https://www.thetimes.co.uk/article/new-golden-age-for-the-holiday-camp-bdl3xq6fz.

81. "Dollar tourist plan fails," *Sunday Herald* (Sydney), November 5, 1950, 12.

82. Pickett, "Rooklyn, Israel (Jack)."

83. "Union Bans the Ballet Girls," *Sydney Morning Herald*, October 6, 1950, 6.

84. "Round the Wax Circle; Chicago," *The Cash Box*, July 7, 1951, 7.

85. Gregg Huff and Gillian Huff, "The Second World War Japanese Occupation of Singapore," *Journal of Southeast Asian Studies*, 51 (1–2), 2020, 243–44.

86. "Coin Operated Radios Coming; An Australian Enterprise," *Straits Times*, June 8, 1954, 12.

87. "And Now Dogs; Government to Hear Proposal For Night Greyhound Racing in Singapore," *Straits Times*, June 25, 1955, 5.

88. "Butlin Camp for Millionaires?" *Singapore Free Press*, July 2, 1948, 3.

89. "And Now Dogs," 5.

90. "Going to the dogs: Two views—yes, no," *Straits Times*, June 29, 1955, 4.

91. Peter Corris, "Miller, Henry Lawrence (Harry) (1913–1972)," *Australian Dictionary of Biography* (Canberra, ACT: Australian National University, 2000), https://adb.anu.edu.au/biography/miller-henry-lawrence-harry-11124.

92. Cyril Pearl, "John Wren: Gambler, His Life and Times [review]," *Sydney Morning Herald*, December 18, 1971, 18.

93. James Griffin, "Wren, John (1871–1953)," *Australian Dictionary of Biography* (Canberra, ACT: Australian National University, 1990), https://adb.anu.edu.au/biography/wren-john-9198.

94. "Cohen gains world bantam title," *Advocate* (Tasmania), September 20, 1954, 15.

95. Pickett, "Rooklyn, Israel (Jack)"; Rooklyn, interview [audio].

96. Pickett, "Rooklyn, Israel (Jack)."

97. Evan Whitton, "Trial by Voodoo: Why the Law Defeats Justice and Democracy; How to Investigate the Truth," *Networked Knowledge*, http://netk.net.au/Whitton/TBV27.asp.

98. Ong Chit Chung, "The 1959 Singapore General Election," *Journal of Southeast Asian Studies*, 6 (1), 2011, 61–62.

99. C. J. W. L. Wee, "'Asian values,' Singapore, and the Third Way: Re-Working Individualism and Collectivism," *Sojourn: Journal of Social Issues in Southeast Asia*, 14 (2), 1999, 332–33.

100. Tony Reeves, *The Real George Freeman: Thief, Race-Fixer, Standover Man and Underworld Crim* (Melbourne, VIC: Penguin Australia, 2011), 100.

3

1. Charles Pickett, "Rooklyn, Israel (Jack) (1908–1996)," *Australian Dictionary of Biography* (Canberra, ACT: Australian National University, 2021), https://adb.anu.edu.au/biography/rooklyn-israel-jack-30530/text37850; Jack Rooklyn, interview [audio], October 15, 1984, National Library of Australia, http://nla.gov.au/nla.obj-216953128.

2. Alexander Smith, *They Create Worlds: The Story of the People and Companies That Shaped the Video Game Industry, Vol I: 1971–1982* [online] (Boca Raton, FL: CRC Press, 2020).

3. Allan Victor Maxwell, *Report of the Royal Commission on Liquor Laws in New South Wales* (Sydney, NSW: Government Printer, 1954), 1–3.

4. Walter Phillips, "'Six o'clock swill': The introduction of early closing of hotel bars in Australia," *Historical Studies*, 19 (75), 1980, 250.

5. Shane Robert Homan, "The mayor's a square: A regulatory history of Sydney's rock venues, 1957–1997" (BA (Hons) thesis, University of Western Sydney, 1999), 133.

6. Michael Sturma, "Gordon, Lee Lazer (1923–1963)," *Australian Dictionary of Biography* (Canberra, ACT: Australian National University, 1996), https://adb.anu.edu.au/biography/gordon-lee-lazer-10332.

7. Ibid.

8. Rooklyn, interview [audio].

9. "Cohen gains world bantam title," *Advocate* (Tasmania), September 20, 1954, 15.

10. Lucy Desoto, *Australia Rocks: Remembering the Music of the 1950s to 1990s* [ebook] (East Gosford, NSW: Exisle Publishing, 2016), Chapter 1.

11. Arthur L. Reuter, *Report on the Activities and Associations of Persons Identified as Present at the Residence of Joseph Barbara, Sr., at Apalachin, New York, on November 14, 1957, and the Reasons for Their Presence: Appendix C* (Albany, NY: State of New York Executive Department, 1958), 13.

12. Mary Helen Gillespie, "Three Men Convicted in Federal Extortion-Conspiracy Trial," *Associated Press*, May 26, 1988, https://apnews.com/article/f9a700ba8684d580095e773c961b5de4.

13. Louis Nowra, *Kings Cross: A Biography* (Sydney, NSW: NewSouth, 2013), 312–13.

14. Sturma, "Gordon, Lee Lazer."

15. Tony Reeves, *Mr Sin: The Abe Saffron Dossier* (Crows Nest, NSW: Allen and Unwin, 2007), 7.

16. Ibid., 8–9.

17. Ibid., 14–17.

18. "Abe Saffron's place still going strong; Sly grog 5'6 a bottle at the Roosevelt," *The Sun* (Sydney), November 25, 1951, 5.

19. Reeves, *Mr Sin*, 36.

20. "Decision reserved on indictment," *Daily Telegraph*, November 12, 1952; Reeves, *Mr Sin*, 46–47.

21. Reeves, *Mr Sin*, 58–59.

22. "Scandalous behaviour charges," *Central Queensland Herald*, November 1, 1956, 15; "Three to face trial on morals charge," *Canberra Times*, February 19, 1957, 8.

23. Reeves, *Mr Sin*, 67.

24. Jack Rooklyn, "252 Pitt St. J. Rooklyn (Rooklyn Investments Pty. Ltd.). To use ground floor for purposes of an amusement arcade and to carry out alterations," October 15, 1959 to January 4, 1960, City of Sydney Archives IDA-00130680, 1.

25. April Hersey, "The Sub-Teens," *The Bulletin*, February 10, 1968, 23.

26. Ibid.

27. *Bally's Park Place, Inc., In the Matter of the Application for a Casino License and the Application of Bally's Manufacturing Corporation for a Casino Service Industry License* [1978] 10 NJAR 356, 16.

28. Evan Whitton, "Allan, Norman Thomas (1909–1977)," *Australian Dictionary of Biography* (Canberra, ACT: Australian National University, 1993), https://adb.anu.edu.au/biography/allan-norman-thomas-9333.

29. Denis Freney, "Exposing the dirty underside of NSW politics," *Tribune* (Sydney), April 17, 1985, 10.

30. David Hickie, *The Prince and the Premier* (Sydney, NSW: Harper Collins Australia, 1985), 59.

31. Kate McClymont, "Saffron's son: Dad paid off Askin and lent Packer money," *Sydney Morning Herald*, July 28, 2008, https://www.smh.com.au/national/saffrons-son-dad-paid-off-askin-and-lent-packer-money-20080728-gdso04.html.

32. David Hickie, "The Askin Legacy: How organized crime became a Sydney institution," *Canberra Times*, March 24, 1985, 36.

33. Murray Goot, "Askin, Sir Robert William (Bob) (1907–1981)," *Australian Dictionary of Biography* (Canberra, ACT: Australian National University, 2007), https://adb.anu.edu.au/biography/askin-sir-robert-william-bob-12152.

34. Ibid.

35. Hickie, "The Askin Legacy," 37.

36. Bob Bottom, "The Mafia Connection," *The Age*, September 9, 1985, 11.

37. Ibid.

38. "Lansky indicted by Las Vegas jury," *New York Times*, October 23, 1971, 16; Bottom, "The Mafia Connection," 11.

39. Bottom, "The Mafia Connection," 11.

40. *Bally's Park Place, Inc.*, 19–20.

41. Bottom, "The Mafia Connection," 11.

42. Tony Reeves, *Mr Big: Lennie McPherson and His Life of Crime* (Crows Nest, NSW: Allen and Unwin, 2005), 160.

43. Michael Corbitt, testimony, August 13, 1997, Office of the Independent Hearing Officer, Laborers' International Union of North America, Chicago City Counsel Docket No. 97–30T, http://laborers_chicago.tripod.com/Corbitt_testimony.html.

44. Bob Bottom, "The Mafia Connection," 11.

45. Michael Newton, *The Mafia at Apalachin* (Jefferson, NC: McFarland and Company, 2012), 99.

46. Carl Sifakis, *The Mafia Encyclopedia* (New York City, NY: Da Capo Press, 2005), 177.

47. Corbitt, testimony; Reeves, *Mr Big*, 159.

48. James Mateja, "Hit Trailer Court Expansion Plans," *Chicago Tribune*, September 24, 1967, 370.

49. Ann McFeatters, "Ousted Official to Appeal," *Chicago Tribune*, June 23, 1968, 63.

50. Corbitt, testimony.

51. Tony Reeves, *The Real George Freeman* (Melbourne, VIC: Hybrid Publishers, 2013), 73–74.

52. David Hickie, "The Illegal Casinos under Askin: How they became the criminals' laundromat," *Sydney Morning Herald*, March 25, 1985, 6–7.

53. Hickie, "The Askin Legacy," 36.

54. Bottom, "The Mafia Connection," 11.

55. Reeves, *Mr Big*, 11–12.

56. Malcolm Brown, "McPherson, Leonard Arthur (Lenny) (1921–1996)," *Australian Dictionary of Biography* (Canberra, ACT: Australian National University, 2020), https://adb.anu.edu.au/biography/mcpherson-leonard-arthur-lenny-23076.

57. Reeves, *Mr Big*, 59.

58. Ibid., 78.

59. Brown, "McPherson, Leonard Arthur."

60. Reeves, *The Real George Freeman*, 44–45.

61. Malcolm Brown, "Smith, Stanley John (Stan) (1937–2010)," *Obituaries Australia* (Canberra, ACT: Australian National University, 2010), https://oa.anu.edu.au/obituary/smith-stanley-john-stan-16917.

62. Richard Hall, *Disorganized Crime* (St Lucia, QLD: University of Queensland Press, 1986), 81.

63. G. P. Walsh, "Freeman, George David (1935–1990)," *Australian Dictionary of Biography* (Canberra, ACT: Australian National University, 2007), https://adb.anu.edu.au/biography/freeman-george-david-12512; Reeves, *The Real George Freeman*, 44–45.

64. Ibid., 62–64.

65. Nowra, *Kings Cross*, 333.

66. John Lawrence Jiggens, "Marijuana Australia: Cannabis Use, Popular Culture, and the Americanisation of Drugs Policy in Australia, 1938–1988" (PhD thesis, Queensland University of Technology, 2004), 166.

67. Nowra, *Kings Cross*, 333–34.

68. Hall, *Disorganized Crime*, 44; Meredith H. Lair, *Armed with Abundance: Consumerism and Soldiering in the Vietnam War* (Chapel Hill, NC: University of North Carolina Press, 2011), 111.

69. "'Cocaine blamed' responsible for Sydney's crimes?" *Daily Telegraph*, August 31, 1928, 4; Larry Writer, *Razor: A True Story of Slashers, Gangsters, Prostitutes and Sly Grog* (Sydney, NSW: Macmillan, 2001), 38.

70. Alvin M. Shuster, "G.I. Heroin Epidemic in Vietnam," *New York Times*, May 16, 1971, 1.

71. Jiggens, "Marijuana Australia," 166–67.

72. Peter Butt, *Merchants of Menace: The True Story of the Nugan Hand Bank Scandal* (Sydney, NSW: Blackwattle Press, 2015), 35–36.

73. Ibid., 26–27, 35–36.

74. Reeves, *Mr Big*, 104–5.
75. "Underworld War; 80 See Hired Gunman Die," *Canberra Times*, May 29, 1967, 3.
76. Reeves, *The Real George Freeman*, 88–90.
77. Ibid., 89–90.
78. Ibid., 131.
79. David Armstrong, "George Freeman Speaks Out: 'Why Haven't They Charged Me?'" *The Bulletin*, June 21, 1983, 22; Evan Whitton, "Biographies," *Can of Worms II*, http://netk.net.au/Whitton/Worms28.asp.
80. "Ex-Strip Club Owner Denies 'Mr Sin' Label," *Sydney Morning Herald*, December 5, 1973, 3; Reeves, *The Real George Freeman*, 95–96.
81. Bottom, "The Mafia Connection," 11; Reeves, *The Real George Freeman*, 96–97.
82. Bottom, "The Mafia Connection," 11.
83. "'Family' Welcome for Joe," *Sydney Morning Herald*, September 9, 1979, 4.
84. Hall, *Disorganized Crime*, 80.
85. Peter Spooner, "New Poker Machines to Beat Club Cheats," *Sydney Morning Herald*, December 22, 1968, 13; Whitton, "Biographies."

4

1. Jack Rooklyn, interview [audio], October 15, 1984, National Library of Australia, http://nla.gov.au/nla.obj-216953128.
2. Matt Condon, "Rooklyn's final curtain," *Sydney Morning Herald*, May 24, 1992, 15.
3. April Hersey, "The Sub-Teens," *The Bulletin*, February 10, 1968, 23.
4. Peter Spooner, "New poker machines to beat club cheats," *Sydney Morning Herald*, December 22, 1968, 13.
5. Ken Miller, "How Bally Manufacturing Cleaned Up Its Act," *Reno Gazette-Journal*, March 30, 1986, 20.
6. Spooner, "New poker machines," 13.
7. Evan Whitton, "Trial By Voodoo: Why the Law Defeats Justice and Democracy; How to Investigate the Truth," *Networked Knowledge*, http://netk.net.au/Whitton/TBV27.asp.
8. Tony Reeves, *The Real George Freeman* (Melbourne, VIC: Hybrid Publishers, 2013), 103.
9. Bob Bottom, "The Mafia Connection," *The Age*, September 9, 1985, 11.
10. Ibid.
11. Anna Sergi, "'Polycephalous 'ndrangheta: Crimes, behaviours and organisation of the Calabrian mafia in Australia," *Australian and New Zealand Journal of Criminology* 52 (1), 2019, 4.
12. Bottom, "The Mafia Connection," 11.
13. Reeves, *The Real George Freeman*, 105.
14. Tony Reeves, *Mr Big: Lennie McPherson and His Life of Crime* (Crows Nest, NSW: Allen and Unwin, 2005), 119.
15. Alfred W. McCoy, *Drug Traffic: Narcotics and Organised Crime in Australia* (Artarmon, NSW: Harper and Row, 1980), 235.
16. Ibid., 235–37.

17. "Merv Wood quits top sculling," *The Argus*, November 28, 1956, 11.
18. Warren Owens, "How the NSW Untouchables snared a rogue cop," *Sydney Morning Herald*, October 15, 1978, 63.
19. McCoy, *Drug Traffic*, 216.
20. Ibid., 220.
21. Ibid., 232.
22. Ibid., 237.
23. Ibid.
24. Reeves, *Mr Big*, 125–26.
25. McNeill's views recorded in a letter by Commonwealth Police officer designated "Sergeant B" on October 9, 1972, several weeks before the final report was released; Athol Moffitt, *Report of the Honourable Mr Justice Moffitt Appointed to Inquire in Respect of Certain Matters Relating to Allegations of Organised Crime in Clubs* (Sydney, NSW: Government Printer, 1974), 85.
26. Ibid.
27. Ibid., 86.
28. Ibid., 89.
29. "Poker machine profits 'ideal target,'" *Sydney Morning Herald*, August 15, 1974, 12; Whitton, "Trial by Voodoo."
30. McCoy, *Drug Traffic*, 241.
31. Moffitt, *Report of the Honourable Mr Justice Moffitt*, 91; McCoy, *Drug Traffic*, 241.
32. Whitton, "Trial by Voodoo."
33. Bob Wiedrich, "Firm doesn't want help of 'salesman,'" *Chicago Tribune*, September 17, 1973, 26; *Bally's Park Place, Inc., In the Matter of the Application for a Casino License and the Application of Bally's Manufacturing Corporation for a Casino Service Industry License* [1978] 10 NJAR 356, 31.
34. Moffitt, *Report of the Honourable Mr Justice Moffitt*, 80–81.
35. Ibid.; Reeves, *The Real George Freeman*, 138–39.
36. Moffitt, *Report of the Honourable Mr Justice Moffitt*, 81–82.
37. Ibid., 80; Reeves, *The Real George Freeman*, 140–41.
38. Reeves, *Mr Big*, 184.
39. Moffitt, *Report of the Honourable Mr Justice Moffitt*, ii.
40. "Moffitt, Athol Randolph (1914–2007), *Obituaries Australia* (Canberra, ACT: Australian National University, 2007), https://oa.anu.edu.au/obituary/moffitt-athol-randolph-16100.
41. Ibid.
42. Moffitt, *Report of the Honourable Mr Justice Moffitt*, 1.
43. Reeves, *Mr Big*, 188.
44. Ibid., 199–200.
45. Ibid., 210.
46. Tony Reeves, *Mr Sin: The Abe Saffron Dossier* (Crows Nest, NSW: Allen and Unwin, 2007), 161.
47. Reeves, *Mr Big*, 207.

48. John Lawrence Jiggens, "Marijuana Australia: Cannabis Use, Popular Culture, and the Americanisation of Drugs Policy in Australia, 1938–1988" (PhD thesis, Queensland University of Technology, 2004), 177.

49. Wiedrich, "Firm doesn't want help," 26.

50. "Crime Inquiry; Former informer gives evidence," *Canberra Times*, February 23, 1974, 7.

51. Reeves, *Mr Big*, 168.

52. "Marcel Francisci shot dead; tied to 'French Connection,'" *New York Times*, January 16, 1982, 23.

53. "'Mafia article shattered me'—Cyril Shack tells High Court hearing," *Coin Slot*, July 3, 1971, 14.

54. Moffitt, *Report of the Honourable Mr Justice Moffitt*, 94.

55. *Bally's Park Place, Inc.*, 19.

56. Ronald Waterhouse, *Child of Another Century: Recollections of a High Court Judge* (London, UK: The Ratcliffe Press, 2013), 158.

57. Evan Whitton, "Doubts about leadership, supervision and political subversion; A force that has failed to win the public's faith," *Sydney Morning Herald*, October 17, 1984, 16.

58. Moffitt, *Report of the Honourable Mr Justice Moffitt*, 132.

59. Ibid.

60. Ibid., 133.

61. Ibid., 134.

62. Ibid.

63. Ibid., 135.

64. "Legislation move for club control," *Canberra Times*, August 16, 1974, 7.

65. Ibid.

66. Whitton, "Doubts about leadership," 16.

67. Ibid.

68. McCoy, *Drug Traffic*, 242.

69. Jiggens, "Marijuana Australia," 177.

70. "Moffitt, Athol Randolph (1914–2007)."

71. Matthew Condon, *The Night Dragon* (Brisbane, QLD: University of Queensland Press, 2019), 44.

72. Reeves, *The Real George Freeman*, 159–60.

73. Wiedrich, "Firm doesn't want help," 26.

74. SAC Los Angeles to FBI Director, memorandum, March 23, 1964, FBI Record Number 124–10199–10436, 2; Carl Sifakis, *The Mafia Encyclopedia*, 3rd ed. (New York City, NY: Facts on File, 2005), 7.

75. Michael Corbitt, testimony, August 13, 1997, Office of the Independent Hearing Officer, Laborers' International Union of North America, Chicago City Counsel Docket No. 97–30T, http://laborers_chicago.tripod.com/Corbitt_testimony.html.

76. Richard Hall, *Disorganised Crime* (St Lucia, QLD: University of Queensland Press, 1986), 100.

77. Ibid., 94.

78. Ibid., 80–81.
79. "'Family' Welcome for Joe," *Sydney Morning Herald*, September 9, 1979, 4.
80. "Legislation move for club control," 7.
81. Neil Mercer, "The mild man, the Mafia and Mr Big," *Sydney Morning Herald*, April 1, 2012, https://www.smh.com.au/national/the-mild-man-the-mafia-and-mr-big-20120331-1w52b.html.

5

1. Athol Moffitt, *Report of the Honourable Mr Justice Moffitt Appointed to Inquire in Respect of Certain Matters Relating to Allegations of Organised Crime in Clubs* (Sydney, NSW: Government Printer, 1974), 91.
2. Jack Rooklyn, advertisement, *Secretaries and Managers Journal of Australia*, 15 (9), 1974, 20.
3. "Luck Leaves the Poker Game," *Sydney Morning Herald*, January 10, 1983, 184.
4. Tony Reeves, *Mr Big: Lennie McPherson and His Life of Crime* (Crows Nest, NSW: Allen and Unwin, 2005), 218.
5. Ibid., 219.
6. Ibid., 220.
7. Jack Rooklyn, interview [audio], October 15, 1984, National Library of Australia, http://nla.gov.au/nla.obj-216953128.
8. David Payne, "Lexcen, Benjamin (Ben) (1936–1988)," *Australian Dictionary of Biography* (Canberra, ACT: Australian National University, 2012), https://adb.anu.edu.au/biography/lexcen-benjamin-ben-14154.
9. "Race History," *Sydney-Hobart and Southern Cross Cup 1973 Official Program* (Rushcutters Bay, NSW: Modern Magazines, 1973), 88–90.
10. Rooklyn, interview [audio].
11. "Race History," 93.
12. Rooklyn, interview [audio].
13. Tony Reeves, *The Real George Freeman* (Melbourne, VIC: Hybrid Publishers, 2013), 130.
14. "Pioneer Las Vegas gaming figure Stein dies at 87," *Las Vegas Sun*, June 9, 2004, https://lasvegassun.com/news/2004/jun/09/pioneer-las-vegas-gaming-figure-stein-dies-at-87/.
15. Ibid.
16. "From the Pigeon Pen," *Las Vegas Sun*, March 7, 1966, 10.
17. Reeves, *The Real George Freeman*, 131.
18. Denis Freney, "Caesar's Palace Casino, Bally pokies: allegations past & present," *Tribune* (Sydney), November 11, 1981, 8.
19. Ibid.
20. Alfred W. McCoy, *Drug Traffic: Narcotics and Organised Crime in Australia* (Artarmon, NSW: Harper and Row, 1980), 251.
21. David Hickie, "The illegal casinos under Askin," *Sydney Morning Herald*, March 25, 1985, 6.

22. Errol Simper, "Legalisation of Casinos in N.S.W.; Mr Wran indulges in an 'exercise in gradualism,'" *Canberra Times*, March 16, 1979, 2.

23. Evan Whitton, "Doubts about leadership, supervision and political subversion; A force that has failed to win the public's faith," *Sydney Morning Herald*, October 17, 1984, 16.

24. "Police watched casino party guests; But Caesar's Palace was after business," *Sydney Morning Herald*, November 7, 1981, 6.

25. Neil Mercer, "The mild man, the Mafia and Mr Big," *Sydney Morning Herald*, April 1, 2012, https://www.smh.com.au/national/the-mild-man-the-mafia-and-mr-big-20120331-1w52b.html.

26. Ibid.

27. Bob Bottom, *Connections II* (Melbourne, VIC: Sun Books, 1987), 16.

28. Evan Whitton, *Can of Worms II: Citizen's Reference Book to Crime and the Administration of Justice* (Broadway, NSW: Fairfax Library, 1987), http://netk.net.au/Whitton/Worms10.asp; James Wood, *Final Report of the Royal Commission into the New South Wales Police Service*, Vol. 1 (Sydney, NSW: NSW Government, 1997), 26.

29. Wood, *Final Report*, 53; Paul Lynch, *Research Report on Trends in Corruption* (Sydney, NSW: Committee on the Office of the Ombudsman and the Police Integrity Commission, 2002), 30.

30. Lynch, *Research Report*, 30.

31. Whitton, "Doubts about leadership," 16.

32. Malcolm Brown, "A cut above a common criminal," *Sydney Morning Herald*, August 29, 1996, 4.

33. Ibid.

34. Donald G. Stewart, *Final Report of the Royal Commission of Inquiry into Alleged Telephone Interceptions*, Vol. 1 (Sydney, NSW: Australian Government and Governments of New South Wales and Victoria, 1986), 142.

35. Freney, "Caesar's Palace Casino," 8.

36. Clive Small and Tom Gilling, *Smack Express: How Organised Crime Got Hooked on Drugs* (Crows Nest, NSW: Allen and Unwin, 2009), 43.

37. Ibid., 45.

38. Bob Bottom, "The Mafia Connection," *The Age*, September 9, 1985, 11.

39. Ovid Demaris, *The Last Mafioso: The Treacherous World of Jimmy Fratianno* (New York City, NY: Bantam Books, 1981), 199; Bottom, "The Mafia Connection," 11.

40. Peter Butt, *Merchants of Menace: The True Story of the Nugan Hand Bank Scandal* (Sydney, NSW: Blackwattle Press, 2015), 35–40.

41. Bottom, "The Mafia Connection," 11; Butt, *Merchants of Menace*, 40–41.

42. Demaris, *The Last Mafioso*, 27–30.

43. Lee Server, *Handsome Johnny: The Life and Death of Johnny Roselli; Gentleman Gangster, Hollywood Producer, CIA Assassin* (New York City, NY: St. Martin's Press, 2018), 230–31.

44. Demaris, *The Last Mafioso*, 93; Server, *Handsome Johnny*, 253.

45. Federal Bureau of Investigations (FBI), "La Cosa Nostra; AR—Conspiracy," interoffice memo, June 9, 1967, 7.

46. Demaris, *The Last Mafioso*, 199.

47. Federal Bureau of Investigations (FBI), "La Cosa Nostra; AR—Conspiracy," inter-office memo, August 9, 1967, 1.

48. Ibid., 1–2.

49. Demaris, *The Last Mafioso*, 233.

50. "Knights in Tarnished Armor," *The Age*, August 3, 1985, 164.

51. Ralph Blumenthal, "Mobster makes offer on French Connection case," *New York Times*, February 21, 2009, https://www.nytimes.com/2009/02/22/nyregion/22french.html.

52. "Knights in Tarnished Armor," 164; Bottom, "The Mafia Connection," 11.

53. John Lawrence Jiggens, "Marijuana Australia: Cannabis Use, Popular Culture, and the Americanisation of Drugs Policy in Australia, 1938–1988" (PhD thesis, Queensland University of Technology, 2004), 230–32.

54. Jonathan Kwitny, *The Crimes of Patriots: A True Tale of Dope, Dirty Money, and the CIA* (New York City, NY: W. W. Norton, 1987), 238.

55. Butt, *Merchants of Menace*, 27.

56. Ibid., 26.

57. McCoy, *Drug Traffic*, 461–72.

58. Denis Freney, "Police report on Nugan Hand; Nugan Bank—deep in CIA network and arms trading," *Tribune* (Sydney), April 13, 1983, 11.

59. Bottom, "The Mafia Connection," 11.

60. Butt, *Merchants of Menace*, 41–42.

61. Jiggens, "Marijuana Australia," 185–86.

62. Kwitny, *The Crimes of Patriots*, 240.

63. Jiggens, "Marijuana Australia," 186.

64. Kwitny, *The Crimes of Patriots*, 240; Jiggens, "Marijuana Australia," 186.

65. Bob Bottom, *The Godfather in Australia: Organised Crime's Australian Connections* (Dunedin, NZ: Reed, 1979), 73.

66. "Evidence Mafia already has a toehold in Australia," *Sydney Morning Herald*, September 16, 1979, 32; Richard Hall, *Disorganised Crime* (St Lucia, QLD: University of Queensland Press, 1986), 85.

67. Jiggens, "Marijuana Australia," 187.

68. Freney, "Police report on Nugan Hand," 11; Bottom, "The Mafia Connection," 11; Kwitny, *The Crimes of Patriots*, 39.

69. Jiggens, "Marijuana Australia," 185.

70. Attila Urmenyhazi, "Abeles, Sir Peter (1924–1999)," *Obituaries Australia* (Canberra, ACT: Australian National University, 2011), https://oa.anu.edu.au/obituary/abeles-sir-peter-14141.

71. Steve Vines, "Mafia riddle of Murdoch trucks," *Observer* (London), February 9, 1986, 7.

72. Denis Freney, "TNT, Jimmy the Weasel, Benny Eggs, and the Mafia," *Tribune* (Sydney), August 4, 1982, 11.

73. Larry McShane, "Venero (Benny Eggs) Mangano, longtime underboss of the Genovese family, dead at 95," *New York Daily News*, August 18, 2017, https:

//www.nydailynews.com/new-york/manhattan/venero-benny-eggs-mangano-genovese-underboss-dead-95-article-1.3423874.

74. "Jury frees Gigante in Costello shooting," *New York Times*, May 28, 1958, 1; McShane, "Venero (Benny Eggs) Mangano."

75. Vines, "Mafia riddle," 7; Jiggens, "Marijuana Australia," 260.

76. Freney, "TNT, Jimmy the Weasel," 11.

77. Tony Reeves, *Mr Sin: The Abe Saffron Dossier* (Crows Nest, NSW: Allen and Unwin, 2007), 86.

78. Moffitt, *Report of the Honourable Mr Justice Moffitt*, 103–7.

79. "Six jailed for attempt to import buddha sticks," *Canberra Times*, July 26, 1979, 8; Jiggens, "Marijuana Australia," 181.

80. Small and Gilling, *Smack Express*, 50.

81. Philip Morgan Woodward, *Further Report of the Royal Commission into Drug Trafficking* (Sydney, NSW: Government Printer, 1980), 2; "The Life of Riley," *Sydney Morning Herald*, November 21, 1981, 40; Kate McClymont and Colleen Ryan, "The Labor heavy with big business mates," *Sydney Morning Herald*, October 25, 1994, 6.

82. "Six jailed for attempt," 8; Small and Gilling, *Smack Express*, 51.

83. "Police told cannabis filled crew's bunks," *Canberra Times*, August 24, 1978, 6; "Six jailed for attempt," 8.

84. "Six jailed for attempt," 8; Jiggens, "Marijuana Australia," 180.

85. Jiggens, "Marijuana Australia," 180–81.

86. Ibid., 181–83.

87. Woodward, *Further Report*, 58; Bob Bottom, "Woodward's tougher stand on Australia's Drug Peril," *The Bulletin*, 101 (5226), 1980, 27.

88. Woodward, *Further Report*, 235.

89. "Six jailed for attempt," 8; Small and Gilling, *Smack Express*, 51–52.

90. "Csidei jailed for 15 months," *Canberra Times*, September 28, 1978, 16.

91. Demaris, *The Last Mafioso*, 372.

92. Ibid., 505.

93. Ibid., 512.

94. John C. Keeney, *Statement of John C. Keeney Before the Permanent Subcommittee on Investigations Committee on Governmental Affairs United States Senate Concerning Organized Crime in the Great Lakes Region on January 31, 1984* (Washington, DC: US Department of Justice, 1984), 2–3; Demaris, *The Last Mafioso*, 535.

95. Ray Loynd and Jean Merl, "'Jimmy the Weasel' Fratianno; Mob Figure, Informant," *Los Angeles Times*, July 1, 1993, https://www.latimes.com/archives/la-xpm-1993-07-01-mn-8855-story.html; Joseph P. Fried, "Ex-Mob Underboss Given Lenient Term for Help as Witness," *New York Times*, September 27, 1994, 1.

96. Reeves, *Mr Big*, 230–31.

97. Ibid., 233.

98. Bob Bottom and Greg Sheridan, "Lennie on money and the Press," *The Bulletin*, 103 (5384), 1983, 30.

99. Malcolm Brown, "Smith, Stanley John (Stan) (1937–2010)," *Obituaries Australia* (Canberra, ACT: Australian National University, 2010), https://oa.anu.edu.au/obituary/smith-stanley-john-stan-16917.

100. Reeves, *The Real George Freeman*, 207–8.

101. Ibid., 211.

102. "Meet Sydney's latest 'head honcho' of crime," *Sydney Morning Herald*, December 21, 1996, 8.

103. G. P. Walsh, "Freeman, George David (1935–1990)," *Australian Dictionary of Biography* (Canberra, ACT: Australian National University, 2007), https://adb.anu.edu.au/biography/freeman-george-david-12512.

104. "Hobart line honours to Ballyhoo," *Canberra Times*, December 30, 1976, 14.

105. Charles Pickett, "Rooklyn, Israel (Jack) (1908–1996)," *Australian Dictionary of Biography* (Canberra, ACT: Australian National University, 2021), https://adb.anu.edu.au/biography/rooklyn-israel-jack-30530/text37850.

6

1. "Christmas sports car in crash," *Canberra Times*, January 1, 1977, 3.

2. Ken Miller, "How Bally Manufacturing cleaned up its act," *Reno Gazette-Journal*, March 30, 1986, 20.

3. Ibid.

4. Ibid.

5. Gregory H. Smith, letter, September 1, 1982, quoted in William V. Roth, *State Lotteries: An Overview* (Washington, DC: US Government Printing Service, 1984), 215–17.

6. Ibid., 216.

7. Ibid., 217.

8. Brendan Riley Carson, "Extend Bally's Probation, Board Says," *Nevada State Journal*, October 13, 1977, 29; Evan Whitton, "Trial by Voodoo: Why the Law Defeats Justice and Democracy; How to Investigate the Truth," *Networked Knowledge*, http://netk.net.au/Whitton/TBV27.asp.

9. Whitton, "Trial by Voodoo."

10. "Rooklyn buys back pokie firm," *Canberra Times*, December 20, 1977, 7.

11. "A quiet woman in Rooklyn's chair," *Sydney Morning Herald*, October 5, 1978, 13.

12. "Rooklyn buys back pokie firm," 7.

13. Matt Condon, "Rooklyn's final curtain," *Sydney Morning Herald*, May 24, 1992, 15.

14. Neville Harper, "In-line Machines," *Parliamentary Debates [Hansard]*, March 7, 1984, LA, QLD, 1899.

15. Wayne Goss, "In-line Gambling Machines," *Parliamentary Debates [Hansard]*, March 7, 1984, LA, QLD, 1914.

16. "Big American Centre Open," *Courier-Mail*, July 5, 1943, 3; "Upkeep of Lavish American Centre Was £2,000 Weekly," *Courier-Mail*, January 3, 1945, 3.

17. Rae Wear, *Johannes Bjelke-Petersen: The Lord's Premier* (Brisbane, QLD: University of Queensland Press, 2002), 6.

18. Ibid., 45.

19. John Wanna and Tracey Arklay, *The Ayes Have It: The History of the Queensland Parliament 1957–1989* (Canberra: ANU E Press, 2010), 230; Rae Wear, "Chalk, Gordon William (Chalkie) (1913–1991)," *Australian Dictionary of Biography* (Canberra, ACT: Australian National University, 2014), http://adb.anu.edu.au/biography/chalk-gordon-william-chalkie-15168.

20. Evan Whitton, *The Hillbilly Dictator* (Crows Nest, NSW: ABC Books, 1989), 10

21. W. Ross Johnston, "Bischof, Francis Erich (Frank) (1904–1979)," *Australian Dictionary of Biography* (Canberra, ACT: Australian National University, 1993), http://adb.anu.edu.au/biography/bischof-francis-erich-frank-9513.

22. Phil Dickie, *The Road to Fitzgerald* (Brisbane, QLD: University of Queensland Press, 1988), 5.

23. Glendon Patrick Hallahan, statutory declaration—appendix H, October 19, 1988, Queensland State Archives Item ID2548831, Commission of Inquiry—legal advice, 1.

24. Matthew Condon, *Three Crooked Kings* (Brisbane, QLD: University of Queensland Press, 2013), 87.

25. Queensland Police Union of Employees to Francis Bischof, letter, July 16, 1963, Queensland State Archives Item ID373745, Administration file, police, 1.

26. Steve Bishop, *The Most Dangerous Detective: The Outrageous Glen Hallahan* (Charleston, SC: CreateSpace, 2012), 27–30.

27. Condon, *Three Crooked Kings*, 70.

28. Ibid., 85.

29. Glendon Patrick Hallahan, statutory declaration—appendix C, October 19, 1988, Queensland State Archives Item ID2548831, Commission of Inquiry—legal advice, 1; Bishop, *The Most Dangerous Detective*, 215; Condon, *Three Crooked Kings*, 283–84.

30. Gerald E. Fitzgerald, *Report of a Commission of Inquiry Pursuant to Orders in Council* (Brisbane, QLD: Commission of Inquiry into Possible Misconduct and Associated Police Misconduct, 1989), 32.

31. Ibid.

32. Ibid., 33.

33. Fitzgerald, *Report of a Commission*, 33; Condon, *Three Crooked Kings*, 182.

34. Dickie, *The Road to Fitzgerald*, 268.

35. "An 'Outsider' with Inside Experience," *Canberra Times*, January 19, 1970, 2; Condon, *Three Crooked Kings*, 206.

36. Raymond Whitrod, *Before I Sleep* (Brisbane, QLD: University of Queensland Press, 2001), 135.

37. Ibid., 93.

38. Ibid., 137.

39. "Decision on Charge Deferred," *Canberra Times*, May 20, 1972, 8; Condon, *Three Crooked Kings*, 271–73.

40. Bishop, *The Most Dangerous Detective*, 183–84; Condon, *Three Crooked Kings*, 293–94.

41. Dickie, *The Road to Fitzgerald*, 270.

42. Ibid., 49.

43. Fitzgerald, *Report of a Commission*, 61.

44. Alexander Smith, *They Create Worlds: The Story of the People and Companies That Shaped the Video Game Industry, Vol I: 1971–1982* [online] (Boca Raton, FL: CRC Press, 2020).
45. Evan Whitton, "A fresh oath every day for tale-telling Tilley," *Sydney Morning Herald*, June 28, 1988, 8.
46. Colin Bennett, "Information supplied by Police Department on Playboy Club; Alleged Passing of Forged Currency by Police Officers," *Parliamentary Debates [Hansard]*, November 28, 1968, LA, QLD, 1874.
47. Colin Bennett, "Committee—Financial Statement—Resumption of Debate," *Parliamentary Debates [Hansard]*, October 14, 1971, LA, QLD, 1157.
48. Dickie, *The Road to Fitzgerald*, 277; Fitzgerald, *Report of a Commission*, 116; Ross Fitzgerald, "Judicial Culture and the Investigation of Corruption: A Comparison of the Gibbs National Hotel Inquiry 1963–64 and the Fitzgerald Inquiry 1987–89," in Scott Prasser, Rae Wear, and John Nethercote (eds.), *Corruption and Reform: The Fitzgerald Vision* (Brisbane, QLD: University of Queensland Press, 1990), 65.
49. Donald Lane, "Alleged Political Interference in Police Force Administration," *Parliamentary Debates [Hansard]*, November 30, 1976, LA, QLD, 1932.
50. Nigel Powell, "Gig Boss Recalls QLD Police Action," *Australian Financial Review*, June 28, 1988, https://www.afr.com/politics/gig-boss-recalls-qld-police-action-19880628-k2tvc.
51. Fitzgerald, *Report of a Commission*, 37.
52. "Lawyer Says a Clean Police Force Wanted," *Canberra Times*, May 20, 1976, 3.
53. Fitzgerald, *Report of a Commission*, 37.
54. "$1,500 a Month Bribe Offer Alleged," *Canberra Times*, September 2, 1975, 7.
55. G. A. G. Lucas, *Report of the Committee of Inquiry into the Enforcement of Criminal Law in Queensland* (Brisbane, QLD: Committee of Inquiry into the Enforcement of Criminal Law in Queensland, 1977), Queensland State Archives Item ID2236744, Commission of Inquiry—reports, 22–23.
56. Fitzgerald, *Report of a Commission*, 39.
57. Lucas, *Report of the Committee*, 22–23.
58. Ibid., 29.
59. Fitzgerald, *Report of a Commission*, 39.
60. Ibid., 40.
61. Dickie, *The Road to Fitzgerald*, 69.
62. Whitrod, *Before I Sleep*, 170.
63. Raymond Wells Whitrod to David Longland, letter, January 3, 1973, Queensland State Archives Item ID373748, Administration file, police, 1; Condon, *Three Crooked Kings*, 252.
64. Matthew Condon, *Jacks and Jokers* (Brisbane, QLD: University of Queensland Press, 2015), 26; Owen Kelly to Johannes Bjelke-Petersen, letter, August 10, 1976, Queensland State Archives Item ID540963, Protest demonstrations—general, 1.
65. Whitrod, *Before I Sleep*, 180.
66. Ibid., 184–85.
67. Fitzgerald, *Report of a Commission*, 45–46.

68. Ibid., 61.
69. Ibid.
70. Max Bingham, *Report on Gaming Machine Concerns and Regulations* (Brisbane, QLD: Criminal Justice Commission, 1990), 21.
71. Carson, "Extend Bally's Probation," 29.
72. "Rooklyn buys back pokie firm," 7.
73. Fitzgerald, *Report of a Commission*, 62.
74. Ibid.
75. "Rooklyn buys back pokie firm," 7.

7

1. "Rooklyn buys back pokie firm," *Canberra Times*, December 20, 1977, 7.
2. Phil Dickie, *The Road to Fitzgerald* (Brisbane, QLD: University of Queensland Press, 1988), 282.
3. Gerald E. Fitzgerald, *Report of a Commission of Inquiry Pursuant to Orders in Council* (Brisbane, QLD: Commission of Inquiry into Possible Misconduct and Associated Police Misconduct, 1989), 62.
4. Dickie, *The Road to Fitzgerald*, 252.
5. Ibid.; Fitzgerald, *Report of a Commission*, 62.
6. Dickie, *The Road to Fitzgerald*, 252.
7. Ibid.
8. Fitzgerald, *Report of a Commission*, 62.
9. Ibid.
10. Ibid., 63.
11. Terence Lewis, notebook, January 3, 1978, Queensland State Archives Item ID ITM2548771, Commission of inquiry–legal advice, 1.
12. Terence Lewis, diary entry, March 20, 1978, Queensland State Archives Item ID ITM2549194, Commission of inquiry–legal advice, 1.
13. Dickie, *The Road to Fitzgerald*, 252.
14. Lewis, notebook, January 3, 1978, 1; Fitzgerald, *Report of a Commission*, 62.
15. Fitzgerald, *Report of a Commission*, 62.
16. Wayne Goss, "In-line Machines," *Parliamentary Debates [Hansard]*, March 28, 1984, LA, QLD, 2141.
17. Ibid., 2141–42.
18. Peter Duncan, "Ministerial Statement: Mr. A. G. Saffron," *Parliamentary Debates [Hansard]*, March 7, 1978, HoA, SA, 1972; Tony Reeves, *Mr Sin: The Abe Saffron Dossier* (Crows Nest, NSW: Allen & Unwin, 2007), 142.
19. Reeves, *Mr Sin*, 142.
20. Duncan, "Ministerial Statement," 1971–73.
21. Parliamentary Joint Committee on the National Crime Authority, *The National Crime Authority and James McCartney Anderson* (Canberra, ACT: Parliament of Australia, 1994), 162–63.
22. Ibid., 181.

23. Max Bingham, *Report on Gaming Machine Concerns and Regulations* (Brisbane, QLD: Criminal Justice Commission, 1990), 41.

24. Ibid.; Fitzgerald, *Report of a Commission*, 61.

25. Bingham, *Report on Gaming Machine Concerns*, 42.

26. Salvatore Di Carlo, testimony, May 17, 1988, Queensland State Archives Item ID ITM2548522, Commission of inquiry–legal advice, 9286–87.

27. Matthew Condon, *The Night Dragon* (Brisbane, QLD: University of Queensland Press, 2019), 67.

28. Athol Moffitt, *Report of the Honourable Mr Justice Moffitt Appointed to Inquire in Respect of Certain Matters Relating to Allegations of Organised Crime in Clubs* (Sydney, NSW: Government Printer, 1974), 80–81.

29. Condon, *The Night Dragon*, 69.

30. *R v O'Dempsey* [2018] QCA 364, s10.

31. Condon, *The Night Dragon*, 76–77.

32. Bingham, *Report on Gaming Machine Concerns*, 42.

33. Ibid., 97.

34. Fitzgerald, *Report of a Commission*, 62.

35. Serge Pregliasco, testimony, May 12, 1988, Queensland State Archives Item ID ITM2548520, Commission of inquiry–legal advice, 9105; Tony Reeves, *The Real George Freeman* (Melbourne, VIC: Hybrid Publishers, 2013), 95–96.

36. Fitzgerald, *Report of a Commission*, 62.

37. Ibid.

38. Evan Whitton, *The Hillbilly Dictator: Australia's Police State* (Crows Nest, NSW: ABC Enterprises, 1989), 63.

39. Ibid.

40. Ibid., 63–64.

41. "#42 Len Ainsworth," *Forbes*, n.d., https://www.forbes.com/profile/len-ainsworth/; Bingham, *Report on Gaming Machine Concerns*, 25.

42. Bingham, *Report on Gaming Machine Concerns*, 26.

43. Trade Practices Commission, *Annual Report 1982–83* (Canberra, ACT: Australian Government Publishing Service, 1983), 78–79.

44. Bingham, *Report on Gaming Machine Concerns*, 27.

45. Ibid.

46. Whitton, *The Hillbilly Dictator*, 63.

47. Ibid., 54.

48. Cameron Atfield, "Corrupt Queensland police escaped 1970s investigation, author claims," *Brisbane Times*, October 7, 2015, https://www.brisbanetimes.com.au/national/queensland/corrupt-queensland-police-escaped-1970s-investigation-author-claims-20151001-gjzeiq.html.

49. Harvey Bates to Wal Fife, letter, September 17, 1979, National Library of Australia MS7626, Papers of Wal Fife, 1.

50. John McLeay, "Royal Commission Into Drugs," September 9, 1980, *Parliamentary Debates [Hansard]*, HoR, PoA, 1004.

51. Fitzgerald, *Report of a Commission*, 63.

52. Evan Whitton, "Trial by Voodoo: Why the Law Defeats Justice and Democracy; How to Investigate the Truth," *Networked Knowledge*, http://netk.net.au/Whitton/TBV27.asp.

53. Ibid.

54. Fitzgerald, *Report of a Commission*, 51.

55. Ibid., 52.

56. G. A. G. Lucas, *Report of the Committee of Inquiry into the Enforcement of Criminal Law in Queensland* (Brisbane, QLD: Committee of Inquiry into the Enforcement of Criminal Law in Queensland, 1977), Queensland State Archives Item ID2236744, Commission of Inquiry—reports, 214.

57. Fitzgerald, *Report of a Commission*, 54.

58. Ibid., 55.

59. "Three Machine Operators Allegedly Ordered to Pay $50,000 Each," *Canberra Times*, May 17, 1988, 7; Fitzgerald, *Report of a Commission*, 55.

60. Dickie, *The Road to Fitzgerald*, 276.

61. Whitton, *The Hillbilly Dictator*, 53.

62. Fitzgerald, *Report of a Commission*, 67.

63. Noel Dwyer, testimony, May 19, 1988, Queensland State Archives Item ID2548524, Commission of Inquiry–legal advice, 9515.

64. Jack Rooklyn, interview [audio], October 15, 1984, National Library of Australia, http://nla.gov.au/nla.obj-216953128.

65. "Loss of Apollo," *Yachting*, July 1980, 24.

66. Duncan Van Woerdan, "Apollo's final hour," *Offshore* (54), 1980, 10.

67. Charles Pickett, "Rooklyn, Israel (Jack) (1908–1996)," *Australian Dictionary of Biography* (Canberra, ACT: Australian National University, 2021), https://adb.anu.edu.au/biography/rooklyn-israel-jack-30530/text37850.

68. Michael Corbitt, testimony, August 13, 1997, Office of the Independent Hearing Officer, Laborers' International Union of North America, Chicago City Counsel Docket No. 97–30T, http://laborers_chicago.tripod.com/Corbitt_testimony.html.

69. Ibid.

70. Ibid.

71. Corbitt, testimony; "Reputed Mafia associate Joseph Testa had his right leg blown off," *United Press International*, June 27, 1981, https://www.upi.com/Archives/1981/06/27/Reputed-Mafia-associate-Joseph-Testa-had-his-right-leg/1672362462400/.

72. Ray Gibson, "FBI hears of links to DuPage killings," *Chicago Tribune*, November 2, 1999, https://www.chicagotribune.com/news/ct-xpm-1999–11–02–9911020141-story.html.

73. Ibid.

74. Bob Bottom, "The Mafia Connection," *The Age*, September 9, 1985, 11.

75. "Caesar's Palace executive arrested in Australia," *United Press International*, November 4, 1981, https://www.upi.com/Archives/1981/11/04/Caesars-Palace-executive-arrested-in-Australia/9480373698000/.

76. Peter Rees, *Killing Juanita* (Crows Nest, NSW: Allen & Unwin, 2004), 224.

77. Richard Hall, *Disorganized Crime* (Brisbane, QLD: University of Queensland Press, 1986), 211.
78. Ibid.
79. Rees, *Killing Juanita*, 224–25.
80. Evan Whitton, "A force that has failed to win the public's faith," *Sydney Morning Herald*, October 17, 1984, 16.
81. Ibid.; Hall, *Disorganized Crime*, 212.
82. "'Whiter than white' poker-machine firm," *Canberra Times*, October 8, 1983, 15.
83. Bingham, *Report on Gaming Machine Concerns*, 15.
84. Fitzgerald, *Report of a Commission*, 85.

8

1. Phil Dickie, *The Road to Fitzgerald* (Brisbane, QLD: University of Queensland Press, 1988), 267; Gerald E. Fitzgerald, *Report of a Commission of Inquiry Pursuant to Orders in Council* (Brisbane, QLD: Commission of Inquiry into Possible Misconduct and Associated Police Misconduct, 1989), 54.
2. Domenico Cacciola and Ben Robertson, *Who's Who in the Zoo? A Story of Corruption, Crooks and Killers* (Brisbane, QLD: University of Queensland Press, 2014), 188.
3. Fitzgerald, *Report of a Commission*, 76–77.
4. Ibid., 61.
5. Dickie, *The Road to Fitzgerald*, 84–85.
6. Fitzgerald, *Report of a Commission*, 64–65.
7. Dickie, *The Road to Fitzgerald*, 274.
8. Max Bingham, *Report on Gaming Machine Concerns and Regulations* (Brisbane, QLD: Criminal Justice Commission, 1990), 22.
9. Ibid.
10. "Men on trial on pokies conspiracy charges," *Canberra Times*, April 28, 1983, 10.
11. Terence Lewis, diary extract, April 5, 1982, quoted in Bingham, *Report on Gaming Machine Concerns*, 90.
12. Bingham, *Report on Gaming Machine Concerns*, 90.
13. Gerald E. Fitzgerald, *Report of a Commission of Inquiry Pursuant to Orders in Council: List of Appendices* (Brisbane, QLD: Commission of Inquiry into Possible Misconduct and Associated Police Misconduct, 1989), A165.
14. Fitzgerald, *Report of a Commission*, 33; Bingham, *Report on Gaming Machine Concerns*, 90.
15. Evan Whitton, "Names keep dropping as Herbert tells story," *Sydney Morning Herald*, September 6, 1988, 5.
16. Fitzgerald, *Report of a Commission: List of Appendices*, A146; Matthew Condon, *Jacks and Jokers* (Brisbane, QLD: University of Queensland Press, 2014), 393; Steve Bishop, "Chapter 4: Campbell's War Attracts TV Coverage," *Bob Campbell's War*, n.d., http://www.stevebishop.net/chapter-4-campbells-war-attracts-tv-coverage.html.
17. Terence Lewis, diary extract, April 6, 1982, quoted in Bingham, *Report on Gaming Machine Concerns*, 90.
18. Bingham, *Report on Gaming Machine Concerns*, 90.

19. Ibid., 90–91.
20. Ibid., 92.
21. Ibid., 94.
22. Jack Taylor, "Poker machine exports in doubt as two men wait for trial," *Sydney Morning Herald*, August 15, 1983, 4; Bingham, *Report on Gaming Machine Concerns*, 22.
23. Bingham, *Report on Gaming Machine Concerns*, 29.
24. Condon, *Jacks and Jokers*, 429–30.
25. Denis Reinhardt, "Death threats in machine racket alleged," *The Bulletin*, April 24, 1984, 30.
26. Neville Harper, "In-line Machines," *Parliamentary Debates [Hansard]*, March 7, 1984, LA, QLD, 1899.
27. Denis Reinhardt, "Mish-mash of lies—Rooklyn," *The Bulletin*, April 24, 1984, 29.
28. Peter Coaldrake, "Coalition crisis and the Queensland state election of 1983," *Politics* 19 (1), 1984, 85.
29. "Liberals in move for new vote in Merthyr," *Canberra Times*, November 25, 1986, 14.
30. Fitzgerald, *Report of a Commission*, 116.
31. Ibid., 85.
32. Phil Dickie, "A year after Sturgess, sex for sale business thrives unchallenged," *Courier-Mail*, January 12, 1987, 1.
33. Phil Dickie, "Brisbane's casinos flourish despite Gunn's vow to close them," *Courier-Mail*, April 13, 1987, 1–2.
34. Matthew Condon, *All Fall Down* (Brisbane, QLD: University of Queensland Press, 2015), 260.
35. Ibid., 261.
36. Ibid., 147.
37. James Slade and Alan Barnes, transcript, February 7, 1985, Queensland State Archives Item ID1276355, Commission of Inquiry—exhibit, 1–2.
38. Chris Masters, "The Moonlight State [video]," *Four Corners*, ABC Australia, May 11, 1987.
39. Ibid.
40. Ibid.; Dickie, *The Road to Fitzgerald*, 172.
41. Christine Jennett, "Political Review," Australian Quarterly 59 (1), 1987, 102.
42. Fitzgerald, *Report of a Commission*, 3.
43. Condon, *All Fall Down*, 311.
44. Ibid.
45. Fitzgerald, *Report of a Commission*, 70; Condon, *All Fall Down*, 302.
46. Fitzgerald, *Report of a Commission*, 70.
47. Ibid.
48. Ibid.
49. Ibid.
50. Dickie, *The Road to Fitzgerald*, 194.
51. Ibid., 196.
52. Ibid., 202.

53. Masters, "The Moonlight State"; Dickie, *The Road to Fitzgerald*, 204–5.
54. Fitzgerald, *Report of a Commission*, 71.
55. Dickie, *The Road to Fitzgerald*, 208.
56. Fitzgerald, *Report of a Commission*, 71.
57. Graeme Robert Parker, testimony, November 4, 1987, Queensland State Archives Item ID ITM1273356, Commission of Inquiry—Transcript; Dickie, *The Road to Fitzgerald*, 220–21.
58. Dickie, *The Road to Fitzgerald*, 188.
59. "Herberts not wanted for inquiry," *Canberra Times*, February 13, 1988, 3.
60. Condon, *All Fall Down*, 402–3.
61. Fitzgerald, *Report of a Commission*, 72.
62. Jack Herbert, quoted in Condon, *All Fall Down*, 423.
63. Fitzgerald, *Report of a Commission*, 62; Condon, *All Fall Down*, 425.
64. Dickie, *The Road to Fitzgerald*, 278.
65. "Disgraced Lewis forfeits super," *Canberra Times*, May 6, 1995, 7.
66. "Lane the corruption 'pipeline,'" *Canberra Times*, September 14, 1988, 1.
67. "Herbert's former boss weeps at bribes inquiry," *Canberra Times*, September 20, 1988, 3.
68. Ibid.
69. "Tragedy and Farce," *Canberra Times*, November 27, 1987, 2; Condon, *All Fall Down*, 376.
70. "Tragedy and Farce," 2; "Sad End for Sir Joh," *Canberra Times*, December 2, 1987, 2.
71. Masters, "The Moonlight State [video]."
72. Condon, *All Fall Down*, 444.
73. Chris Masters, "Beyond Bethany [video]," *Four Corners*, ABC Australia, March 3, 2008.
74. Fitzgerald, *Report of a Commission*, 4.
75. Ibid., 116; Condon, *All Fall Down*, 450.
76. "Disgraced Lewis forfeits super," 7.
77. "Summonses for Lewis, Rooklyn and 18 others," *Canberra Times*, July 27, 1989, 1; Condon, *All Fall Down*, 467.
78. "Summonses for Lewis," 1.
79. "Rooklyn set for trial on corruption charges," *Sydney Morning Herald*, April 1, 1990, 21.
80. Condon, *All Fall Down*, 467–68.
81. "Rooklyn set for trial," 21.

Conclusion

1. Matthew Condon, *All Fall Down* (Brisbane, QLD: University of Queensland Press, 2015), 478.
2. Ibid., 478–79.
3. "Jury locked up after judge tells of 'untarnished' Lewis," *Canberra Times*, August 1, 1991, 1; Condon, *All Fall Down*, 486.
4. Jack Herbert, quoted in Condon, *All Fall Down*, 487.

5. *The Queen v. Terence Murray Lewis* [1992] QCA 223, 52; Bob Mulholland, quoted in Condon, *All Fall Down*, 489.

6. "Jury locked up," 1.

7. Rhyll Cronin, "5 days' deliberations; 15 charges proved," *Canberra Times*, August 6, 1991, 1.

8. Condon, *All Fall Down*, 525–26.

9. "Qld newspaper report not a contempt of court," *Canberra Times*, January 9, 1992, 12.

10. Matthew Condon, "Rooklyn's final curtain," *Sydney Morning Herald*, May 24, 1992, 15.

11. Ibid.

12. Ibid.

13. "Rooklyn, 84, avoids jail; $1/3m fine," *Canberra Times*, May 26, 1992, 3.

14. Condon, *All Fall Down*, 516.

15. Condon, "Rooklyn's final curtain," 15.

16. Condon, "Rooklyn's final curtain," 15; "Rooklyn, 84, avoids jail," 3.

17. "Rooklyn, 84, avoids jail," 3.

18. Ibid.

19. Ibid.

20. "Notice of intended distribution of estate," *Government Gazette of State of New South Wales* (22), February 28, 1997, 1351; Charles Pickett, "Rooklyn, Israel (Jack) (1908–1996)," *Australian Dictionary of Biography* (Canberra, ACT: Australian National University, 2021), https://adb.anu.edu.au/biography/rooklyn-israel-jack-30530/text37850.

21. Condon, *All Fall Down*, 528–30.

22. Pickett, "Rooklyn, Israel (Jack)."

23. John Patrick Kimmins, *Report of the Inquiry into Allegations of Misconduct in the Investigation of Paedophilia in Queensland* (Brisbane, QLD: Criminal Justice Commission, 1998), 20–21.

24. Ibid., 36.

25. Condon, *All Fall Down*, 539–40.

26. Glendon Patrick Hallahan, statutory declaration, October 19, 1988, Queensland State Archives Item ID2548831, Commission of Inquiry—legal advice, 2.

27. Evan Whitton, *The Hillbilly Dictator: Australia's Police State* (Crows Nest, NSW: ABC Enterprises, 1989), 54.

28. Condon, *All Fall Down*, 491–92.

29. Gerald E. Fitzgerald, *Report of a Commission of Inquiry Pursuant to Orders in Council* (Brisbane, QLD: Commission of Inquiry into Possible Misconduct and Associated Police Misconduct, 1989), 77.

30. Condon, *All Fall Down*, 505–9.

31. Anthony Murphy, writ of summons, November 15, 1990, Queensland State Archives Item ITM1072369, Writ, 1–2; Condon, *All Fall Down*, 509.

32. Condon, *All Fall Down*, 545.

33. "Fitzgerald Inquiry whistleblower dies," *ABC News*, April 8, 2004, https://www.abc.net.au/news/2004-04-08/fitzgerald-inquiry-whistleblower-dies/166630.

34. Condon, *All Fall Down*, 546–47.

35. "Ex-Minister Lane jailed on 27 charges," *Canberra Times*, October 4, 1990, 1.
36. Condon, *All Fall Down*, 518–19.
37. "Jury foreman worshipped Sir Joh: claim," *Canberra Times*, May 6, 1993, 16.
38. Tony Stephens, "Farewell, Sir Joh, the great divider," *Sydney Morning Herald*, April 25, 2005, https://www.smh.com.au/national/from-the-archives-2005-farewell-sir-joh-the-great-divider-20200406-p54hk1.html.
39. Parliamentary Joint Committee on the National Crime Authority, *The National Crime Authority and James McCartney Anderson* (Canberra, ACT: Parliament of Australia, 1994), 19.
40. *Saffron v The Queen* (1989) 17 NSWLR, 407–17.
41. "Sydney 'identity' Abe Saffron dies," *Sydney Morning Herald*, September 16, 2006, https://www.smh.com.au/national/sydney-identity-abe-saffron-dies-20060916-gdoefq.html.
42. Caro Meldrum-Hanna, "Episode 3 [video]," *Exposed: The Ghost Train Fire*, ABC Australia, March 30, 2021.
43. Ibid.
44. Cindy Jones, "Victor Camilleri: His interesting career," *Sydney Morning Herald*, March 8, 1992, 20.
45. Malcolm Brown, "Police took sides in gang wars: Smith," *Sydney Morning Herald*, August 12, 1993, 3.
46. Ibid.
47. Ibid.; Tony Reeves, *Mr Big: Lennie McPherson and His Life of Crime* (Crows Nest, NSW: Allen and Unwin, 2005), 245.
48. "Flannery 'frightened' before disappearance," *Canberra Times*, February 3, 1994, 2; Adam Shand, "Ganglands: Part 2," *Sunday*, Nine Network Australia, February 22, 2004.
49. G. P. Walsh, "Freeman, George David (1935–1990)," *Australian Dictionary of Biography* (Canberra, ACT: Australian National University, 2007), https://adb.anu.edu.au/biography/freeman-george-david-12512.
50. Tony Reeves, *The Real George Freeman* (Melbourne, VIC: Hybrid Publishers, 2013), 212.
51. Malcolm Brown, "McPherson, Leonard Arthur (Lenny) (1921–1996)," *Australian Dictionary of Biography* (Canberra, ACT: Australian National University, 2020), https://adb.anu.edu.au/biography/mcpherson-leonard-arthur-lenny-23076.
52. Malcolm Brown, "Smith, Stanley John (Stan) (1937–2010)," *Obituaries Australia* (Canberra, ACT: Australian National University, 2010), https://oa.anu.edu.au/obituary/smith-stanley-john-stan-16917.
53. Clive Small and Tom Gilling, *Smack Express: How Organised Crime Got Hooked on Drugs* (Crows Nest, NSW: Allen and Unwin, 2009), 51–52.
54. Ibid., 127–28.
55. Ibid., 52.
56. Ibid.
57. Jamie McDowell, "'Prince of Promises': Flamboyant Oz crime lord Murray Stewart Riley who ran counterfeiting op with Provos dies," *Sunday World*, January 6, 2021, https:

//www.sundayworld.com/crime/world-crime/flamboyant-oz-crime-lord-murray-stewart-riley-who-ran-counterfeiting-op-with-provos-dies-39934067.html.

58. Small and Gilling, *Smack Express*, 52–53.

59. McDowell, "'Prince of Promises.'"

60. John C. Keeney, *Statement of John C. Keeney Before the Permanent Subcommittee on Investigations Committee on Governmental Affairs United States Senate Concerning Organized Crime in the Great Lakes Region on January 31, 1984* (Washington, DC: US Department of Justice, 1984), 2–3; Ovid Demaris, *The Last Mafioso: The Treacherous World of Jimmy Fratianno* (New York City, NY: Bantam Books, 1981), 535.

61. Ray Loynd and Jean Merl, "'Jimmy the Weasel' Fratianno; Mob Figure, Informant," *Los Angeles Times*, July 1, 1993, https://www.latimes.com/archives/la-xpm-1993-07-01-mn-8855-story.html; Joseph P. Fried, "Ex-Mob Underboss Given Lenient Term for Help as Witness," *New York Times*, September 27, 1994, 1.

62. Loynd and Merl, "'Jimmy the Weasel.'"

63. Bob Bottom, *Connections II* (Melbourne, VIC: Sun Books, 1987), 16.

64. "Pioneer Las Vegas gaming figure Stein dies at 87," *Las Vegas Sun*, June 9, 2004, https://lasvegassun.com/news/2004/jun/09/pioneer-las-vegas-gaming-figure-stein-dies-at-87/.

65. John Wilkinson, *NSW and Gambling Revenue* (Sydney, NSW: NSW Parliamentary Library, 1997), 37–38.

66. *Bally's Park Place, Inc., In the Matter of the Application for a Casino License and the Application of Bally's Manufacturing Corporation for a Casino Service Industry License* [1978] 10 NJAR 356, 44–45, 50–51.

67. Ibid., 16–17.

68. Richard W. Stevenson, "Bally-MGM Grand Deal Announced," *New York Times*, November 18, 1985, Section D, 1.

69. David Dishneau, "Bally gambling its games will outperform its gyms: Company sheds health clubs to focus on casinos," *Akron Beacon Journal*, May 18, 1994, B8.

70. Barry Meier, "Hilton Hotels to Buy Bally Entertainment for More Than $2 Billion," *New York Times*, June 7, 1996, Section D, 1.

Index

About the Author

Paul Bleakley is an assistant professor of criminal justice at the University of New Haven in Connecticut. He is also vice chair of the American Society of Criminology's Division of Historical Criminology. Paul completed his doctorate in criminology at the University of New England in 2019 and has worked at universities in Australia, the United Kingdom, and the United States. Before entering the academic world, Paul was a journalist working in both London and Sydney. He is the author of two books on historical crime in Australia: *Under a Bad Sun* (2021) and *Policing Child Sexual Abuse* (2022).

www.ingramcontent.com/pod-product-compliance
Lightning Source LLC
Chambersburg PA
CBHW030301100426
42812CB00002B/525

* 9 7 8 1 5 3 8 1 7 7 0 8 2 *